The Logical Structure of English

The Logical Structure of English

computing semantic content

Allan Ramsay

Professor of Artificial Intelligence
University College, Dublin

PITMAN PUBLISHING
128 Long Acre, London WC2E 9AN

A Division of Longman Group UK Limited

© A. Ramsay 1990

First published in Great Britain 1990

British Library Cataloguing in Publication Data

Ramsay, Allan
  The logical structure of English.
  1. Natural language. Syntax. Logic
  I. Title
  415

  ISBN 0-273-03287-9

ISBN 0 273 03287 9

PREFACE

The work reported in this book was prompted by a feeling that there were a lot of potentially useful fragments of formal analysis of English syntax and semantics around, and that it might be interesting to try to glue them all together. It turned out that this feeling was entirely justified. There are a lot of potentially useful fragments around, and trying to glue them together was *extremely* interesting. So interesting, in fact, that by the time I'd glued a few of them together they had changed so as to be almost unrecognisable.

This work falls within the general framework of **Montague grammar** [Dowty et al. 1981, Chierchia et al. 1989]. It is an attempt to elicit the "logical content" of an utterance on the basis of the "logical contents" of its constituents. A large part of the book is devoted to examining what logical content is like, and any attempt to summarise it here would certainly be inadequate. Perhaps the suggestion that it concerns what you could infer from an utterance if you did not know what any of the words in it meant — what, for instance, you could glean from the statement that *Frumious bandersnatches gimbled mimsily* — gives a glimpse of what it is about.

The discussion draws on syntactic theory, since the way the meanings of the constituents contribute to the meaning of the whole must depend on the way they are organised; it draws on formal semantics and formal logic, since we need precise descriptions of what utterances entail; and it draws on discourse theory, since it turns out that a large part of the meaning of most utterances depends on what has been said before and contributes to what will be said next. The interesting thing, for me at least, was the changes that were forced on me when I tried to combine explanations which had been proposed for different phenomena and which seemed perfectly satisfactory in isolation. How, for instance, could I combine an explanation of the relation between restrictive and attributive relative clauses with an explanation of the relation between definite and indefinite noun phrases?

The shape of the book reflects these varied sources of information. Chapter 1 attempts to characterise the task itself, to explain the point of view taken in the rest of the book, and to present some examples. Chapter 2 presents a formal language for talking about meanings, and Chapter 3 presents a formal language for talking about syntactic rules and develops a grammar for a fragment of English. These chapters draw extensively on existing work, in order to provide a framework for the detailed discussion in Chapters 4 and 5. Chapters 4 and 5 contain a set of rules which describe the meanings of English sentences in terms of the meanings of their parts. Chapter 4 presents a partial analysis which takes us as far as we can go without considering the internal structure required for understanding the relationship between words like *die* and *kill*. Chapter 5 considers how to extend the analysis of Chapter 4, making some minimal assumptions about this internal structure. Chapter 6 is concerned with the real-world effects of utterances. There would be no reason for using language if it did not affect the world in various ways, and the discussion in Chapters 4 and 5 does not explain how this can happen. Unfortunately, nor does the discussion in Chapter 6, which just suggests that the current standard approach to this phenomenon is unlikely to be successful.

The rules that are presented in Chapters 3 – 5 are all in a form which makes them amenable to computer processing. This is partly because I believe that this helps ensure that the rules are not underspecified, and partly because I hope that the programs may actually be useful for practical tasks. These programs, including a parser which is not discussed in the book, run under QUINTUS Prolog. As far as I can tell they do not rely on any special QUINTUS facilities, so they should run under almost any standard PROLOG without changes. They are available, on a 720K 3.5inch MS-DOS disk, for £IR15, from:

Allan Ramsay
Dept. of Computer Science
University College Dublin,
Belfield, DUBLIN 4
IRELAND

Acknowledgements

A lot of people have helped me, in various ways, in the writing of this book — by introducing me to aspects of syntax and semantics that I was not aware of, by explaining things to me over and over again, by telling me when I was wrong, ... I owe particular debts to Roger Evans and Gerald Gazdar, for their patience when I asked the same questions about syntax a hundred times, and to Ray Turner for introducing me to property theory, intensional logic and discourse representation theory.

I would also like to thank Digital Equipment Corporation and the Department of Computer Science at University College Dublin for providing me with some time to spend on writing this book. I hope I haven't wasted it.

Allan Ramsay
February 1990
Dublin

CONTENTS

1 LOGICAL SEMANTICS

In *Alice through the looking-glass*, Alice asks Humpty Dumpty to explain the following verse to her:

> *'Twas brillig, and the slithy toves*
> *Did gyre and gimble in the wabe.*
> *All mimsy were the borogoves,*
> *And the mome raths outgrabe.*

He does so by explaining what toves are, what it's like to be slithy, what you do when you gyre and gimble, and so on. The remarkable thing about the way he does it is that he feels no need to tell her that brillig is a time, toves are things, slithy is an attribute, gyring and gimbling are actions. He assumes that she can obtain this information for herself, that it is somehow implicit in the way the verse is organised.

What is it about the verse that enables Alice to extract this basic information? Some of what she needs is encoded in the syntactic structure, in the way the words are put together. Some of it is encoded in the meanings of function words like *the, in, all* and *did*. Between them these two sources convey a picture of the way the world is organised — how many objects there are in it, how they are related to one another, how they are organised into groups, what the relations between groups are, and so on. The task of **logical semantics** is to describe the ontological commitment that lies behind such pictures; and to show in detail how particular structures encode particular pictures.

If we look again at our verse, we see that we can find out quite a lot about what the world would have to be like for it to be a true narrative, even without Humpty Dumpty's help. We know, for instance, that the actions it describes must have happened at some time in the past, and that they must now have stopped. We know something about the speaker's view of the world, namely that they are aware of some particularly salient sets of toves, borogoves and raths. We may know enough about the speaker's view of the world to decide that they know of some other toves which did not gyre and gimble, but which can be distinguished from those that did on the grounds that they were not slithy. These general properties of the way the world would be if the verse described it correctly are built on some global picture of what the world is like, and of the relationship between language, speakers and the world. Our task in this book is to try to describe this global picture, and to show how texts correspond to configurations of elements of the world.

Logical semantics by itself is not enough for us to understand how language carries messages about the world to people, or how it affects their behaviour. Before we could claim to understand how language does its job we would have to address at least two other topics. (i) We would have to do what Humpty Dumpty did for Alice: we would have to explain how words correspond to objects, classes, properties and actions. (ii) We would have to describe the relation between the information that a message carries and the behaviour that it evokes in a listener.

The first of these other tasks can itself be split into two parts. To explain how words correspond to objects, classes, etc. we would need to start by describing what objects and classes there are (or at any rate what objects and classes users of the language in question are aware of). Before we could claim to understand the word *man* properly, for instance, we would need to know about the properties of being animate, male, human, two-legged, rational, and so on, and we would need to be able to describe the relationships between them. To understand the word *unmarried* we would need to know about social institutions, contracts, emotional states, religious systems, ... In other words we would have to know about the conceptual categories that members of our culture use for representing the world to themselves. If we wanted to address this aspect of language, we would have to describe the concepts and relations between concepts that are shared by all native English speakers. There are various ways of approaching this task. It might be achieved by setting out a set of primitives and axioms that relate them [Carnap 1936, Schank 1972]; or by presenting a set of relations whose structure mirrors the structure of the relevant conceptual system [Quine 1960, Quillian 1968, Eco 1976]. This is a major task which we will not tackle, though we will occasionally call on the notion of **meaning postulates** when we need to call on some intrinsic property of the meaning of some word.

In addition to our language users' underlying conceptual systems, we would need to specify the relationships between words and concepts. To understand what *buy* means, for instance, we need to know about ownership, about money, and about control. *Buy* corresponds to some particular set of changes in control of money and other objects by animate agents standing in particular relations to one another. Describing the correspondence between words and concepts is another very substantial task. Even an apparently simple word like *buy* involves some very subtle distinctions. It is not just a matter of A being in control of some money, and B of some object X, at time T, followed by A being in control of X and B of the money at some later time T'. If someone takes my bicycle and leaves me money which would pay for an identical replacement, they have not bought it from me, though this sequence of events would fit most naive characterisations of *buy*ing. Indeed, if the meaning of *buy* were a simple matter then solicitors would lose a large part of their income.

We will return to these matters when we come to consider thematic relations in Chapter 5. It seems that some facets of our shared conceptual framework manifest themselves in the structure of our language. Consider, for instance, the following pair of sentences:

(1) *Steven caught the ball.*
(2) *The ball was caught by Steven.*

It is clear that these two describe the same event, though they presumably emphasise different aspects of what happened. This connection between **active** and **passive** forms is very regular, and applies to any transitive verb (and any ditransitive one, and to verbs that take certain kinds of sentential complement). Well, to almost any transitive verb. The verb *open* in

(3) *The key opened the door.*

looks like a transitive verb. However

*(4) *The door was opened by the key.*

seems ugly, if not downright unacceptable. The explanation seems to be that only NPs which refer to **agents** can appear in the PP(by) of a passive form, and that agents are usually **animate** entities. The decision to encode a message in a passive sentence involves a grammatical rule. Nonetheless, it is constrained by deep-rooted properties of our conceptual system — that certain kinds of action involve agents, that there is a distinction between animate and inanimate objects, and that agents are generally animate. We will return to this interaction between our conceptual systems and the structure of English in Chapter 5, but even there we will not attempt a detailed description of the meanings of particular words, or of the conceptual system that any native English speaker may be assumed to possess.

The second task that logical semantics fails to address concerns the use of texts to produce effects. Our main aim is to describe the propositions that someone who sincerely produces some utterance must be committed to. If someone sincerely says

(5) *The milk's boiling.*

then we can assume certain things about their beliefs. We can assume, for instance, that they believe that there is some milk which is boiling. Furthermore, we can assume that they believe we know which milk it is that is boiling. We might say that these are the **truth conditions** for (5). Saying that they are truth conditions, however, commits us to a rather specific view of the nature of meaning, and of the relationship between language and the world. We therefore prefer to call them the **commitments** of (5).

We can see what the commitments of an utterance are even if we know nothing about the circumstances in which it was produced. Suppose, however, that someone who had just made some coffee, and was now buttering a pile of toast, said (5) to you. You would then infer that they wanted you to do something about it — to take the pan off the cooker and pour the milk into a jug, for instance. If utterances did not produce effects like this then there would be very little point in making them.

Any explanation of the way that linguistic actions affect people's behaviour will require a theory of rational action, and a theory of **epistemic** and **dochastic** reasoning (reasoning about one's own and other people's knowledge and beliefs). In Chapter 6 we will consider AI planning theory as a theory of rational action, and we will see how it applies to linguistic actions. We will at this point require some analysis of epistemic reasoning, since a lot of the "real world" effects of linguistic actions are in fact effects on other people's knowledge. We will, however, require a treatment of epistemic reasoning even to describe the commitment of an utterance. We noted above that anyone who sincerely uttered (5) must believe that their listener knows what milk they are talking about. Thus even to represent the commitment of an utterance we need to be able to represent statements about knowledge and belief. We will therefore need to make some decisions about the way we will treat knowledge and belief in Chapter 2, when we present the language we will be using for describing commitments.

1.1 Compositionallty

Our main task, then, is to characterise commitments. We place two constraints on the way that we do this. The first is that we want our treatment to be **compositional**. We assume that texts are built by constructing groups of words, and then collecting these into larger groups, and then collecting these into yet larger ones, until complete meaningful utterances are produced. This grouping process is governed by **syntactic rules**, which specify when and how groups may be joined together. Compositionality is the requirement that the meanings of complex groups are simple combinations of the meanings of their parts.

We have several reasons for wanting to obey this principle. The most important is that it shows the distinction between syntax and semantics to be largely illusory. If we are to provide a compositional analysis of meaning, we will have to show that every semantic distinction corresponds to some combination of constituents which is permitted by a syntactic rule. If we also managed to show that every combination of constituents that is permitted by a syntactic rule generates a unique commitment then the distinction between syntax and semantics would largely disappear. There would just be one set of organising principles, which would cover both the way language is organised and the way that its organisation carries messages.

This is a very attractive prospect. If we could do it, we could explain the genesis of syntactic structures in terms of basic properties of the way people experience the world. We could use it as a probe for discovering semantic distinctions — if there is a 1-1 correspondence between syntactic constructions and semantic distinctions, for instance, then the active/passive distinction between (1) and (2) must correspond to some difference in meaning. We would, in fact, understand the real reason why people want to study syntax: because it encodes the structure of our view of the world.

Quite apart from this, trying to keep our treatment compositional will make our task much simpler. Consider the following sentences:

(6) *Who borrowed my tennis racket?*

(7) *I saw the woman who borrowed my tennis racket going to the courts.*

(8) *I saw the woman, who borrowed my tennis racket, going to the courts.*

(9) *I know who borrowed my tennis racket.*

Each of them contains the phrase *who borrowed my tennis racket.* In each case it seems to contribute something different to the meaning of the overall sentence. Looking at these sentences, we see that they each require different syntactic analyses, with the phrase *who borrowed my tennis racket* almost certainly making a different contribution in each case. Since we need different syntactic descriptions, we can expect the meaning of this phrase to be used differently in each example, so we will need different semantic rules corresponding to each of the syntactic ones. The phrase itself, however, looks the same in each case. We would therefore like to have a single description of its syntactic structure in each case, and hence a single description of its commitment. If our treatment of the relation between syntax and semantics is compositional we will have just one rule for any unambiguous phrase, though we may of course need different explanations of how that phrase fits into different contexts.

Our emphasis on compositionality suggests that when we come to explain what texts mean we will depend heavily on their syntactic structures. This in turn means that we will need some way of describing syntactic structures. We will present the framework for our discussion of syntax in Chapter 3. At that point we will have a language for describing commitments, and a language for describing syntactic structures. In Chapter 4 we will combine these to present a detailed analysis of the logical structure of a fragment of English.

1.2 Computational Representation

In addition to trying to keep our treatment compositional, we will insist that it be amenable to processing by computer. This does not mean that we are going to present algorithms for manipulating text — for extracting a representation of its semantic content, say, and investigating the consequences of this representation. Our aim is rather to present the backgound information that such algorithms draw on in order to perform their tasks. We will present syntactic and semantic rules which could be used by a range of existing programs, without any particular commitment to specific approaches. As it happens we use a fairly orthodox left-corner chart parser for applying syntactic rules and constructing a representation of semantic content, and a variant of Manthey and Bry's [1988] model generation approach to theorem proving for investigating the consequences. We believe these to be the best available techniques. The analysis in this book, however, does not depend upon the use of these techniques. What we want is a description of the knowledge required for understanding English texts. We want this description to be sufficiently precise and sufficiently detailed for it to be usable by a computational system. The rules we present below could equally well be processed via some other parsing technique, such as Matsumoto et al.'s [1983] bottom-up parser, and the consequences could be investigated via some other theorem-proving technique such as resolution [Robinson 1965] or path elimination [Bibel 1982]. What matters to us here is that our rules can be used at all by such programs, not the details of how they get used. We will therefore concentrate largely on the rules themselves, and will say nothing more about the algorithms that we use for applying them.

We have two reasons for wanting our rules to be precise enough to be used by computational systems. Firstly, we believe that theories which are embodied in computer programs are more precise and more testable than ones which are not. Expressing your theory as a program does not guarantee that it will be perfectly precise, nor that it will be completely testable (let alone completely tested). It does, however, provide some extra rigour, and some indication of how we might go about testing a theory.

How would we test our theory? The rules we will develop in Chapters 4 and 5 will express relationships between the way texts are organised and the propositions their speakers are committed to. It is clear, then, how we would test them — we would just see whether the propositions they predicted were the ones that a speaker would indeed be committed to.

The problem is that it is very hard to find out just what someone who produces an utterance actually would be committed to. If we embody our theory as a program, we can at least find out what descriptions of the commitment of an utterance it generates (if any). We still have to find out whether what it generates does describe the right propositions, and having it expressed as a program will not help with that. A computer program can be useful for enumerating the analyses that a theory assigns to a given text. Deciding whether those analyses correspond to what the text "really" means is another problem.

The only real way to test whether some description of the meaning of a text is correct is to see if it entails the same things as the text itself. Suppose that D is some expression which purports to be a description of:

(10) *Edith ate a peach and an apple.*

D will not be a satisfactory representation of (10) unless it entails the propositions that Edith ate a peach and that she ate an apple. It will be impossible to find out whether this is so unless the language of which D is an expression itself has a semantics which supports the notion of entailment. We will therefore take considerable care in Chapter 2 to ensure that our language for describing commitments has a well-defined semantics.

Suppose we have a program which is guaranteed to enumerate the semantic descriptions generated by our theory, and we understand the semantics of the description language well enough to be able to tell whether one proposition in it entails another. We still have the task of ascertaining the set of propositions that a sentence of English entails. This is in fact simply beyond us. For any given utterance we can specify some of what it entails — that (10), for instance, entails that there was at least one peach and one apple, that there are now one less of each, that at some time Edith had an apple in her tummy, and so on. We can also specify various things that it does not entail. (10) does not entail that there was ever a tomato, or that Rachel lives in Cambridge, or ... We therefore have two negative tests: do we know of something that the description fails to entail even though it ought to, and do we know of something that it entails which it ought not to.

We would also like to use our program for checking entailments. Unfortunately, it is clear that any language which is rich enough to provide a description of the semantics of language will be at least as expressive as **first-order predicate calculus** (FOPC). It is well-known that FOPC is **semi-decidable**. We can see what this means by imagining a program that was supposed to decide whether D_1 entailed D_2. For FOPC, and indeed for the language we will present in Chapter 2, you could write a program that would take two expressions and say yes if and only if the first did entail the second. The problem is that you could not guarantee that it would also say no if the first did not entail the second. It might simply keep looking for a proof of the second from the first, without ever realising that it was not going to find one. This well-known result puts a limit on the use of programs for testing our theory. We can have a program which will enumerate all the descriptions of commitments the theory generates for a given text; and we can have a program which we can rely on when it tells us that some description does or does not entail some proposition, but which may sometimes simply fail to tell us anything. When it fails to say anything, we do not know whether it was because we did not wait long enough or because the entailment does not hold. And even when it does specify that the entailment does or does not hold, we have to rely on our intuitions to decide whether it ought to.

We see then that if we embody our theory as a computer program, we can do some tests that would otherwise be beyond us. In particular, given an English text we can generate an expression in some formal language which is supposed to have the same consequences; and we can enumerate some of those consequences, and use them to judge whether our analysis is right. We said, however, that we had two reasons for wanting to have our theory embodied as a program. The second one is simply that we believe such a program may have practical applications. There is little more to be said about this, apart from the following warning. It will become apparent as we proceed that English enables us to make some very subtle distinctions. Native English speakers make these distinctions despite the fact that they are seldom consciously aware of them. Consider the following sentence:

(11) *I want to speak to a salesman.*

If you think about it you will see that there are two ways of reading this sentence. It could be that the speaker has some particular salesman in mind — the one that called on her yesterday, for instance. If we interpret (11) this way, then it entails that there must actually be a salesman. On the other hand, we could interpret it as a general request to speak to anyone who happens to be a salesman. If our speaker meant it this way then she need not be committed to the proposition there are any salesman. We will see numerous examples of this kind. Very few current computer systems are capable of making inferences based on such subtle distinctions, or even of recognising that they exist. Until such time as applications require this degree of sophistication, it may be that natural language systems will be of very limited use. Nonetheless, we may as well hope that we can find some practical use for our programs, since we are writing them anyway in order to help us see exactly what our theory predicts.

1.3   Examples

We now have a general picture of the phenomena we want our theory to deal with and the way we want it to deal with them. We end this general discussion with some examples illustrating these phenomena (some of these examples echo topics we have remarked on already. It seems, nonetheless, worth gathering them all together for future reference). The specific rules we present in Chapters 4 and 5 will cover some of these, and will leave others either partially or completely unexplained. They all, however, illustrate important distinctions. For the moment we will just point out the problems involved in their interpretation without saying how we intend to deal with them, or indeed whether we can or not.

Discourse representation

(12) *The man works in Dublin.*

(13) *A man works in Dublin.*

In (12) the speaker assumes that the listener will know what man is being talked about. (13), on the other hand, seems to introduce a new man into the conversation. We therefore see from this very simple pair of sentences that meaning representations must refer to both the speaker's and the listener's knowledge and beliefs, and to the state of the discourse. More complex examples show this to be a very subtle matter indeed:

(14) *I bought an apple and a pear for my friend, who ate the apple but threw the pear away.*

*(15) *I bought an apple and a pear for my friend who ate the apple but threw the pear away.*

(14) seems much more acceptable than (15). The difference seems to be that somehow the information that an apple and a pear have been mentioned is available at the point when the relative clause in (14) is encountered, but not when the one in (15) is. We will have to work quite hard to get a precise description of what is going on here.

Parameterised adjectives

It is often assumed that adjectives modify nominal groups by adding constraints. In

(16) *I saw a grey elephant.*

for instance, we generally interpret *a grey elephant* as a reference to something which is an elephant and which is grey. In

(16′) *I saw a big grey elephant.*

however, we cannot just think in terms of something which is an elephant, and is grey, and is big. The problem is that *big* does not specify an objectively defined property. Something that was big for an elephant could be tiny for a battleship; something that was not big for an elephant might still be enormous for a mouse. We seem to need to distinguish between adjectives which specify simple properties, and adjectives whose meaning depends on the kind of object they are applied to.

Plurals

(17) *John eats the peaches.*
(18) *John eats peaches.*
(19) *John eats some peaches.*

(17) clearly refers to some well-defined set of peaches. To represent the commitment of (17) we would need to be able to talk about sets as objects, but there should be no problem with that. (19) also has a reading where there is a set of peaches that John eats, though the listener is not expected to know which ones they are. The commitment of (18), however, is rather difficult to characterise. It expresses a general tendency rather than a specific event. (19) also has an interpretation like this. You could elaborate (19) to:

(19') *John eats some peaches. He eats Italian ones, but not the ones from the market.*

(18), and the interpretation of (19) evoked by (19'), require us to talk about some relation between John and the property of being a peach, rather than between John and some particular peaches. It is worth noting here that since (19) seems to have two different interpretations, the principle of compositionality requires that either there are two different syntactic analyses or that there is a lexical ambiguity. We will propose later on that the word *some* is ambiguous, generating either an **extensional** interpretation (the one where there is some particular, though unknown, set of peaches) or a **generic** one (the one evoked by (19')). Even the indefinite article *a* seems to have both an extensional and a generic interpretation:

(20) *Mary loves a sailor.*
(21) *Every nice girl loves a sailor.*

The most obvious interpretation of (20) is that there is some particular sailor that Mary loves. (21), on the other hand, seems to state some general relation between nice girls and sailors. There is not one sailor that all nice girls love; rather, nice girls are generally attracted to sailors.

Opaque contexts

(22) *I'm looking for a unicorn.*

Again we have two possible interpretations. The first is brought out by:

(22') *I'm looking for a unicorn. I saw it in the castle garden this morning.*

Under this interpretation there clearly is some unicorn which I am looking for. The second interpretation arises when we elaborate (22) to:

(22") *I'm looking for a unicorn. I want to make unicorn pie.*

(22″) could be true even if I do not have any particular unicorn in mind. It could even be true if there are no unicorns. As in the previous example, the second interpretation seems to require us to talk about a relationship between me and the general property of unicornhood, rather than between me and some specific unicorn. This second interpretation is often called the **intensional** reading of (22). It is worth noting that this semantic ambiguity, which does not seem to reflect any underlying syntactic ambiguity, can often be resolved within the sentence itself:

(23) *John is looking for a man who he thinks is a unicorn.*

does not seem to have an intensional reading. There must be some man X such that John thinks X is a unicorn, and John must be looking for X. In

(24) *John is looking for a man who thinks he is a unicorn.*

on the other hand, not only can the sentence be given an intensional reading, it is also ambiguous in terms of whether *he* refers to John or to the man who is doing the thinking.

Relative clauses and complex NP's

(25) *One of your friends who plays tennis rang me up.*
(26) *One of your friends who play tennis rang me up.*
(27) *One of your friends, who plays tennis, rang me up.*
(28) *One of your friends, who play tennis, rang me up.*

(25) – (28) illustrate two points. The first is the different roles we have already noted for relative clauses. In (25) and (26) the relative clause contributes information to help identify the person being talked about. In (25) it is somebody who is a friend of the listener and who plays tennis, and in (26) it is somebody who is a member of the set of people who are friends of the listener and play tennis. In (27) and (28), on the other hand, the relative clause contributes new information. (27) could be paraphrased as:

(27′) *One of your friends plays tennis. She rang me up.*

(28) could be paraphrased as:

(28′) *Your friends play tennis. One of them rang me up.*

(25) – (28) also emphasise the role of changes in syntactic structure. The presence or absence of commas, and the form of the word *play*, lead to four different syntactic analyses for the subject NPs in these sentences. We need to understand exactly what the relative clause is grouped with in each case, and hence what its commitment is to be combined with, if we want to understand how (25) – (28) convey their different messages.

WH-complements

(29) *I don't know much about art but I know what I like.*

(30) *I ate what I was given.*

The problem in (29) and (30) lies with the WH-clauses. They seem to be essentially relative clauses, except that there is nothing for them to modify. It seems likely that the best way to deal with them is to treat them exactly as though they were restrictive relative clauses modifying some vacuous NP, as in:

(29') *I don't know much about art, but I know the things which I like.*

(30') *I ate the things which I was given.*

Alternative presentations

(31) *Peter cooked dinner for Joan.*

(32) *Peter cooked Joan dinner.*

(33) *Joan was cooked dinner by Peter.*

(34) *Dinner was cooked for Joan by Peter.*

(31) – (34) are simply a reminder that you can say very much the same thing in a variety of different ways. We believe that syntactic differences always correspond to semantic differences, so we believe that (31) – (34) all mean different things. The differences in these examples, however, are almost certainly concerned with the organisation of large texts, and as such are outside our scope. We will therefore simply aim to derive a single description of the commitment of (31) – (34).

The following group of sentences seem to be instances of much the same phenomenon:

(35) *John opened the door with his key.*

(36) *John's key opened the door.*

(37) *The door opened.*

It is worth noting, however, that

*(38) *The door opened with John's key.*

looks rather odd. Detailed examination of cases like these suggests that we share very deeply ingrained assumptions about the relations between individuals and actions or events, and about basic conceptual categories.

The fact that we believe (31) – (34) to mean very much the same thing indicates that the *for* in (31) and (34) is largely redundant. It looks as though *cook* is an action which centrally involves three entities — someone doing the cooking, something being cooked, and someone who it is cooked for. The person being cooked for is often omitted, but the near equivalence of (31) and (32) indicates that their existence is somehow an intrinsic part of the meaning of the verb. In

(39) *I'll make Jenny a toy boat for her birthday.*

on the other hand, *for her birthday* seems to be a rather general addition to the meaning of the basic sentence. To deal with cases like this we will probably want to be able to refer to the event or action described by the core of the sentence as though it were a simple object. We see a similar situation in:

(40) *Quickly, Jones telephoned every customer.*

This seems to refer to a situation in which Jones performed the action of telephoning every customer, where not much time elapsed between his call to the first customer and his call to the last. This contrasts with

(41) *Jones telephoned every customer quickly.*

which can be interpreted as saying that it did not take him long to call any particular customer, though it may have taken him a very long time to get through all his calls. (39) prompted us to suggest that we may need to be able to refer to the event or action described by some sentence as though it were an object; but Pulman's [1987] examples (40) and (41) force us to worry about the nature of events such as telephoning every customer. Is there one grand event consisting of a lot of phone calls, or is there some implicit collection of little events?

Coordination

Connectives like *and* and *or* are usually taken to operate on propositions, i.e. on the meanings of sentences. We can follow this approach when dealing with

(42) *Jack or Jill built a house.*

since it seems to be equivalent to a disjunction of a pair of sentences:

(42′) *Jack built a house or Jill built a house.*

However if we apply this line of argument to

(43) *Jack and Jill built a house.*

we are forced to suppose that it means the same as:

(43′) *Jack built a house and Jill built a house.*

(43′) does not seem to capture the obvious interpretation of (43), since in (43) there is a single house which Jack and Jill built together whereas in (43′) there are two houses — the one that Jack built and the one that Jill built. It seems that the relationship between the English words *and* and *or* and the standard logical connectives ∧ and ∨ is not entirely straightforward.

The situation becomes even less clear when we consider the relation between the English *If ... then ...* and the logical relation of implication:

(44) *If Pedro owns a donkey he beats it.*
(45) *If Pedro owns a donkey Manuel wants it.*

The problem here concerns the relationship between *a donkey* and *it*. We do not want to describe the meaning of (44) as though it were:

(44′) *There is a donkey which Pedro beats if he owns it.*

Yet it seems hard to see how a purely compositional approach to semantics can connect the donkey whose existence is hypothesised in the antecedent of (44) with the *it* which Pedro beats in the consequent. The connection between *If ... then ...* and logical implication is further confused by:

(46) *Either Pedro does not own this donkey or Manuel wants it.*
*(47) *Either Pedro does not own a donkey or Manuel wants it.*

With the **material implication** of ordinary logic, $\neg P \vee Q$ is regarded as being identical to $P \rightarrow Q$. Yet so far from being identical to (45), (47) actually seems to be more or less meaningless. There is certainly something wrong with it, though (46) does not seem to be anything like as odd.

Category shifts

It is very common for English words to belong to more than one lexical class. For example, in

(48) *She walked to Bray.*

the word *walk* seems to denote an action. In

(49) *She went for a walk.*

it is playing the role of a noun, i.e. the sort of word that denotes an object. Many English words seem capable of this kind of category switch. In fact people can usually understand what is meant the first time it is done for a given word:

(50) *He Nixoned the tapes.*
(51) *We went to the canteen for eats.*

In order to describe what it going on here, we will yet again have to be able to switch between viewing something as an event, an action or a relation and viewing it as an object. We will also need some notion of its dominant properties. Why does (50) mean anything? Because one of Richard Nixon's best-known actions was to erase incriminating material from tape-recordings of private conversations. An explanation of how (50) comes to be meaningful would have to be able to draw on this sort of information.

Category switches of this kind are often explained by suggesting that the item belongs to two or more different categories. Present participles in English, for instance, often occur in places where you would expect to find adjectives or nouns:

(52) *It's hard to get a good shot at a running deer.*
(53) *We just bought a new washing machine.*
(54) *Running a youth hostel involves a lot of cooking and cleaning.*

In (52) it seems clear that *running* is performing very much the same task as an ordinary adjective, adding information about the kind of deer that is hard to shoot. In (54) *cooking* and *cleaning* seem to be playing the same sort of role as *work* in:

(55) *Running a youth hostel involves a lot of work.*

Washing in (53), however, seems a little more difficult. It is rather like an adjective, but the information it supplies is not simply additive in the way that *running* was in (52). *Washing machine* seems to be rather more like a noun-noun compound, like *bottle opener* or *paper clip*. *Washing* in (53), in fact, seems to be playing the role of a noun playing the role of an adjective. We will emphasise that the word in each case is the same, with the same meaning, but that the role it is playing requires the meaning to be used differently. This contrasts with the view that there are different classes — things like gerunds and gerundives — which just happen to always have exactly the same form as present participles.

Tense and aspect

English provides facilities for making quite subtle temporal distinctions. The following examples, for instance, carry information both about the time of the reported event and about its duration:

(56) *Henry is working in Paris.*
(57) *Henry works in Paris.*
(58) *Henry has worked in Paris.*
(59) *Henry worked in Paris.*

(56), for instance, says that at the moment Henry's place of employment is in Paris, but that this is not a permanent state of affairs. (57) says that at the moment Henry's permanent place of employment is in Paris (though he need not in fact be working there at the moment — if he was on temporary secondment to Milan you would still say that he works in Paris). (58) and (59) say much the same kind of thing, except that they refer to some past (temporary or permanent) state of affairs.

The mechanisms that English provides for placing events in time are extremely subtle, and can be combined to produce quite unexpected effects. Winograd [1983], for instance, develops a series of sentences involving complex auxiliary sequences to express particular points of view, ending with:

(60) *I was going to have to have been fixing radios for a century to get my pension.*

The effects of auxiliary sequences can be combined with other temporal modifiers to obtain even more complex effects:

(61) *If he caught the train he wanted he will be in London by now.*
(62) *If I am not in my office when you ring I'll be in the lab.*

We see here a sentence which seems to have a future marker (*will*) and yet which refers to something which is believed to be the case at the time of utterance; and one which seems to have a present marker (*am*) and yet which refers to something which may be the case at some future time.

We will not manage to deal with all the subtleties of the facilities English provides for talking about time. We cannot, however, ignore the problem without completely trivialising our treatment. We will therefore need to ensure that our language for describing commitments allows us to talk about time, and we will need at the very least to give some account of the way that auxiliary sequences position the speaker with respect to the reported event. We will not, however, do much about examples like (61) and (62).

Many of the examples above exemplify well-known problems. In Chapters 4 and 5 we will develop a set of rules to try to account for some of them. These rules draw upon work in the tradition of Montague grammar, notably on [Dowty 1989, Kamp 1984, Chierchia & Turner 1987]. The theory embodied in these rules will not solve all the problems we have introduced. It will deal with a substantial fraction of them, and where we have some understanding of why we fail to deal with others we will discuss what needs to be done. In Chapter 6 we will discuss the further problem of examples like:

(63) *Do you know the time?*
(64) *The milk's boiling.*

(63) and (64) are clearly intended to have an effect on the listener which goes beyond what they actually say. In order to explain how an utterance can have this kind of **indirect** effect, we will need to consider how utterances can have effects at all.

This will lead us into a consideration of rational action in general in terms of AI planning theory. We will not offer any particular planning algorithm, but we will look very closely at the notion of **speech act** to see whether it adds anything to our understanding of the problem or whether we can get everything we need from the semantic descriptions discussed in Chapters 4 and 5.

At the end of all this we will have a very partial description of the way uttering sentences can affect other people's behaviour. The merit of this description will be that it will be fully specified as far as it goes, so that it should be easy to see what it fails to account for. The demerit will be its incompleteness.

2 SEMANTIC FRAMEWORK

We now have a picture of our overall goal. We want to show the relationship between the commitment of an utterance and its syntactic structure, and we want to show how producing utterances with particular commitments can induce other people to do what we want. In order to describe the relationship between commitment and syntactic structure we need to have languages in which to describe commitments and syntactic structures. Exactly what these languages will be like depends on our general view of the nature of commitments and of syntactic structures. These are substantial matters, and we will devote the next two chapters to describing how we see them and to the details of the languages we will be using. We start by considering commitments and the language we will use for describing them.

The examples in Section 1.3 emphasised four things about the nature of commitments.

(i) When we talk about commitments, we need considerable freedom in our attitude to things like properties and propositions. This is clear from the problems we saw earlier when we considered WH-clauses, where the same thing can function as a question, or as a proposition, or as a modifier. If the same object can have all these functions, we need to be fairly flexible in the way we view it. We cannot, for instance, simply equate clauses with their truth values if we sometimes want to treat them as questions, sometimes as statements, and sometimes as qualifications.

The need for flexibility becomes even clearer when we look at the way verbs like *know* or *believe* work. These verbs can take either sentences (which presumably denote propositions) or NPs (which presumably denote objects) as their arguments. How could the same verb denote a relation to propositions and objects unless there is very little difference between them? Furthermore, when we think about such "verbs of propositional attitude", we see again that we cannot simply equate their meanings with their truth values. Suppose that it is true at the moment that Margaret Thatcher is the prime minister of the United Kingdom, and that Mikhail Gorbachev is the president of the USSR. If we were to take the meaning of a proposition to be its truth value we would be forced to conclude that the sentences

(65) *Martha knows Margaret Thatcher is the prime minister of the UK.*
(66) *Martha knows Mikhail Gorbachev is the president of the USSR.*

mean the same thing. This is clearly false. It seems unlikely that replacing truth values by sets of truth values, corresponding to situations in which the proposition is true, will solve the problem. It seems implausible that

(67) *Johnny knows every number has a successor.*
(68) *Johnny knows there are an infinite number of primes.*

are equivalent, though the situations in which every number has a successor are exactly the same as the ones in which there are an infinite number of primes.

We see the same need again when we look at the way expressions like *look for* work. The intensional reading of

(69) *I'm looking for a unicorn.*

seems to involve a relationship between me and the proposition that I am in the presence of a unicorn. The intensional reading of (69) undoubtedly requires us to be able think of this proposition as an object to which I would like to be able to ascribe a particular truth value, namely that it be true.

We will be very wary of being too precise about what we think propositions are. We will sketch some properties we believe them to possess — that they are the kinds of things to which truth values can be assigned, for instance — but we will avoid equating them with their truth values or truth conditions. Propositions are objects whose properties necessarily include the possession of truth values and truth conditions, just as human beings are objects whose properties necessarily include possession of gender characteristics. But just as human beings and gender characteristics are not the same kind of thing, so propositions and truth conditions are not the same kind of thing. Inextricably linked, yes, but not identical.

We will therefore require the language we develop in this chapter to allow us to talk about propositions as simple objects, and to talk about truth as a property. We will say as little as we can about the relations between propositions — about whether the proposition corresponding to the formula $A \wedge B$ is the same as the one corresponding to $B \wedge A$, for instance. We will not need to commit ourselves to a particular view on this. The formalism we will be using can be elaborated in various directions to support different views. We will remain as neutral as we can, leaving readers with specific views on the issue to interpret what we say in their own way.

(ii) The commitment of an utterance concerns the speaker's view of the world. The speaker's view of the world includes many things, notably a view of the listener's view and a view of the state of the discourse. All linguistic communication depends on a common understanding of what the speaker and listener already know about each other; and all linguistic communication involves the augmenting of that common understanding. Our entire presentation will be couched in terms of what the speaker must believe the listener to know if the utterance is to make sense, and what they must believe if it is to be true. We will therefore make extensive use of the predicates *BELIEVE* and *KNOW*, which express particular relationships between people and propositions.

The distinction between what the speaker must believe about the listener if the utterance is to make sense, and what they must believe in general if it is to be true, is fundamental. We will build this into our notation, splitting the commitment of an utterance into a presupposition and a content.

The presupposition is some proposition which the speaker believes that the hearer already believes. If the hearer does not believe it, the utterance will make no sense to them. The speaker can make assumptions about the process of verifying the presupposition. In particular, if the verification of some presupposition involves identifying objects with particular properties then the speaker can assume that the listener will identify those objects, or will say that they do not understand the utterance.

The suggestion that the speaker believes the hearer *already* believes the presupposition begs the following question: when is "already"? Presuppositions are closely connected with the use of definite references and pronouns, where the verification of some presupposition identifies the referent of a definite reference as a side-effect. The information required for verifying such a presupposition is often provided within the same sentence as the reference that draws on it, as in:

(70) *John wants his boss to give him a pay-rise.*

We will therefore have to be careful when talking about the point at which presuppositions get evaluated.

The content is simply a proposition which the speaker believes. The listener is entitled to assume that the speaker wants them to become aware of this belief.

This division of commitments into presuppositions and contents is central to our presentation. We will generally write commitments as

Presupposition: ...
Content: ...

It is important to remember that an utterance will make no sense to a listener unless they can verify its presupposition; that the speaker may make assumptions about side-effects of this verification; and that the listener may assume that the speaker intends that they should be aware that the speaker believes the content. We will not spell this out every time we describe a commitment, but it will always be true.

(iii) The speaker's view of the world also includes their view of various past and future states. We will not attempt to provide a characterisation of the "real" nature of time. If time has a real nature it will be discovered by physicists, who will analyse it in terms of irreversible processes like entropy and in terms of the improbability of various sub-atomic events such as spontaneous collisions between particles of matter and anti-matter [Reichenbach 1956]. What we need is a way of representing the intuitive notions we use in everyday discourse. Everyday discourse deals with instants and intervals and the notions of before and after, so it seems that at the very least we need to be able to talk about instants and intervals, and about one instant or interval being before or after another. If we were trying to develop a logic of time we would need to take specific views on various other issues — how many instants are there, are they finite, countable, dense, are intervals open or closed, etc. For our purposes in attempting to extract the content of English utterances we do not need to commit ourselves to particular answers to these questions. We doubt that they have unique "correct" answers anyway. It seems far more plausible that different answers will be appropriate for solving different kinds of problem. We will therefore simply leave it that the ontology of temporal reasoning includes instants and intervals, and that these objects have properties which are irrelevant to our current purposes.

For the same sort of reason, we will refuse to commit ourselves to a view on the "reality" of alternative pasts and futures. We will, however, certainly want to be able to represent alternative pasts and futures, since otherwise we will have no way of representing the meanings of sentences like the following:

(71) *If I do not apply for this post I will not get it.*
(72) *If I had not read the paper yesterday I would not have seen the advert.*

Yet again, the fact that we will be working with a language which enables us to treat propositions as though they were just objects will make it easier for us to fit temporal notions into our formal treatment. To represent the fact that something is true now, for instance, we will simply relate the proposition that expresses the fact to the object which represents now. Our formal framework will not help us discover the properties of instants and intervals, nor will it help us investigate how English encodes temporal viewpoints. It will, however, at least minimise the extra formal complexity that arises as soon as we introduce these notions at all.

(iv) The information you gain when interpreting a text puts constraints on the discourse situation. This information may be used later on, for example when you come to verify the preconditions of some subsequent utterance. Consider the following brief discourse:

(73) *John ate a peach. He enjoyed it.*

He and *it* in the second sentence are clearly connected to John and the peach he ate. If we want to represent this kind of **anaphoric reference** formally, we need some way of deciding exactly what is to be connected to what. But before we can attempt to calculate such connections we need to have a representation of the connected items. We can manage this with named individuals such as John. It is less obvious what we should do about entitities which are introduced via existential and universal quantifiers, such as the peach referred to in (73). The worst problems occur when the scope of the quantifiers in question does not reach as far as the anaphoric reference, as in:

(74) *If Pedro owns a donkey he beats it.*

(75) *If everyone from Madrid owns a donkey they beat them.*

We will deal with these cases by looking at the constraints that commitments place on discourse situations. Before we come to deal with discourse situations and anaphoric references, we will need to see how to describe commitments themselves; and before we can do that we will need to see how to talk about properties and propositions.

2.1   Properties and Propositions

Our first requirement, then, is for a language for talking about properties and propositions. We would like this to be a language with a precisely specified semantics, since we are going to use it for describing commitments. The only test we have for seeing if our description of a commitment is correct is, does it entail the right things? Entailment is not a clearly defined notion for languages without well-defined semantics. Thus if we are to have any hope of telling whether our descriptions are correct, the language we state them in must have a precisely specified semantics.

We also presume that people can perform inferences on the basis of their recognition of these commitments, and we would like to investigate the nature of such inferences. If we are to get any practical benefits from our computer implementation of our theory then we will need a mechanised proof theory; but even if we just want to speculate about how people might use commitments we will need some proof theory for our language.

This means that our language must be a **logic**. It must be a language for which we have a precise semantics, and hence have some clear notion of entailment. We would also like to have some syntactic characterisation of the notion of proof, and we would be even happier if we could automate the process of constructing proofs. This is less important than the existence of a precise semantics and a clear notion of entailment.

Logics that deal with properties are prone to serious problems. Consider the λ-calculus. The λ-calculus consists of a language of terms, an operation for abstraction, and an operation of application. The result of abstracting a term P containing a variable x is denoted by $\lambda x P$, and the result of applying a term Q to a term t is denoted by $Q.t$. The relation between abstraction and application is characterised by the following axiom:

($\lambda\beta$-equivalence) $(\lambda x P).t \equiv P_{t/x}$

You would hardly expect anything else. Abstraction removes detail, application supplies it. So if $\lambda x P$ has had the details of x removed, and $(\lambda x P).t$ has had them replaced by the details of t, you would expect the result to be the same as if you literally replaced x by t throughout P.

λ-calculus is not itself a logic, at least not a logic in the sense that we introduced above. Terms of λ-calculus denote functions rather than propositions, so we cannot easily develop a notion of consequence between the objects denoted by such terms. Suppose, however, that we introduce the logical connectives of FOPC into λ-calculus in such a way that we can use them to combine λ-calculus terms. The resulting language, FOPC$_\lambda$, will contain expressions like $\lambda Q(P \rightarrow Q)$, which is clearly intended to denote the property of being something which is implied by P.

Let us consider in particular the formula $\lambda P(\neg P.P)$. Its denotation seems to be the property of being some property which is not true of itself. Let us use the name $\mathcal{F}$ for this property. Since $\mathcal{F}$ is a property, we can reasonably wonder whether it applies to itself. In other words, we want to think about $\mathcal{F}.\mathcal{F}$. This is identical to $(\lambda P(\neg P.P)).\mathcal{F}$. The axiom of $\lambda\beta$-equivalence allows us to turn this into $\neg(\mathcal{F}.\mathcal{F})$. In other words $\mathcal{F}.\mathcal{F}$ is true if and only if $\neg(\mathcal{F}.\mathcal{F})$ is. This is inherently self-contradictory. We cannot countenance propositions that are true if and only if their own negations are true, i.e. if and only if they are false. Whatever else propositions are, they are things which are either true or false; and whatever else true and false are, they are mutually exclusive.

There is nothing wrong with allowing the symbols that are normally used as connectives of FOPC to be used for building complex terms out of simpler ones. Problems only arise if we continue to *interpret* them as truth functional connectives. The language FOPC$_\lambda$ is not of itself inconsistent. It can't be, since of itself it is not even a logic. The inconsistency only arises when we try to interpret it as though it were one, by interpreting its primitive terms as though they were prime formulae of FOPC and reading the symbols that are used for building complex terms as though they were in fact truth functional connectives.

The problem we have just seen with $\mathcal{F}$ is a formal version of the **Liar Paradox**, the sentence *This sentence is false*. Paradoxes of this kind arise very frequently once you combine abstraction with truth functional operations. They are generally known as **paradoxes of self-reference**, since they nearly always depend on finding some expression that encodes some general property of formulae, and then applying that expression to itself. We will just consider one other example, namely the paradox of **Russell's set**. Suppose $x \in s$ holds if and only if x is a member of the set s. The property $\lambda p(p \notin p)$ denotes the property of being something which is not a member of itself. This seems to be a fairly reasonable property. There are lots of sets which are not members of themselves — the set of all red things, for instance, is not a red thing; and there also seem to be sets which are members of themselves, such as the set of all sets. If we consider $\lambda p(p \notin p)$ a bit more carefully, however, we see that we have a problem again. Let $\mathcal{R}$ be defined as $\{x : \lambda p(p \notin p).x\}$, the set of all x which are not members of themselves. Is $\mathcal{R}$ a member of itself? Clearly it is if and only if it is not.

These paradoxes seem to undermine the basis of logic and mathematics. In order to develop a solid foundation for mathematics we need to be able to talk about sets and properties, and we need to be able to construct truth functional relations between statements about such things. Yet as soon as we combine truth functional operations and abstraction we run into these paradoxes. There seem to be two ways out. Either we can put restrictions on the application of abstraction and set formation; or we can change the nature of our view of truth and falsity. The first option appears more immediately appealing. Whitehead and Russell [1925], for instance, restricted abstraction by imposing a hierarchy on sets, in which each abstraction induced a move up the hierarchy. Application of an abstraction was then restricted to terms of lower order than the abstraction, so that self-reference became impossible. Later versions of set theory, such as Zermelo-Fraenkel set theory (see e.g. [Jech 1971]), restricted abstraction by constraining the **Axiom of Comprehension**. The unconstrained version of this axiom says that any property P defines a set, namely the set of all objects that satisfy P:

$$\forall P \exists s \forall u(u \in s \equiv P.u)$$

This version of the axiom leads immediately to exactly the kinds of problems we saw above. The property of being a set which is not a member of itself is a well-defined property, so the Axiom of Comprehension says that Russell's set is indeed a set. In order to avoid this kind of paradox, we restrict this axiom so that it is only used for forming *subsets* of things which are already known to be safe:

$$\forall P \forall s \exists s' \forall u((u \in s') \equiv ((u \in s) \wedge P.u))$$

This says that for any property P and any set s, the set of elements of s which satisfy P forms a well-defined set s'. This essentially restricts abstraction so that it can only be used to define subsets of sets which have been constructed by other operations which are known to be non-paradoxical. We can, for instance, talk about the set of all subsets of the integers which are not members of themselves without any fear of running into problems. The set of all subsets of the integers can be defined without reference to the Axiom of Comprehension, and hence will not involve us in any paradoxes; and the use of this axiom, even with a potentially dangerous property like Russell's property, can never lead from a well-behaved set to a paradoxical one.

These restrictive moves do indeed rule out the paradoxes. Unfortunately they also prevent us from saying things that we would like to be able to say. Turner [1989] points out that the following pair of sentences seem perfectly compatible:

(76) *John knows he knows everything Peter knows.*

(77) *Peter knows he knows everything John knows.*

These two are unlikely to strike a native English speaker as paradoxical. You might wonder how John and Peter came to be in this privileged position with respect to one another's knowledge, but this is not much more mysterious than the question of how anyone ever comes to know anything at all. Propositions like the one embodied in the conjunction of (76) and (77) may even be essential if we need to talk about mutual belief when dealing with the effect of a linguistic act on its speaker and hearer. Yet restrictions of the kind required for ruling out the paradoxes of self-reference will also make it impossible for us to produce formal equivalents of (76) and (77).

If we decide that we cannot afford to rule out propositions like these, we will have to find some other way of coping with the paradoxes. We can identify the source of the problem as the axiom of $\lambda\beta$-equivalence. If we weaken this, however, we find that our ordinary notions of truth and falsity no longer work. Turner [1989] surveys a number of closely related theories of truth which enable us to make sense of weakened versions of this axiom. We present Turner's own [1987] proof and model theories to illustrate what is going on; and we follow this with an alternative semantic treatment of exactly the same proof theory. We will use the notation of this theory as the basis of our language for describing commitments. The choice between the two semantic analyses of this notation is left open. All that really matters is that it should make some coherent sense.

2.2 Revision-based Theories of Truth

We are looking for a language in which we can talk about propositions and properties both in terms of their truth and applicability, and as though they were just objects. We define the expressions of our language, which we will call **property theory** (PT), as follows:

(i) PT is built on top of some ordinary first-order language, which we will call L. If t is a term of L then t is a term of PT, and if A is a formula of L then A is a formula of PT. We include the absurd statement, $\perp$, as a formula of PT.

(ii) If $t_1, \ldots, t_k, t$ are terms of PT then $\pi_k(t_1, \ldots, t_k, t)$ is a formula.

(iii) If A is a formula of PT then $\bullet[x_1, \ldots, x_n, A]$ is a term.

(iv) The usual logical operators $(\vee, \wedge, \rightarrow, \equiv, \neg, \forall, \exists)$ may used for making compound formulae.

$\bullet[x_1, \ldots, x_n, A]$ is intended to correspond to the abstraction of A with respect to $x_1, \ldots, x_n$. In this notation the axiom of $\lambda\beta$-equivalence would look as follows:

(Tarski biconditional (TB)) $\qquad \pi_k(t_1, \ldots, t_k, \bullet[x_1, \ldots, x_k, A]) \equiv A_{t_1/x_1, \ldots, t_k/x_k}$

We will refer to $\bullet[x_1, \ldots, x_k, A]$ as the **objectification** of A with respect to $x_1, \ldots, x_k$ to emphasise that its role is to enable us to talk about propositions and properties as objects. The axiom (TB) suggests that objectification is very like abstraction. However we know from the earlier discussion that we cannot have (TB) without restricting the formulae to which we are prepared to apply objectification; and we do not want to do this. The task for property theory is to provide a coherent interpretation of objectified formulae without reintroducing the paradoxes. The semantics we will develop will restrict the application of (TB), which is named after Tarski's definition of truth, that "P" is true if and only if P.

Before we present Turner's semantics for PT, we will note that the intuitive interpretation of the operators π_k is that they assert that the object which is their final argument holds of their first k arguments. We will refer to $\pi_k(t_1, \ldots, t_k, t)$ as the **instantiation** of t by $t_1, \ldots, t_k$. We will use π_0 and π_1 particularly frequently, and we introduce the suggestive abbreviations $T(A)$ and $t \in p$ for $\pi_0(A)$ and $\pi_1(t, p)$ respectively.

Turner follows Gupta [1982] and Herzberger [1982] in defining the semantics of PT in terms of a series of models. The construction is as follows:

(i) Start with a simple model $\mathcal{M}_0$ of the base language L, with a designated set P_k^0 of k-tuples of members of the domain of $\mathcal{M}_0$ for every integer k. $\mathcal{M}_0$ assigns one of the values T and F to sentences of PT by the following rules, using the convention that $[[E]]_V$ denotes the object that the semantic interpretation V associates with the expression E:

(i-a) If A is an atomic formula of the base language L then $[[A]]_{\mathcal{M}_0}$ is T if $\mathcal{M}_0 \models A$, F otherwise.

(i-b) $[[\pi_k(t_1, \ldots, t_k, t)]]_{\mathcal{M}_0}$ is T iff. the $k+1$-tuple $\langle [[t_1]]_{\mathcal{M}_0}, \ldots, [[t_k]]_{\mathcal{M}_0}, [[t]]_{\mathcal{M}_0} \rangle$ is in P_k^0.

(i-c) $[[A \wedge B]]_{\mathcal{M}_0}$ is T iff. $[[A]]_{\mathcal{M}_0}$ and $[[B]]_{\mathcal{M}_0}$ are both T, and likewise for the other standard truth functional connectives.

(ii) Given a model $\mathcal{M}_i$, build a new model $\mathcal{M}_{i+1}$ as follows.

(ii-a) Atomic formulae of L get the same interpretation as they had in $\mathcal{M}_i$ (so in fact they always have the same value as they had in $\mathcal{M}_0$).

(ii-b) The sets P_k^i of $k+1$-tuples of elements of the domain of $\mathcal{M}_0$ are replaced by sets P_k^{i+1}, where $\langle [\![t_1]\!]_{\mathcal{M}_{i+1}}, \ldots, [\![t_k]\!]_{\mathcal{M}_{i+1}}, [\![t]\!]_{\mathcal{M}_{i+1}} \rangle$ is in P_k^{i+1} iff. t is some $\bullet[x_1, \ldots, x_k, A]$ and $[\![A_{t_1/x_1,\ldots,t_{k-1}/x_k}]\!]_{\mathcal{M}_i}$ is T.

(ii-c) The denotation of any other formula is determined by the usual recursive rules (i.e. $[\![A \wedge B]\!]_{\mathcal{M}_{i+1}}$ is T if and only if $[\![A]\!]_{\mathcal{M}_{i+1}}$ and $[\![B]\!]_{\mathcal{M}_{i+1}}$ are both T, and so on).

The crucial part of this definition is step (ii-b). This defines the value at stage $i+1$ of terms which denote propositions, on the basis of the truth or falsity of the denoted propositions at stage i, and likewise for terms denoting properties.

To see what all this means, consider the formula $P(x) \to P(x)$. We will call this formula A, and we will use the abbreviation $\bullet[x, A] \in \bullet[x, A]$ for $\pi_1(\bullet[x, A], \bullet[x, A])$. The rules above fail to specify a value for $[\![\bullet[x, A] \in \bullet[x, A]]\!]_{\mathcal{M}_0}$. Nonetheless, we can see that $\mathcal{M}_0 \models A_{\bullet[x,A]/x}$ must hold, since A is a valid formula of FOPC. Therefore (ii-b) specifies that $[\![\bullet[x, A] \in \bullet[x, A]]\!]_{\mathcal{M}_1}$ will be T, and likewise for all $\mathcal{M}_i$ for i greater than 0.

This contrasts with what happens when we consider the formula $x \notin x$. We will call this formula B, and consider the proposition $\bullet[x, B] \in \bullet[x, B]$. This is another presentation of Russell's paradox: does the property denoted by $\bullet[x, \neg(\pi_1(x, x))]$ apply to itself? Suppose the pair $\langle [\![\bullet[x, B]]\!]_{\mathcal{M}_0}, [\![\bullet[x, B]]\!]_{\mathcal{M}_0} \rangle$ is in P_1^0. Then $[\![\bullet[x, B] \in \bullet[x, B]]\!]_{\mathcal{M}_0}$ will be T, by (i-b). Consider the formula $B_{\bullet[x,B]/x}$. This turns out to be $\bullet[x, B] \notin \bullet[x, B]$, i.e $\neg(\bullet[x, B] \in \bullet[x, B])$. This must have the value F at $\mathcal{M}_0$, since $\bullet[x, B] \in \bullet[x, B]$ has the value T. From this and (ii-b) we see that

$$\langle [\![\bullet[x, B] \in \bullet[x, B]]\!]_{\mathcal{M}_1}, [\![\bullet[x, B] \in \bullet[x, B]]\!]_{\mathcal{M}_1} \rangle$$

will not be in P_1^1. A similar argument will enable us to show from this that

$$\langle [\![\bullet[x, B] \in \bullet[x, B]]\!]_{\mathcal{M}_2}, [\![\bullet[x, B] \in \bullet[x, B]]\!]_{\mathcal{M}_2} \rangle$$

will be in P_1^2, and then that the corresponding pair will not be in P_1^3, and so on. Thus if we start from the assumption that

$$\langle [\![\bullet[x, B] \in \bullet[x, B]]\!]_{\mathcal{M}_0}, [\![\bullet[x, B] \in \bullet[x, B]]\!]_{\mathcal{M}_0} \rangle$$

is in P_1^0 then we see that the value assigned to $\bullet[x, B] \in \bullet[x, B]$ alternates at each revision. Exactly the same argument will show that it also alternates if we start from the assumption that

$$\langle [\![\bullet[x, B] \in \bullet[x, B]]\!]_{\mathcal{M}_0}, [\![\bullet[x, B] \in \bullet[x, B]]\!]_{\mathcal{M}_0} \rangle$$

is not in P_1^0. It seems that some formulae, like $\bullet[x, A] \in \bullet[x, A]$, keep the same value during the revision process, whereas others keep switching. We can construct formulae which switch values for some finite series of revisions and then settle down. We can also invent formulae which switch values over arbitrarily complex cycles. The critical difference is between ones which do eventually settle down and ones which do not.

Semantic theories based on model revision, then, concentrate on what happens to formulae when you consider **limit** models. The discussion above looked at what happened after finite numbers of steps of the revision process. Classical set theory allows you to talk about **limit ordinals**, which are essentially the "last" members of infinite sequences. The ordinal ω, for instance, is the "last" integer (more precisely, the first integer after all the ordinary finite ones). This is not the place to consider the ramifications of this notion in detail. We will simply note that if we decide to use ω as a name for some integer that comes after all the numbers that you get by starting at 0 and adding 1 a finite number of terms, then there will be another series that starts with ω and moves on through $\omega + 1, \omega + 2, \ldots$, with presumably another limit ordinal at the end of this series. And that furthermore there will be an infinite series of such limit ordinals, and therefore there will be a limit ordinal at the end of this series, and so on.

The rules for constructing models that we gave above explained how we obtain one model from another, and thus how we can generate an infinite sequence of models. We can define the model that we get at the "end" of such a sequence by saying that if λ is a limit ordinal then P_k^λ contains the $k + 1$-tuple $\langle a_1, \ldots a_k, a \rangle$ if and only if there is an ordinal β such that $\langle a_1, \ldots a_k, a \rangle$ is in every P_k^α for every α between β and λ. In other words, P_k^λ contains everything which has eventually settled down during the sequence which culminates with $\mathcal{M}_\lambda$. Items may go through an initial period of oscillation before they settle down, but there must be some point β after which they are permanently in P_k^α.

Ordinary propositions eventually settle down to a stable value during this revision process. Paradoxes like the Liar and Russell's Paradox keep changing value no matter how far you go. Turner replaces our ordinary notion of **truth in a model** with **stable truth**. The resulting treatment contains **truth gaps**, since not all formulae which look as though they ought to have truth values turn out to be stably true or stably false. The idea that not all expressions have truth values is not all that revolutionary — if a is a constant of some first-order language L then the expression consisting just of a will not have a truth value, though it will be perfectly meaningful and can appear as an element of more complex expressions which do have truth values. All that has happened in our present treatment is that it has become rather harder to tell whether an expression has a truth value.

There are numerous semantic theories based on this approach. Aczel [1980], for instance, introduces a predicate P which is true of precisely those objects which are either true or false, and then develops an axiomatisation of the characteristics of P. Turner [1987] assumes that the Tarski biconditional (TB) is the defining characteristic of propositionhood, and analyses the circumstances under which it holds. Turner [1989] provides a comprehensive survey of the relations between these theories. For the moment we will simply note that the notation of [Turner 1987] looks extremely suitable for our task of describing commitments. Readers who are happy with theories of truth based on limiting properties of infinite series of models can therefore accept that we have a well-founded notation for our task, and can skip to Section 2.4.

2.3 Game Theoretic Semantics for Property Theory

Revision-based theories of truth may be technically satisfactory. It can be argued, however, that they do not correspond very closely to our intuitions. In particular, the revision process seems more closely related to reasoning and inference than to any pre-theoretical notions about truth. Can we make more sense of what is going on if we think more in terms of the properties of infallible reasoners than in terms of necessary truth?

At this point it is worth recalling that all our descriptions of the meanings of English phrases are going to be couched in terms of the speaker's knowledge and belief about various aspects of the discourse situation, and in particular about the listener's knowledge and belief. We will therefore want our language to be well-suited to the expression of statements about knowledge and belief.

It has been widely noted that **possible worlds** semantics for epistemic and dochastic logic is more or less satisfactory as a technical device, but fails to provide any real characterisation of knowledge or belief. We suggest that here also it might be better to think in terms of ideal reasoners rather than necessary truth. We therefore propose an alternative semantics for PT in terms of the **game theoretic semantics** proposed by Lorenz [1961] and Lorenzen [1959]. We start by considering a game theoretic treatment of ordinary first-order epistemic logic, and then extend this to deal with objectification and instantiation.

Epistemic logic aims to capture the properties of what people know about their own knowledge and the knowledge of other people. In particular, we want to characterise the circumstances under which one statement about an agent's knowledge entails another. This is the same task as the one we are faced with whenever we want to develop a logic of X—what are the circumstances under which one statement about X entails another? Most successful attempts to answer questions of this kind develop interpretations of statements about X in terms of structures which share, as far as possible, the properties of X. Temporal logics interpret statements about time in terms of structured sets of instants or intervals [Allen 1984, McDermott 1982], modal logics interpret statements about necessity and possibility in terms of possible alternative states of affairs [Hughes & Cresswell 1968], nonmonotonic logics interpret defeasible statements in terms of worlds that contain precisely what is needed to make them come out true [Reiter 1980]. The same should be true for epistemic logics. If an epistemic logic is to be an effective characterisation of the relations between statements about knowledge, its semantics should be based on objects which have, as far as possible, the same properties as bits of knowledge.

Of course if we really knew what properties "bits of knowledge" had, we would hardly need to develop an epistemic logic at all. And if we do not know what properties they have, we cannot construct an abstract domain whose components have the same ones. Nonetheless, we have to do the best we can. We have to choose what we think bits of knowledge are like, and we then have to develop some precise description of how they behave. Once we have a tentative picture of the behaviour of bits of knowledge, we can sensibly try to develop a language whose expressions refer to such things, and a proof theory that relates statements of this language to one another. The first thing to do, then, is to commit ourselves to some view on the nature of bits of knowledge.

Most existing epistemic logics take one of two views on this. They either characterise them as sets of sentences in some knower's mind; or they describe them indirectly in terms of sets of possible worlds, suggesting that you know P if you are attuned to a partition of the ways the world might be into ones where P is true and ones where it is not. This is not the place to recount the voluminous literature which attacks and defends these positions (see for example [Stalnaker 1984] for a clear discussion of their merits and demerits). They both have attractive features, and they also both have apparently fatal weaknesses. The attractive features and the fatal weaknesses both arise because of the particular properties of knowledge which the objects in question share. They are not going to be right, since it seems that neither sets of sentences nor sets of possible worlds actually have exactly the same properties as bits of knowledge, but they are revealing about the consequences of the properties they do share. Our intention here is to develop a logic whose semantics is focussed on other properties of bits of knowledge. This logic is not going to be right, any more than the others are; the best we can hope for is that it will also be revealing, and hence will help shape the next round of the debate.

So what are the properties we intend to focus on? The critical one is that knowledge is something that **agents** have. We will therefore want our semantics to capture the behaviour of agents. What do agents do with their knowledge? They may act on it, they may manipulate it in order to make it grow, and they may get it from other agents or give it to them. Following Hintikka and Kulas [1983], we might say that when they act on it they are playing a game with nature. Exactly what game they are playing will depend on how they act, but it will be a game in which the agents' success depends on what they know. Furthermore, since we are talking about knowledge rather than belief it is a game they cannot lose. There is more to the difference between knowledge and belief than simply the fact that knowledge is bound to be true whereas beliefs can turn out to be false, but this is at least part of it. It follows that if in your game with nature you make a move which is based on something you know, that move cannot lead you to lose the game.

We can also think in terms of playing a game, this time against yourself, when we consider the act of manipulating your knowledge in order to make it grow. In this case it is easier to see what the game must be. It is a game in which you argue with yourself about some proposition. You win if you show that you can defend the proposition in question against any possible attack. In order to show that you can defend a proposition against all possible attacks, of course, you have to be able to show that you have indeed anticipated all possible attacks. This puts some sharp limits on what knowledge is. In particular, it has to be something which you can represent to yourself in such a way that you can know how it might be attacked. It is worth noting that not all agents need be equally good at this game. It seems unlikely that goldfish, for instance, are very good at it—they certainly know some things, particularly things about the environment which affect the well-being of goldfish, so they can play some games with nature, but they probably cannot play the kinds of games with themselves which underly human introspection. Any logic of knowledge will clearly have to reflect the abilities of the agent in question.

We can view actions which provide other people with knowledge, or which obtain it from them, in very much the same way. If you give someone else some knowledge, the effect is to put them in a position to win games that they had not previously been able to win. If you get knowledge from someone else, you can win games that you would otherwise have lost. Constructive argument can be seen as a way of playing a game with someone else in the hope that you may be able to win a game using your combined knowledge that each of you separately would have lost—in other words, as a way for both of you to extend your knowledge.

We therefore want a theory of knowledge which puts agents and their ability to play games with nature, with themselves, and with each other at the centre. This means that the basic objects that underly our semantics are going to be not sets of sentences, not sets of possible worlds, but games. To develop our semantic theory we have to describe the objects that are used in these games, and then explore the rules that cover what you can do with these objects.

Stegmuller's [1964] presentation of game theoretic semantics, which is based on work by Lorenz [1961] and Lorenzen [1959], clearly takes formulae to be the objects which are used in games. The rules of attack and defence take different forms depending on the main connective of the formula being attacked or defended—to attack $P \wedge Q$, for instance, you would challenge one of P and Q, whereas to attack $\neg(\neg P \vee \neg Q)$ you would claim $\neg P \vee \neg Q$. If two formulae were logically equivalent, they would be equally defensible, but the form of the defence would be different. This seems to suggest that we will be identifying bits of knowledge with sets of sentences. We prefer to take a slightly weaker line. The best way to see the essential nature of knowledge is to see what games we can win; but the way we represent our knowledge to ourselves is clearly a factor in our ability to win games with it.

2.4   A Language for Epistemic Logic

We therefore start by presenting a language whose formulae are to correspond to representations of bits of knowledge. As with PT, this language will be built on top of some ordinary first-order language L. This time we extend L to a language EL (epistemic logic) by including **viewpoints**, which are used to encode information about whose knowledge is being described. The detailed formation rules are as follow:

(i) If A is a formula of L then A is a formula of EL.

(ii) If $t_1, \ldots, t_n$ are terms of L then we say that $[t_1, \ldots, t_N]$ is a *viewpoint*. If A is a formula of EL and $[t_1, \ldots, t_N]$ is a viewpoint then $A@[t_1, \ldots, t_n]$ is a formula of EL. The intended reading of a formula like $(p(a,b) \wedge q(c))@[a_1, a_2]$ is that a_1 knows that a_2 knows that $p(a,b)$ and $q(c)$ are both true. There is no restriction on the terms which may appear in a viewpoint—$\forall x((\exists y(mother(y,x)))@[x])$ is a perfectly acceptable formula which says that everyone knows they have a mother. We write $\emptyset$ to denote the "empty view", which is in some sense the viewpoint of the person who is thinking about the formulae under consideration.

We make our intended reading of formulae of this language precise in the following way. We say that a set of formulae Γ **supports** a formula A, written $\Gamma \models A$, if A can be defended using elements of Γ against all possible attacks. The rules for attacking and defending ordinary formulae of L are as follow:

(GTS-i) If A is a member of Γ, you can defend against an attack on A by pointing out that it is an agreed hypothesis.

(GTS-ii) If A is $B \wedge C$, you can attack it by claiming $\neg B$ or $\neg C$. If the attack is of the form $\neg C$ then the attacker is presumed to have conceded B, in which case B is added to the set of assumptions, and can therefore be used in the defence of C. You can defend against these attacks by counter-attacking your opponent's new claim.

(GTS-iii) If A is $B \vee C$, you can attack it just by stating that you doubt its validity. To defend it you have show that you can defend one of B and C.

(GTS-iv) If A is $B \to C$, you can attack by claiming B. There are two ways of defending against this attack. The first is to show that C holds, with B added to the set Γ of formulae you can use for defending things. The second is to attack B.

(GTS-v) If A is $\forall x B$, you can attack it by suggesting a constant c to be substituted for x in B. The defence is to claim $B_{c/x}$.

These are exactly the rules given in [Stegmuller 1964]. They are moderated by constraints on the situations in which particular players are allowed to use particular rules. Stegmuller shows that different constraints correspond to different axiomatisations of FOPC. For the sake of argument we will take the constraints he develops for classical FOPC. These are stated in terms of the principal roles of the two participants in the game. WHITE is taken to be the person who is defending the original claim that Γ supports A, BLACK is the person who is trying to attack it. The constraints are as follow:

Basic rule:
WHITE is only allowed to use prime formulae, for either attack or defence, if BLACK has already used them or they are members of Γ. Prime formulae are taken to be direct claims about the world, which could only be evaluated independently by stepping outside the game. WHITE can therefore only use them within the game if BLACK has already conceded them. It is worth noting that $\bot$ is a prime formula.

Structural rule:
(SR-a) BLACK can attack a formula that has been claimed by WHITE exactly once.
(SR-b) WHITE can attack a formula that has been claimed by BLACK as many times as she likes, so long as the attacks are all different.
(SR-c) Either player may defend against an attack so long as all subsequent attacks have already been dealt with. This imposes a stack-like discipline on games. Suppose WHITE has claimed $P \to Q$, where P and Q are some complex formulae, and BLACK has responded by claiming P. WHITE could continue either by attacking P or by defending with a claim of Q. If she decides to attack P she cannot subsequently defend with Q until her attack on P has been dealt with.

Stegmuller shows that with these rules WHITE can defend all and only those formulae which can be derived according to the proof theory of classical FOPC, i.e. that they provide a semantics for which the proof theory of classical FOPC is sound and complete. We need to adapt them to allow for formulae which refer to viewpoints.

> (GTS-vi) You can attack a formula $P@[a_1, a_2, \ldots, a_n]$ (where n is at least 1) by doubting it.

There are two ways to defend against such an attack. The most important way is by starting a new game, in which you take the role of WHITE. In this new game you have to defend $P@[a_2, \ldots, a_n]$ on the basis of a new set Γ' of hypotheses. Γ' is derived from the original set of hypotheses Γ as follows. You take each member of Γ which is of the form $Q@V$, where a_1 is a member of V. Suppose V is $[b_1, \ldots, b_k, a_1, c_1, \ldots, c_l]$, where none of the b_i is in fact a_1. Since viewpoints are supposed to represent knowledge, and knowledge is necessarily true, anyone who has access to the fact represented by $P@[b_1, \ldots, b_k, a_1, c_1, \ldots, c_l]$ should have access to the entailed fact represented by $P@[a_1, c_1, \ldots, c_l]$. If such a person were to want to pretend to be the person represented by a_1, they would know that they could draw on the fact represented by $P@[c_1, \ldots, c_l]$. In other words, $P@[c_1, \ldots, c_l]$ would be an appropriate item to include in Γ'. We refer to this kind of defence as a **change of viewpoint**, and we will call Γ' the **projection** of Γ at the viewpoint $[a_1]$, written $proj([a_1], \Gamma)$. We define *proj* more precisely as follows:

(proj-i): $proj(\emptyset, \Gamma) = \Gamma$.

(proj-ii): $proj([a, a, a_1, \ldots, a_n], \Gamma) = proj([a, a_1, \ldots, a_n], \Gamma)$.

(proj-iii): given a viewpoint $[a_1, \ldots, a_n]$ where $a_1 \neq a_2$ and a set of hypotheses Γ, let Γ' be $proj([a_2, \ldots, a_{n-1}], \Gamma)$. $proj([a_1, \ldots, a_n], \Gamma)$ is then obtained from Γ' by taking every element of Γ' of the form $P@[b_1, \ldots, b_k, a_n, c_1, \ldots, c_l]$, where none of the b_i is a_n, and replacing it by $P@[c_1, \ldots, c_l]$. If c_1 is in fact a_n then we delete it as well, and in that case if c_2 is also a_n then we delete it, and so on.

The other way to defend against an attack on a formula of the form $P@[a_1, \ldots, a_n]$ is to replace it by one in which either one of the a_i is repeated, or in which consecutive appearances of some a_i are collapsed. These defences depend on the fact that you can introspect on your knowledge. An agent that could not reflect on its own knowledge would be unable to make these moves. They are both justified on the grounds that an agent knows P if and only if they know they know it; and that all agents are aware of this fact, and hence can make the appropriate moves. If we had agents who could not do this sort of introspection, e.g. goldfish, this defence would not be permissible.

(GTS-vii) You can attack a formula $P@\emptyset$ by attacking P itself. The only defence is to defend P with the current set of hypotheses. If we take it that $P@\emptyset$ says that the person thinking about the current set of formulae knows P, then they should be able to defend it on the basis of the other things they are assumed to know.

These rules give us an abstract model within which to interpret statements about knowledge. The objects in this model are perfect games players. An epistemic statement A is supported by a set of hypotheses Γ if and only if a perfect games player could refute all possible attacks on it in a finite period of time. We would also like to have a proof theory for such statements, i.e. a formal description of the relations between specific statements of this language. We provide this in the next section, where we also show that this proof theory is sound and complete with respect to the semantics we have just given.

2.5   Proof Theory

All our proofs are constructed relative to a viewpoint. Once you introduce any epistemic notions into your language, it makes little sense to talk about proofs without specifying the agent performing the proof. In many cases this agent is yourself, but it is hard to see how something can be "a proof" without knowing who it is a proof for. We therefore insist that the viewpoint is always specified when a proof is constructed. We write $\Delta \vdash_V P$ to mean "P can be proved from the viewpoint V on the basis of the set of assumptions Δ". Our proof theory is given by the following inference rules:

$$\frac{\Delta \vdash_V P \qquad \Delta' \vdash_V Q}{\Delta \cup \Delta' \vdash_V P \wedge Q} \quad (\wedge\text{-introduction}) \qquad\qquad \frac{\Delta \vdash_V P \wedge Q}{\Delta \vdash_V P} \quad (\wedge\text{-elimination})$$

$$\frac{\Delta \vdash_V P}{\Delta \vdash_V P \vee Q} \quad (\vee\text{-introduction}) \qquad \frac{\Delta \vdash_V P \vee Q \qquad \Delta' \vdash_V P \to \perp}{\Delta \cup \Delta' \vdash_V Q} \quad (\vee\text{-elimination})$$

$$\frac{\Delta \vdash_V P \to \perp}{\Delta \vdash_V \neg P} \quad (\neg\text{-introduction}) \qquad\qquad \frac{\Delta \vdash_V \neg P}{\Delta \vdash_V P \to \perp} \quad (\neg\text{-elimination})$$

$$\frac{\Delta \cup \{P\} \vdash_V Q}{\Delta \vdash_V P \to Q} \quad (\to\text{-introduction}) \qquad \frac{\Delta \vdash_V P \qquad \Delta' \vdash_V P \to Q}{\Delta \cup \Delta' \vdash_V Q} \quad (\to\text{-elimination})$$

$$\frac{\Delta \vdash_V A}{\Delta \vdash_V \forall x A} \quad (\forall\text{-introduction}) \qquad\qquad \frac{\Delta \vdash_V \forall x A}{\Delta \vdash_V A_{c/x}} \quad (\forall\text{-elimination})$$

$$\frac{\Delta \vdash_V A}{\Delta \vdash_V \exists x A_{x/c}} \quad (\exists-\text{introduction})$$

$$\frac{\Delta \vdash_V \exists x A}{\Delta \vdash_V A_{c/x}} \quad (\exists-\text{elimination})$$

$$\frac{\Delta \vdash_{V+V'} P}{\Delta \vdash_V P@V'} \quad (view-\text{introduction})$$

$$\frac{\Delta \vdash_V P@V'}{\Delta \vdash_{V+V'} P} \quad (view-\text{elimination})$$

$$\frac{\Delta \vdash_V P}{\Delta \vdash_{V'} P} \quad (view-\text{compression}, V' \text{ is any subsequence of } V)$$

$$\frac{\Delta \vdash_{[...a...]} P}{\Delta \vdash_{[...aa...]} P} \quad (view-\text{expansion})$$

$V + V'$ in the rules of $view-$introduction and $view-$elimination denotes the concatenation of V and V'.

The rules for the normal logical connectives and quantifiers are fairly standard. The only points worth remarking on are that the constant c which is introduced in the rule for $\exists-$elimination must not appear in A or in Δ; and that the rule for $\rightarrow$ $-$introduction supports "conditional proofs", in which assumptions are introduced for the sake of convenience and later discharged. The interesting rules are the ones concerned with views.

Recall that we intend to use $P@[A]$ as a translation of "A knows that P". $View-$introduction, then, says that from the viewpoint V you can legitimately infer that P could be inferred on the basis of Δ from the viewpoint V' if Δ does in fact support a proof of P from that viewpoint. In other words, to prove that B knows that A knows P, you have try to prove that A knows P using only things which you know B knows.

$View-$elimination is the rule that enables you to pretend to be someone else. It says that if $P@V'$ is known to someone whose viewpoint is represented by V, then P itself would be known to someone whose viewpoint was represented by $V + V'$. We can thus use it to convert problems about knowledge at the user's viewpoint into straightforward problems of FOPC at some other viewpoint.

Finally, $view-$compression and $view-$expansion capture the properties of knowledge that are usually dealt with using constraints on the accessibility relationship between worlds. Suppose that we have $p@[a, b, c, d]$. This means that A knows that B knows that C knows that D knows P. Given the crucial property of knowledge, that you can't know anything which isn't true, we can infer that A knows P, that A knows that C knows P, that A knows that B knows that D knows P, and so on. $View-$compression enables us to unpack nested statements about knowledge to get at any of the component statements. Similarly, $view-$expansion allows us to infer that A knows that B knows that B knows that C knows P from the fact that A knows that B knows that C knows P, and so on.

We illustrate these rules with some simple proofs.

Example 1: show that if A knows P implies Q, and B knows that A knows P, then A knows Q.

Formally, the problem is to show that $\{(p \rightarrow q)@[a], p@[b, a]\} \vdash_\emptyset q@[a]$. Note that problem as a whole is stated in terms of the empty viewpoint.

Proof:

Let $\Delta = \{(p \rightarrow q)@[a], p@[b, a]\}$.

(1)
$$\frac{\Delta \vdash_\emptyset (p \rightarrow q)@[a]}{\Delta \vdash_{[a]} p \rightarrow q} \quad (view-\text{elimination})$$

(2)
$$\frac{\Delta \vdash_\emptyset p@[b, a]}{\Delta \vdash_{[b,a]} p} \quad (view-\text{elimination})$$

(3)
$$\frac{\Delta \vdash_{[b,a]} p}{\Delta \vdash_{[a]} p} \quad (view-\text{compression})$$

(4)
$$\frac{\Delta \vdash_{[a]} p \rightarrow q \qquad \Delta \vdash_{[a]} p}{\Delta \vdash_{[a]} q} \quad (\rightarrow -\text{elimination})$$

(5)
$$\frac{\Delta \vdash_{[a]} q}{\Delta \vdash_\emptyset q@[a]} \quad (view-\text{introduction})$$

Example 2: show that if A knows P implies Q, and A knows that B knows P, then A knows Q.

Proof: the proof is identical to the proof for Example 1, except that the conclusion of step 2 is $\Delta \vdash_{[a,b]} p \rightarrow q$, from which $view-$compression again leads to $\Delta \vdash_{[a]} p \rightarrow q$.

Example 3: show that if A knows that B knows P then B knows that B knows P.

Proof:

Let $\Delta = \{p@[a, b]\}$.

(1)
$$\frac{\Delta \vdash_\emptyset p@[a, b]}{\Delta \vdash_{[a,b]} p} \quad (view-\text{elimination})$$

(2)
$$\frac{\Delta \vdash_{[a,b]} p}{\Delta \vdash_{[b]} p} \quad (view-\text{compression})$$

(3)
$$\frac{\Delta \vdash_{[b]} p}{\Delta \vdash_{[b,b]} p} \quad (view-\text{expansion})$$

(4)
$$\frac{\Delta \vdash_{[b,b]} p}{\Delta \vdash_\emptyset p@[b, b]} \quad (view-\text{introduction})$$

Example 4: show that if A knows that all cats are animals, and A knows B knows C is a cat, then A knows C is an animal.

Proof:

Let $\Delta = \{(\forall x(cat(x) \rightarrow animal(x)))@[a], cat(c)@[a, b]\}$.

(1)
$$\frac{\Delta \vdash_\emptyset (\forall x(cat(x) \rightarrow animal(x)))@[a]}{\Delta \vdash_{[a]} \forall x(cat(x) \rightarrow animal(x))} \quad (view-\text{elimination})$$

(2)
$$\frac{\Delta \vdash_\emptyset cat(c)@[a, b]}{\Delta \vdash_{[a,b]} cat(c)} \quad (view-\text{elimination})$$

(3)
$$\frac{\Delta \vdash_{[a,b]} cat(c)}{\Delta \vdash_{[a]} cat(c)} \quad (view-\text{compression})$$

(4)
$$\frac{\Delta \vdash_{[a]} \forall x(cat(x) \rightarrow animal(x))}{\Delta \vdash_{[a]} cat(c) \rightarrow animal(c)} \quad (\forall-\text{elimination})$$

(5)
$$\frac{\Delta \vdash_{[a]} cat(c) \qquad \Delta \vdash_{[a]} cat(c) \rightarrow animal(c)}{\Delta \vdash_{[a]} animal(c)} \quad (\rightarrow -\text{elimination})$$

(6)
$$\frac{\Delta \vdash_{[a]} animal(c)}{\Delta \vdash_{\emptyset} animal(c)@[a]} \quad (view\text{--introduction})$$

This example illustrates a point about our interpretation of constants. We take it that all proofs start from the empty viewpoint, and that in all contexts all constants have the denotation that they have at that viewpoint. This leaves us to puzzle over the denotation of constants that are introduced by virtue of one person knowing that someone else knows there is something with a specified property. If we had, for some Δ, that $\Delta \vdash_{\emptyset} (\exists x P(x))@[a]$, then we would be able to obtain $\Delta \vdash_{\emptyset} P(c)$ for some c which did not appear in Δ. What does c denote?

There is a considerable literature on the interpretation of constants with respect to possible worlds semantics—is the domain of all worlds supposed to be fixed, do constants denote the same things in every world, ... We assume here that the domain from which constants are allocated interpretations is the set of objects that the agent constructing the proof knows of. We will not address here the question of how we distinguish between knowing that there is an object with some property and knowing what object it is that has it. We will just note that we do not believe that the difference is captured by asking whether we have a uniquely identifying name for the object in question.

2.6 Correctness

We now have a proof theory and a semantics for our language. We need to know that they correspond correctly to one another—that the proof theory is sound and complete with respect to the semantics. Since the rules of the proof theory were all given relative to one or more viewpoints, we will have to find some way of relativising the semantics to a set of viewpoints. Suppose we had an inference rule that licensed a move from $\Delta \vdash_V P$ to $\Delta \vdash_{V'} P'$. To prove that this rule is sound with respect to our semantics, we want to know that if $proj(V, \Delta) \models P$ then $proj(V', \Delta) \models P'$. In other words, if the information in Δ which is available from the viewpoint represented by V supports P, then the information which is available from the viewpoint represented by V' should support P'.

We will assume that Stegmuller's proof of the soundness and completeness of classical FOPC with respect to the rules (GTS-i)–(GTS-v) can be lifted to the case where inference rules are parameterised by a viewpoint, and will simply consider the rules that deal with viewpoints. The soundness proofs for the rules that deal with viewpoints depend on properties of the projection function $proj$. We will not consider them all in detail. The arguments are all very similar, and we will simply illustrate the general form of the argument by showing that $view$–introduction and $view$–expansion are sound.

Proposition: *view*−introduction is sound.

Proof:

We have to show that if $proj(V + V', \Delta) \models P$ then $proj(V, \Delta) \models P@V'$. The proof is by induction on the length of V'.

(i) Suppose V' is $\emptyset$. Then $V + V'$ is just V, so what we have to show is that if $proj(V, \Delta) \models P$ then $proj(V, \Delta) \models P@\emptyset$. But this is exactly what (GTS-vii) says— that the way to defend $P@\emptyset$ is by defending P itself. So if we know that $proj(V, \Delta)$ supports P, i.e. that it contains whatever is required for defending P, then we know that it also supports $P@\emptyset$.

(ii) Suppose we know that *view*−introduction is sound for all V' such that V' is a sequence $[a_1 \ldots a_n]$ with n less than or equal to N. Suppose that for some viewpoints $[a_1, \ldots, a_m]$ and $[b_1, \ldots, b_N, b_{N+1}]$ we know that $proj([a_1, \ldots, a_m, b_1, \ldots, b_N, b_{N+1}], \Delta) \models P$. Then by the inductive hypothesis we know that $proj([a_1, \ldots, a_m, b_1], \Delta) \models P@[b_2, \ldots, b_N, b_{N+1}]$. Applying the inductive hypothesis again we get $proj([a_1, \ldots, a_m], \Delta) \models (P@[b_2, \ldots, b_N, b_{N+1}]) @ [b_1]$. From (GTS-vi) we see that this will be the case if and only if $proj([b_2, \ldots, b_N, b_{N+1}], proj([b_1], proj(a_1, \ldots, a_m], \Delta))) \models P$. But if we look at the definition of $proj$, we see that $proj(V_1, proj(V_2, \Delta)) = proj(V_2 + V_1, \Delta)$, since $proj(V, \Delta)$ simply takes elements of Δ which have prefixes which cover V and reduces them appropriately. So we have that $proj([b_1, b_2, \ldots, b_N, b_{N+1}], proj([a_1, \ldots, a_m], \Delta)) \models P$, which is exactly what we need in order to conclude that $proj([a_1, \ldots, a_m], \Delta) \models P@[b_1, b_2, \ldots, b_N, b_{N+1}]$ ∎

Proposition: *view*−expansion is sound.

Proof:

Suppose we have that $proj([a_1, \ldots, a_i, a, a_{i+1}, \ldots, a_n], \Delta) \models P$. By (GTS-vi) we know that this will be the case if and only if $proj([a, a_{i+1}, \ldots, a_n], \Delta) \models P@[a_1, \ldots, a_i]$ (*). By (proj-ii), $proj([a, a_{i+1}, \ldots, a_n], \Delta) = proj([a, a, a_{i+1}, \ldots, a_n], \Delta)$, so (*) is equivalent to $proj([a, a, a_{i+1}, \ldots, a_n], \Delta) \models P@[a_1, \ldots, a_i]$. Using (GTS-vi) again, we see that this is equivalent to $proj([a_1, \ldots, a_i, a, a, a_{i+1}, \ldots, a_n], \Delta) \models P$, as required ∎

Both these proofs invoked properties of *proj*. These properties in turn are intended to reflect intuitions about knowledge. The proof that *view*−introduction is sound depended on (proj-iii), which is intended to capture people's ability to carry out defences if they have the required material. To prove that *view*−expansion is sound we used (proj-ii), which is supposed to capture the fact that people are capable of reflecting on their own knowledge, and that everyone knows that everyone else knows the rules of epistemic logic. These properties of *proj* play the same role here as properties of the accessibility relationship do in possible worlds approaches. The difference is that *proj* was introduced explicitly as a direct representation of the effect on one's knowledge of a change of viewpoint. It is therefore easier to see what properties of *proj* are plausible, and to argue about the definition of *proj*, than is the case for the more indirect approach via possible worlds.

The proofs of the soundness of the other rules for dealing with views are very similar. To show that the proof theory is complete with respect to the given semantics, we have to show that whenever $proj([a_1, \ldots, a_n], \Delta) \models P$ is true then so is $\Delta \vdash_{[a_1, \ldots, a_n]} P$. We consider two cases, one where P is of the form $Q@V$ and one where it is not.

(i) Suppose $proj([a_1, \ldots, a_n], \Delta) \models P$, where P is not of the form $Q@V$. By (GTS-vi) we know that P can be defended on the basis of appropriate reductions of those elements of Δ that have appropriate prefixes. So by the completeness of classical FOPC with respect to (GTS-i)–(GTS-v) we know that there is a proof of P from a set of such reduced elements. Any such proof must draw on a finite set $\alpha_1, \ldots, \alpha_k$ of elements of $proj([a_1, \ldots, a_n], \Delta)$. We can use the definition of *proj* to show that for each such α_i we have $\Delta \vdash_{[a_1, \ldots, a_n]} \alpha_i$. We can therefore reconstruct the classical proof on the basis of the α_i using (GTS-i)–(GTS-v).

(ii) We assume that if $proj(V, \Delta) \models P@[a_1, \ldots, a_n]$ then $\Delta \vdash_{V+[a_1, \ldots, a_n]} P$ whenever n is less than some N (part(i) gave us this result for $N = 1$). Suppose we know that $proj(V, \Delta) \models P@[a_1, \ldots, a_N]$. Then (GTS-vi) tells us that $proj(V + [a_1], \Delta) \models P@[a_2, \ldots, a_N]$. From the inductive hypothesis we can infer that $proj(V + [a_1], \Delta) \vdash_{[a_2, \ldots, a_N]} P$. As in case(i) we consider the α_i that are extracted from $proj(V + [a_1], \Delta)$ as the basis of the given proof. Just as before, we know that $proj(V, \Delta) \vdash_{[a_1]} \alpha_i$. If we concatenate these proofs of α_i with the steps that derive P from $proj(V + [a_1], \Delta)$ from the viewpoint $[a_2, \ldots, a_N]$ then we will get a proof of P from $proj(V, \Delta)$ from the viewpoint $[a_1, a_2, \ldots, a_N]$ as required ∎

The notation $P@V$ was convenient for the presentation of the inference rules involving knowledge, and for the proofs that these inference rules corresponded to our intuitions about knowledge. It will be less convenient when we come to develop our analysis of the meanings of English sentences, and we introduce $KNOW(X, P)$ as an alternative to $P@[X]$. We will also need to talk extensively about belief rather than knowledge. The treatment of belief is exactly parallel to that for knowledge, save that we cannot assume that P follows from $BELIEVE(X, P)$ in the way that it followed from $KNOW(X, P)$. This affects both the semantics of belief and its proof theoretic characterisation. The change in the semantics just deletes the third clause from the way we defined it for knowledge, since the third clause was there to capture the fact that anything which is known must be true. The change in the proof theory simply restricts *view*−compression so it only applies in cases where the V' is obtained from V by deleting repeated instances of the same term. In other words, if we have a viewpoint $[a, a, a, b, c, c, a, a, e, e, e]$ then the version of *view*−compression that characterises belief would allow us to replace it by for instance $[a, b, c, a, e]$, but not by $[a, b, e]$.

It would be absurd to pretend that the logic described above is a complete characterisation of knowledge, or that the suggestion that belief is just like knowledge apart from a change in the rule of *view*–compression is an adequate description of the relation between the two. The most we can claim is that we have rules which describe some of the inferences you can make if you do know or believe something. These rules will be adequate for our purposes in Chapters 4, 5 and 6. At the very least they indicate how we can use the freedom we get from PT when we want to talk about propositions as objects. The rules we have just seen depend on our ability to talk about relations between individuals and propositions. Even if the particular rules we have presented are inadequate, or even wrong, we have still illustrated how convenient it is to be able to treat propositions as though they were just things, like anything else.

2.7 Mutual Knowledge

The logic described above helps us describe simple propositions about people's knowledge and belief. If we want to use it for formalising the notion that language use is just another form of rational activity, we will also need to be able to deal with **mutual knowledge**. The need for a treatment of mutual knowledge can be seen very clearly if we consider Appelt's [1985] treatment of language use in terms of AI planning mechanisms. Appelt characterises linguistic actions in terms of their effects on the knowledge of the speaker and hearer. Consider the act of informing someone of something. If A successfully informs B of P, then we can draw a number of conclusions about what A and B each subsequently know. In fact we can infer any conclusion of the form "A knows that B knows that ... that P" or "B knows that A knows that ... that P", where the ... stand for any alternating sequence of "A knows that" and "B knows that". We extend our language with an operator μ for mutual knowledge. The intended reading of $P@[\mu(a, b)]$ is that A and B are mutually aware of P. We can capture this intended reading with the following game-theoretic rule:

> (GTS-viii): you can attack a formula of the form $P@[\mu(a, b)]$ by attacking $P@V$, where V is an arbitrary sequence of a's and b's. The only defence is to defend $P@V$.

The inference rules of *view*–introduction and elimination can clearly be used with statements of this kind. We can therefore reason about what A and B mutually know with the proof theory of Section 3. We need, however, to be able to relate statements about mutual knowledge to more ordinary epistemic statements. We need, for instance, to be able to say that if A and B are mutually aware of P then

A knows that B knows P, and that B knows that A knows that B knows P, and so on. The following rule says that if A and B are mutually aware of P then you can infer all the ordinary epistemic statements involving A, B and P.

$$\frac{\Delta \vdash_{[\mu(a,b)]} P}{\Delta \vdash_V P} \quad (\mu\text{--elimination, } V \text{ is any sequence of } a's \text{ and } b's)$$

The most notable thing about μ--elimination is that there is no corresponding rule of μ--introduction. This is as it should be. A rule of μ--introduction would have to be something like

$$\frac{\Delta \vdash_V P}{\Delta \vdash_{[\mu(a,b)]} P}$$

where V is some finite sequence of a's and b's. The conclusion of this rule could then be used, via μ--elimination, to justify inferring that $\Delta \vdash_{V'} P$, where V' is some arbitrary sequence of a's and b's. We would then be able to do things like inferring that A knows that B knows P from the fact that B knows that A knows P, which we clearly do not want to be able to do.

We see, then, that you can never infer that two people are mutually aware of some fact simply by knowing some finite number of statements to the effect that one of them is aware of the other's awareness of ... The rule of μ--elimination tells you what you can do once you realise that you and someone else are mutually aware of something. No rule of logic can tell you when it is reasonable to suppose that this is the case. The most that you can expect sound rules of inference to do for you is to tell you what would follow if you and someone else did have mutual knowledge of some set of facts. You can, however, never be absolutely sure that you do.

2.8 Intensionality

We are now in a position to deal with statements about people's knowledge of particular propositions. We would like, further, to be able to make statements about their knowledge in general. We would like to be able to deal with statements like "John knows everything that Peter knows", or "The teacher knows everything about geography that any of her students know". We therefore need to extend the rules of the game to deal with objectifications and instantiations. We use the notation of PT for talking about these, and introduce a game theoretic rule to interpret them. This rule looks very much like the axiom TB of PT.

(GTS-ix): you can attack a formula of the form $\pi_i(a_1, \ldots, a_i, \bullet[x_1, \ldots, x_i, F])$ by doubting it. The only defence against such an attack is to claim $F_{a_1/x_1,\ldots,a_i/x_i}$.

We introduce two inference rules that correspond to this semantic rule:

$$\frac{\Delta \vdash_V P}{\Delta \vdash_V \pi_i(a_1, \ldots, a_i, \bullet[x_1, \ldots, x_i, P_{x_1/a_1, \ldots, x_i/a_i}])} \quad (\pi-\text{introduction})$$

$$\frac{\Delta \vdash_V \pi_i(a_1, \ldots, a_i, \bullet[x_1, \ldots, x_i, P])}{\Delta \vdash_V P_{a_1/x_1, \ldots, a_i/x_i}} \quad (\pi-\text{elimination})$$

The substitutions of variables for constants in $\pi-$introduction need not replace every occurrence of the given variable with the constant. $\pi-$introduction would, for instance, sanction the inference of $a \in \bullet[x, x = a]$ from the sentence $a = a$.

This all seems very attractive. We can now say the kinds of thing we want to say, and we seem to have a precise characterisation of what they mean. "Mary knows everything her students know", for instance, would translate to $\forall s \forall x (student(s, m) \rightarrow (\mathcal{T}(x)@[s] \rightarrow \mathcal{T}(x)@[m]))$ — everything which can be defended from the viewpoint of one of Mary's students can be defended from Mary's own viewpoint. Furthermore, we have inference rules which correspond almost exactly to the given semantic rule, so that we can construct proofs about formulae containing abstractions and applications. We know, however, that the situation cannot be as clear as it seems. We have already seen that once we have a language which combines the truth functional operators of classical FOPC with mechanisms for objectification and instantiation we are bound to be able to make seemingly paradoxical statements. Consider again the property R defined as $\bullet[x, x \notin x]$. We have placed no restrictions on the use of objectification which would rule it out. There also seems to be no reason why the formula $R \in R$ should not be well-formed. However, if we expand some of the abbreviations in this formula we see that it is in fact $\pi_1(R, \bullet[x, \neg x \in x])$. By (GTS-ix) this can be defended if and only if $R \notin R$ can be defended — we have a formula which is true if and only if it's false.

This is less problematic within the framework of game theoretic semantics than it is for more classical approaches. We simply note that there are a number of formulae, like $R \in R$, for which neither the formula nor its negation can be defended. One consequence of this is that the law of the excluded middle, $P \vee \neg P$, is no longer generally valid. We can capture the situations in which such problems arise by putting the following general constraint on the conduct of the semantic game:

(GTS-x): you may never claim $\neg P$ in the course of a defence of P (this applies to any P, not just to atomic formulae).

The corresponding change to the proof theory is that no branch of a proof may contain both P and $\neg P$. This is a reasonable enough constraint. The only way you could get both P and $\neg P$ occurring on the same branch of a proof is if your original set of assumptions was inconsistent, in which case any proof based on them will be extremely suspect.

We seem to have found a very easy way out of one of the principal problems of semantic theory. Our semantics validates the Tarski biconditional, $P \leftrightarrow T(\bullet[P])$, for a language which is expressive enough for us to state the paradoxes of self-reference. Furthermore, our proof theory is complete with respect to the semantics. Where did all the problems go?

Game theoretic semantics specifies the interpretation of formulae in terms of moves in the semantic game. It specifies the interpretation of prime formulae only in terms of the willingness of the players to introduce them into a game. They can be introduced at any time by BLACK as challenges, and they can be introduced by either player if they are part of the initial set of hypotheses. There is, however, no explanation of the circumstances in which a formula gets to be one of the initial set of hypotheses, nor of the relationship between such formulae and the world. We have therefore sidestepped the question of how basic predicates should be interpreted, and in particular of whether their denotations should be equated with sets of individuals. This is especially significant for the predicates π_i. We have, in fact, given a semantic rule which characterises the meaning of these predicates, namely (GTS-ix), together with the covering principle expressed in (GTS-x) for the overall conduct of semantic games. By refusing to give an independent description of the sets of N-tuples which are denoted by the predicates π_i we avoid having to answer the questions for which approaches via revision procedures are required. We might say that we have an analysis of the notion of "true for an agent" in terms of the way that agent might conceive of possible refutations; but that we have failed to explain the relationship between "true for an agent" and "true of the world". As far as the use of intensional operators within epistemic logic is concerned, this seems to be a reasonable position to take.

Model revision and game theoretic semantics both provide coherent interpretations for a formal language for describing epistemic and intensional relations. We have dealt with the game theoretic approach at rather greater length since it is less well-known, though a similar approach to semantics in terms of ideal proof procedures has recently emerged in computer science in Girard's [1987] **linear logic**. The game theoretic approach seems to us more appropriate in view of our emphasis on knowledge and belief, with the merits of the two approaches as explanations of the paradoxes fairly evenly balanced. Nonetheless, very little in the remainder of our discussion depends on the choice between the two approaches. What matters is that the notation is available and can be given a sensible interpretation. From now on we will simply use PT as a convenient language for describing semantic commitments, with the reader free to choose how PT itself is to be interpreted.

2.9   Commitments

We now consider the distinction between the presupposition of a commitment and its content. This distinction is motivated by two phenomena. The first of these is the relationship between meaning and use. We are intensely aware that what matters about language is not its relation to the world so much as the way it mediates between the speaker's desires and the hearer's actions. Speakers say things because they want their hearers to do things.

Sometimes, of course, the things they want their hearers to do are primarily concerned with changes in the hearers' view of the world. A domestic science teacher, for instance, might say

(5) *The milk's boiling.*

simply to point out to the students the stage that had been reached during the execution of some recipe. In this case the action that is expected of the students is presumably that they should remember this fact about the situation, possibly correlating it with other things they already know about what has happened previously.

Someone else, however, might utter the same sentence as an invitation to their hearer to remove the milk pan from the cooker. It seems most improbable that (5) means different things in the two different situations. (5) is an expression of the speaker's knowledge of the situation (or at any rate, of their beliefs about the situation). Exactly why a speaker might want someone to become aware of their belief about the milk will indeed change from situation to situation. What is common about all situations in which (5) is uttered is that the speaker wants the hearer to accept that the speaker believes the milk to be boiling. This will be true even if the speaker is lying, and does not actually have this belief. Even then, they do want their hearer to accept that they do have it.

We thus believe that if we are to make any sense of the way people use language to bring about desired situations we must emphasise that what is communicated is beliefs about the world. We further note, however, that the beliefs that get communicated play two different roles. Most utterances convey some belief that the speaker believes the hearer does not have already. It is sometimes difficult to see what new information is being conveyed. Suppose I show you the time of our appointment in my diary and point to my watch, and then say:

(78) *You're late.*

My initial non-linguistic actions should convey to you the fact that I believe you to be late. The utterance thus seems to contain no new information. We will return to cases like this in Chapter 6. For the moment we will simply assume that the meaning of most utterances contains a statement about the speaker's beliefs which they believe the hearer to be unaware of. Our description of semantic content, then, will definitely contain a description of some belief of the speaker.

Some utterances, however, seem to be simply uninterpretable without reference to prior beliefs of the hearer. Consider the difference between the following:

(79) *I know someone who baked a chocolate cake.*

(80) *I know someone who baked the chocolate cake.*

(79) would make sense even if it were uttered, as the first sentence of a conversation, by someone you had never met before and about whom you know nothing. (80), however, would not. You would feel that they were assuming too much about you, and that they ought to have ensured that you knew what chocolate cake they were talking about before telling you (80) (they could tell you by extra-linguistic means, such as pointing at it, but they must be satisfied that you know).

Very much the same happens with anaphoric references. In

(81) *Either Pedro does not own this donkey or Manuel wants it.*

the reference to *this donkey* presupposes that speaker and hearer are already focussing on some particular donkey. It is therefore safe to use *it* to refer to it. In

*(82) *Either Pedro does not own a donkey or Manuel wants it.*

on the other hand, there is nothing to guarantee that there is something for *it* to refer to. If Pedro doesn't own a donkey then it cannot be assumed that there is some salient object for *it* to refer to.

We believe this distinction to be so entrenched that we will build it into our semantic descriptions. We will split descriptions into a content and a presupposition, so that the description of

(83) *Robert baked a cake.*

will look something like:

Presupposition : $\emptyset$

Content : $(\exists x : cake(x))baked(R, x)$

The content in this description is described using a **generalised quantifier**. Rather than just saying that there is some x and stating some facts about it, we have constrained the sort of x we are talking about. The content here should be read as "for some x such that x is a cake, Robert baked x". The use of generalised quantifiers makes no difference to the expressive power of our language, since $(\exists x : P(x))Q(x)$ is exactly equivalent to $\exists x(P(x) \wedge Q(x))$, and $(\forall x : P(x))Q(x)$ is exactly equivalent to $\forall x(P(x) \rightarrow Q(x))$. We introduce them because they can make it easier to express our semantic rules compositionally. We also introduce the notation $(\exists! x : P(x))Q(x))$ as an abbreviation for $(\exists x : P(x))(Q(x) \wedge (\forall y : P(y))(Q(y) \rightarrow y = x)) -$ "$Q(x)$ holds for some unique x such that $P(x)$". None of this new notation requires us to change our semantics at all, since it can all be introduced as abbreviations for things we can already say.

The description of (83)'s commitment contrasts with that for

(84) *Robert baked the cake.*

which will look like:

$Presupposition : \{(\exists!x : cake(x))salient(x)\}$
$Content : baked(R, x)$

The presupposition is what the speaker believes the hearer to know already. The speaker believes that the hearer knows about some cake which is "salient". We will return to the exact form of the presuppositions induced by definite NPs in Chapter 4, but we will not attempt to give a precise characterisation of "salience".

The content is some proposition which the speaker believes, and which they want the hearer to know they believe, namely that Robert baked this salient cake. We could have avoided the split into presupposition and content by making these beliefs explicit, using the predicates *BELIEVE* and *KNOW* to express relationships between individuals and objectified propositions. This would lead to translation of (83) as

$BELIEVE(S, \bullet[(\exists x : cake(x))cooked(R, x)])$

and (84) as

$BELIEVE(S, \bullet[KNOW(H, \bullet[(\exists!x : cake(x))salient(x)])])$
$\wedge\ BELIEVE(S, \bullet[cooked(R, x)])$

We could treat expressions involving presuppositions and contents as though they were just abbreviations for complex expressions about beliefs and knowledge of this kind. We prefer to split them up, since we will want to argue that hearers are actually being invited to do different things with them. In particular, hearers are usually expected to verify the presupposition of an utterance, and then to think of some goal that the speaker might have that would be furthered by getting the hearer to understand its content. We will return to these topics in Chapter 6. At the very least we believe that the distinction helps make descriptions easy to read.

2.10   Discourse Entities

In the discussion of commitments above we skipped over a problem with our analysis of (84). The presupposition is a perfectly acceptable formula of PT. The content, however, contains a free occurrence of the variable x. It is clear that we intend this occurrence of x to denote the salient cake whose existence is entailed by the presupposition, but our semantics for PT does not yet support this interpretation.

The problem here is that natural language sentences generally occur within extended texts. The significance of a particular sentence cannot be fully specified until its textual context is known. Sentences of formal languages such as PT, or indeed FOPC, are generally taken to have a fixed meaning no matter what else is in the surrounding context. If we want to provide formal descriptions of the meanings of natural language texts we need to introduce some way of capturing these contextual effects.

In (84) the problem manifested itself in the interpretation of a single sentence, in terms of a free variable in the content which had some connection with a bound variable in the presupposition. It also frequently shows up in connection with multi-sentence discourses:

(85) *Robert baked a cake. Janice ate it.*
(86) *Wimpey built all these houses. They all have timber frames.*

In each of (85) and (86) the first sentence contains an NP whose contribution to the meaning of the relevant sentence would normally be interpreted via a generalised quantifier, $\exists x : cake(x)$ or $\forall x : (house(x) \wedge salient(x))$. In each case the second sentence contains a pronoun which seems to refer back to the meaning of the NP. We would like to say that the interpretations of the initial sentences place constraints on the discourse situation. We then want to use these constraints in order to interpret the representations of the pronouns in the second sentence of each pair.

We deal with this by altering the basic structure of semantic games. Up till now we have been considering semantic games as attempts to attack or defend some formula on the basis of a set of assumptions. We now alter this so that semantic games are attempts to attack or defend formulae on the basis of a set of assumptions and a set of presuppositions. As before, assumptions are facts which are agreed beforehand by the participants in the game, and which may be used directly as defences against particular kinds of attack. Presuppositions are slightly different. A presupposition will always be a formula of the form $(\exists!x : P(x))Q(x)$. Suppose that at some point in the ordinary conduct of the game there is an attack on a formula which contains a free occurrence of x. Such an attack is only allowed if the set of assumptions contains enough information to justify the assignment of x in such a presupposition.

We will sketch the effect of this on an example before providing the formal details. Suppose we are considering the meaning of the formula $(\exists x : donkey(x))(owns(p, x))$ $\rightarrow beats(y, z)$ in the light of the presuppositions $\{(\exists!y : human(y))(salient(y), (\exists!z : \neg human(z))(salient(z))\}$ and assumptions $\{human(p), (\forall x : donkey(x))\neg human(x)\}$. In other words, we are considering the meaning of the sentence *If Pedro owns a don-*

key he beats it (we will see later how we can derive this as the interpretation of this sentence. For now we just want to see what the interpretation itself says).

The meaning of a formula is taken to be the conduct of an ideal game which starts with an attack on it. The only way to challenge the formula we are looking at is to concede the antecedent and doubt the consequent. Conceding the antecedent forces us to add $donkey(c) \wedge owns(p, c)$ to the set of assumptions, where c is some new constant which denotes the donkey which we have accepted that Pedro owns. The antecedent contains free occurrences of y and z. These can now be replaced by p and c on the basis of information that is now available in the set of assumptions, though the original set of assumptions did not include enough information to fix a value for z.

We formalise this by adapting the rules of the semantic game as follows. Games are now conducted subject to assumptions and presuppositions, where a presupposition is a formula of the form $(\exists!x : P(x))Q(x)$. We have a general rule for eliminating free variables:

Free variable rule:

If a formula containing free variables $x_1, x_2, \ldots$ is to be challenged, then the presuppositions must contain formulae $(\exists!x_1 : P(x_1))Q(x_1), (\exists!x_2 : P'(x_2))Q'(x_2), \ldots$ and the assumptions must support defences of these presuppositions which fix constant values for the x_i. The defence of the given formula should be conducted only after substituting in the appropriate values.

If there are no appropriate presuppositions, or if the assumptions do not support appropriate defences, then the game is ill-formed, and the formula which initiated it is meaningless in the context. Note that the two ways for a game to be ill-formed correspond to the anomalies in the following short discourses.

*(87) *John bought a pear and an apple. Mary ate the peach.*

*(88) *John bought a pear and an apple. Mary ate it.*

(87) seems odd because the discourse does not supply anything at all for *the peach* to refer to; (88) seems odd because the discourse supplies two items that *it* could refer to, so that the assumption of uniqueness fails. We would not want to say that *Mary ate the peach* in (87) and *Mary ate it* in (88) are false. They are inappropriate, anomalous, *ill-formed*. This is what we are trying to capture in the above rule.

The only other change we need to make to our existing rules for the semantic game concerns what happens when a player makes a concession. In (GTS-iv) we stated that $B \rightarrow C$ can be defended against attack by defending C with B added to the set of assumptions. We now refine this by saying that if B is of the form $(\exists x : P(x))Q(x)$ then we should add $P(c) \wedge Q(c)$, for some new constant c, rather than B itself. In other words, if I concede that there is an x with some property then I should be prepared to give it a name which can be used in subsequent debate.

This change may seem rather *ad hoc*, rather directly aimed at the specific phenomenon of anaphoric reference in conditional statements. We cannot completely refute this charge, but we can produce some indirect support for our analysis. Classically, $P \to Q$ and $\neg P \vee Q$ are taken to be entirely equivalent. Natural language usage does not seem to support this equivalence, as we have already seen with the following pair of sentences:

(89) *If Pedro owns a donkey Manuel wants it.*

*(90) *Either Pedro does not own a donkey or Manuel wants it.*

This is now hardly surprising. The game which defines the meaning of (89) involves adding the fact Pedro owns some named donkey to the assumptions that are to be used for defending the conclusion that Manuel wants something. The game which defines the meaning of (90) involves no such concession, and as such the occurrence of the clause *Manuel wants it* in (90) is uninterpretable.

This is less than a complete defence of the adaptation of (GTS-iv). At the very least, however, this adaptation plus the rule for dealing with free variables does give us some precise idea of how to talk about the meanings of sentences like (89) and (90). The complexity of cases like

(91) *I bought an apple and a pear for my friend, who ate the apple but threw the pear away.*

*(92) *I bought an apple and a pear for my friend who ate the apple but threw the pear away.*

suggests very strongly that we should not expect to find simple ways of describing what is going on here.

2.11 Temporal Relations

If we are to provide formal counterparts of the meanings of English phrases, we clearly need to be able to talk about time. We have already seen that PT allows us to talk freely about the truth or falsity of propositions, and that we can treat knowledge and belief in terms of relations between propositions and certain kinds of entities. We can take very much the same approach to temporal relations. We posit that the universe of discourse includes various special objects called instants and intervals. These objects are clearly related to one another in various ways — one instant may be before or after another, two intervals may overlap, or one may be before or after another, an interval may contain an instant, or may begin or end with it, and so on. Numerous authors have attempted to describe these relations by providing them with axiomatisations. People have argued that the set of instants is dense, that there is a mapping from the set of instants into the real numbers, that intervals should be described in terms of open and closed sets of instants, that instants should be described in terms of intersections between intervals. We doubt that there is a single correct picture, believing that different characterisations of these objects will be required for different tasks. The most that we are prepared to do is to posit sets of instants and intervals, with relations such as *BEFORE*, *AFTER*, *INCLUDES* and *OVERLAPS*, but without any commitment to the exact nature of these sets or relations. Readers who want a discussion of the range of options are referred to our overview in [Ramsay 1988], or to the sources of some of the proposals [Allen 1984, McDermott 1982]. For now we will just assume that there are such things as instants and intervals, and that they are related to one another.

The important point for us here is that once we have accepted that there are instants and intervals, then we can wonder about their relationships with other objects. In particular we can wonder about the relationships between temporal objects and propositions. We introduce two predicates, *AT* and *DURING*, with the intention that *AT* should be a relationship between instants and propositions, and *DURING* should be one between intervals and propositions. We will need the following properties of these relationships:

(T-i) *AT* induces a standard internal logic. By this we mean that if A is, say, $B \wedge C$ and t is an instant then $AT(t, \bullet[B \wedge C])$ iff. $AT(t, \bullet[B]) \wedge AT(t, \bullet[C]))$, and likewise for the other connectives of PT.

(T-ii) There is a relationship *CONTAIN* between intervals and instants such that if $CONTAIN(i, t)$ and $DURING(i, P)$ for some interval i, instant t and proposition P then $AT(t, P)$. *CONTAIN* is supposed to correspond to the intuition that intervals are sets of instants. It is clear, however, that this intuition is not very well understood, and that it may not be a single intuition but may instead consist of a cluster of notions to be selected from depending on the nature of the problem at hand. We will not attempt to specify the properties of *CONTAIN* any further — whether each interval *CONTAIN*s a first and a last instant; or whether the set of instants *CONTAIN*ed in an interval should be dense or continuous; or whether intervals are actually sets of instants, so that *CONTAIN* is just another name for membership; or any of the other questions that might be asked about the relationship between intervals and instants. All we need is the simple relation that anything which holds *DURING* an interval holds *AT* every instant it *CONTAIN*s.

We make no apologies for being so uncommitted about the nature of time. All we need for our goal of characterising the logical structure of English is the notion that people's pictures of the world contain temporal objects and well-behaved relations between these and propositions. In view of the lack of agreement about the nature of these objects, we have no wish to go beyond what we actually need.

We now have everything we require for describing commitments. Property theory provides us with a language within which we can talk freely about propositions and properties. The game theoretic interpretation of property theory helped us develop a formal account of knowledge. The supposition that there are temporal objects which can be related to propositions will enable us to deal, to some extent, with the temporal messages carried by tense and aspect markers and time adverbials. The split between presuppositions and contents clarifies the distinction between what a speaker assumes their hearer already knows and what they want them to become aware of. The use of presuppositions for instantiating free variables on the basis of what has been established and conceded during a semantic game gives some idea of how we will talk about the way referential expressions work. The next move is to explain how we will describe syntactic structures, so that we can develop compositional rules which specify the meaning of an utterance in terms of the meanings of its parts.

3 SYNTACTIC FRAMEWORK

The syntactic framework presented in this chapter is fairly orthodox. We are not presenting a new approach to English syntax, and we do not claim that any of our syntactic analyses reveal anything new about the way English is organised. Our main aim in this book is to take a standard set of syntactic rules and explain how the meanings of the structures they describe can be combined in order to generate meanings of complex texts. In order to do this, we need a standard set of syntactic rules; and in order to have a standard set of syntactic rules, we need a language for describing syntactic structures.

There is, of course, no agreed standard set of syntactic rules for English, nor even any agreed language for describing syntactic structures. Since we are not arguing here for any particular syntactic theory, we have taken a very pragmatic approach, borrowing whatever notation and whatever rules we needed in order to present a reasonably concise description of the structure of a reasonable fragment of English grammar. Our presentation will be in terms of a **unification grammar**, with terms and analyses borrowed from a number of such grammars (notably from **generalised phrase structure grammar** (GPSG) [Gazdar et al. 1985], unification catego- rial grammar (UCG) [Calder et al. 1988] and **head-driven phrase structure grammar** (HPSG) [Pollard & Sag 1988]). Our aim is not to supplant or extend any of these theories. We just need a description of a fragment of English grammar which will support our semantic theory. The framework in the present chapter is intended simply to provide the infrastructure for the combined syntactic-semantic analyses in Chapters 4 and 5.

We make the following broad assumptions:

(i) Syntactic structures can be described in terms of bundles of complex features.

(ii) Syntactic regularities can be described by families of phrase structure rules. We specify such families by writing rules involving partial specifications of syntactic structures, possibly supplemented by sets of Boolean combinations of constraints on partial specifications.

(iii) As much information as possible should be associated with word

classes. This includes specifying within the description of a word class
the relation between words of that class and other structures.

3.1 Describing Syntactic Structures

The language we are going to use for describing syntactic structures is a formal
language, just like any other formal language. To use it we need to combine its
expressions in various ways, in order to extract information that is only implicit in
what we have written down. And in order to ensure that what is extracted when
we combine expressions is indeed implicit in what they say, we have to demonstrate
the soundness of the combination rules with respect to some precise semantics.

We assume that the purpose of linguistic descriptions is to allocate words or
groups of words to various classes — to say for instance that there is one class
of item which contains the words *running* and *beaten*, and a different one which
contains the word *he* and the phrase *the old man your sister was talking to*. We
might, for instance, assign the first two to a class of *verbal* items, which we will call
the class V, and the second to a class of *nominal* ones, which we will call the class
N. We will say that the set $\{V, N\}$ is a **(partial) classification**, and we will call
the classes that make up a classification its **partitions**.

We could introduce another classification, into words, incomplete phrases and
phrases. Suppose we call the class of words O, the class of incomplete phrases I
and the class of complete phrases II. We could use the first classification to specify
common properties of, say, items which were members of N — that they need to
be marked as subject or object case, or that they have agreement properties. We
could use the second classification to specify common properties of words — that
they can impose idiosyncratic constraints on properties of items they occur next to,
for instance.

These examples suggest that our main reason for wanting classifications is that
we may be able to assign an item to a specific partition, and then attribute to it
properties that are shared by all members of that partition. We may, however,
sometimes want to combine a collection of classifications. We might perhaps believe
that the two classifications we have sketched above can be combined to give a finer
classification which is useful for various purposes. This finer classification would
correspond roughly to the familiar categories of traditional grammar — a *verb* is
something which is in the partition V of the first classification and the partition
O of the second, whereas an NP is something which is in partition N of the first
and partition II of the second. We will refer to such a grouping of classifications
as a **classification structure**. Classification structures provide different views of
objects, in terms of particular combinations of classifications.

Making this precise will prove surprisingly difficult. Readers who believe they already understand how unification grammar can be used for describing syntactic regularities may like to skip to Section 3.2, where we start developing a specific set of syntactic rules. The remainder of the current section is devoted to investigating the semantics of descriptions. We start by characterising classifications and classification structures slightly more precisely:

(i) A classification C of a set S is a function from S to subsets of S such that if $C(x) \neq C(y)$ then $C(x) \cap C(y) = \emptyset$. If $dom(C) = S$ then C is a complete classification of S, otherwise it is a partial one. The elements of $range(C)$ are its partitions.

(ii) A classification structure is either a classification or an N-tuple of classification structures.

We now introduce a language L_D for describing objects in terms of a set of classifications and classification structures. The definition of L_D is very simple.

(L_D-i) Any lower case alphanumeric string is a **constant** of L_D and any upper case alphabetic string is a **variable** of L_D (we will also refer to variables as **place-holders**).

(L_D-ii) If f and k are constants then $f(k)$ is a **simple description**.

(L_D-iii) If v is a variable then v is a **description**.

(L_D-iii) If c is a constant and $d_1, \ldots d_n$ are descriptions then $c(d_1, \ldots, d_n)$ is a **compound description**.

(L_D-iv) Any constant or description is a **term**.

We intend a simple description like $cat(n)$ to fit an item x if $[\![cat]\!]$ is a classification, $[\![n]\!]$ is one of its partitions, and $[\![cat]\!](x)$ is in fact $[\![n]\!]$. In other words, simple descriptions allocate items to partitions of classifications. A compound description like $major(cat(n), bar(0))$ is supposed to fit x if $[\![major]\!]$ is a classification structure whose components are the classification structures corresponding to cat and bar, and if each of $cat(n)$ and $bar(0)$ fits x. A compound description fits an item if it corresponds to some known grouping of classifications and if each of its elements fits the item. Variables are used to constrain separate elements of a description to be the same. The description $major(cat(X), bar(X))$, for instance, would fit an item x if $[\![cat]\!]$ and $[\![bar]\!]$ assigned the same partition to it (This would never in fact happen for this example, since $[\![cat]\!]$ and $[\![bar]\!]$ do not have any common partitions. We will see situations where it is useful later on).

Given this approach to the interpretation of descriptions, we see that any description determines a set. If D is a description, then its **characteristic set** is defined as $\{x : D \text{ fits } x\}$. We take the characteristic set of a description to be its meaning, so that we will write $[\![D]\!]$ for the characteristic set of D. If D and D' are different descriptions then it is likely that $[\![D]\!]$ and $[\![D']\!]$ will also be different, and may well be disjoint. Thus a set of descriptions may define a classification. In that case, we might have a description $k(d)$ where k denotes a classification and d is itself a compound description rather than just a constant. Since d defines a set, it makes sense to ask whether this set is a partition of the classification denoted by k. $k(d)$ will now fit x if $[\![d]\!]$ is a partition of $[\![k]\!]$ and x is a member of $[\![d]\!]$, just as with ordinary simple descriptions. We might, for instance, partition the set of verbs in terms of the items that they will accept as subjects — that some verbs accept NP's as subjects whereas others accept VP's of various kinds. The description $subj(major(cat(n), bar(2)))$ would fit verbs of the first kind if $subj$ denoted this partition and $major(cat(n), bar(2))$ was a description which picked out NP's.

Allowing descriptions to be used for picking out partitions of basic classifications makes the semantics of L_D considerably more complex. An assignment of partitions, classifications and classification structures to constants and variables of L_D will define a characteristic set for each description of L_D. But such a collection of characteristic sets will induce non-empty characteristic sets for descriptions which initially did not fit anything at all, and this extended collection of characteristic sets will then force extensions, and so on. Our definition of the semantics of L_D will thus require us to construct a series of interpretations, with the final interpretation defined as a limit of this series. We make all this precise as follows:

(i) A model of L_D consists of a set S, a valuation function f and an assignment function g. The valuation function f maps constants of L_D to subsets of S, classifications of S and classification structures for S. The assignment function g maps variables of L_D to subsets of S.

(ii) Given a model $M = \langle S, f, g \rangle$ we define a series of functions $[\![\ldots]\!]_0^M$, $[\![\ldots]\!]_1^M, \ldots$ for assigning characteristic sets to descriptions.

(Level 0) Let x be a member of S, and consider a description $k(d_1, \ldots, d_n)$. We want to specify the circumstances under which x is in $[\![k(d_1, \ldots, d_n)]\!]_0^M$. There are two possibilities.

(0-i) $f(k)$ is a classification. Then x is in $[\![k(d_1, \ldots, d_n)]\!]_0^M$ if (a) n is 1; (b) d_1 is a constant or a variable; (c) if d_1 is a constant then $f(d_1)$ is a partition of $f(k)$, and if it is a variable then $g(d_1)$ is; and (d) x is a member of $f(d_1)$ or $g(d_1)$ as appropriate.

(0-ii) $f(k)$ is a classification structure, say $\langle C_1, \ldots, C_m \rangle$. Then x is in $[\![k(d_1, \ldots, d_n)]\!]_0^M$ if (a) $m = n$; (b) if d_i is a variable then x must be a member of $g(d_i)$; (c) if d_i is not a variable it must be a description, say $k_i(d_{i,1}, \ldots, d_{i,n_i})$. In this case $f(k_i)$ must be C_i and x must be a member of $[\![d_i]\!]_0^M$.

(Level $i+1$) We now define $[\![\ldots]\!]_{i+1}^M$ in terms of $[\![\ldots]\!]_i^M$. The definition is exactly parallel to the one for $[\![\ldots]\!]_0^M$ for the cases that are covered above, with $[\![\ldots]\!]_{i+1}^M$ replacing $[\![\ldots]\!]_0^M$ throughout. (0-i) and (0-ii), however, do not cover what happens if we have a description of the form $k(d)$ where $f(k)$ is a classification and d is a compound description. Under these circumstances we say that x is in $[\![k(d)]\!]_{i+1}^M$ if $[\![d]\!]_i^M$ is a partition of $f(k)$ and x is a member of $[\![d]\!]_i^M$.

(iii) For any description d, if $[\![d]\!]_i^M$ is non-empty then $[\![d]\!]_{i+1}^M = [\![d]\!]_i^M$ (Suppose this is not so. d must in fact be $k(d')$ for some constant k and some compound description d', since the interpretations of all other descriptions are fixed by definition. We take i to be the lowest index for which this equivalence fails for any description, and d' to be such that there is no simpler description for which the equivalence fails at stage i. But $[\![k(d')]\!]_{i+1}^M$ depends entirely on $[\![d']\!]_i^M$, so this must be different from $[\![d']\!]_{i-1}^M$, contradicting the inductive hypothesis). We therefore take $[\![d]\!]^M$ to be $[\![d]\!]_i^M$ for the least i for which $[\![d]\!]_i^M$ is non-empty. If there is no such i then $[\![d]\!]^M$ is $\emptyset$.

The above definitions specify the semantics of L_D. We now develop a proof theory for combining descriptions and show that it corresponds correctly to the semantics. We start by defining a **substitution** σ as a partial function from variables to terms such that no member of $dom(\sigma)$ is a component of a member of $range(\sigma)$. We say that $\sigma_1 \ll \sigma_2$ if (a) $dom(\sigma_1) = dom(\sigma_2)$ and (b) $\sigma_1(v) < \sigma_2(v)$ for the least v such that $\sigma_1(v) \neq \sigma_2(v)$, with variables and terms ordered by the standard lexicographic ordering. If D is a description and σ is a substitution whose domain contains all the variables that appear in D then $\sigma(D)$ is the description you obtain by simultaneously replacing each variable v in D by the term $\sigma(v)$ which σ assigns to it. We will say that a model $\langle S, f, g \rangle$ **respects** a substitution σ if $g(v) = [\![\sigma(v)]\!]^{\langle S, f, g \rangle}$ for every v in $dom(\sigma)$. Respecting a substitution corresponds very closely to making it true, so as usual we write $M \models \sigma$ if M respects σ.

If D_1 and D_2 are descriptions then a **unifier** for them is a substitution σ such that $\sigma(D_1) = \sigma(D_2)$. Two descriptions **unify** if they have a unifier. A unifier is a **most general unifier** (m.g.u.) for D_1, D_2 if it has no subset which is a unifier for them.

If D_1 and D_2 have a unifier then they have an m.g.u.; and if they have an m.g.u. then they have a least$_{\ll}$ m.g.u., since $\ll$ is a bounded linear order on the set of substitutions. We denote this least$_{\ll}$ m.g.u. by $mgu(D_1, D_2)$, and we denote $mgu(D_1, D_2)(D_1)$ by $D_1 \oplus D_2$ if it exists. If D_1 and D_2 do not unify then $D_1 \oplus D_2$ is $\perp$. Note that according to this definition $D_1 \oplus D_2$ may not be identical to $D_2 \oplus D_1$, though D will unify with $D_1 \oplus D_2$ if and only if it unifies with $D_2 \oplus D_1$.

Unification produces one precise description from two more general ones. Suppose D_1 and D_2 are descriptions which have an m.g.u., and that M is a model which respects $mgu(D_1, D_2)$. Then $[[D_1 \oplus D_2]]^M$ is the same as $[[D_1]]^M \cap [[D_2]]^M$.

To see this, suppose that D_1 and D_2 unify, with σ as their m.g.u., that M is a model which respects σ, but that $[[D_1 \oplus D_2]]^M \neq [[D_1]]^M \cap [[D_2]]^M$. Clearly D_1 and D_2 cannot be identical, since if they were then $D_1 \oplus D_2$ would just be D_1. We are therefore only interested in cases where D_1 and D_2 unify but are not identical. We assume without loss of generality that there are no smaller descriptions than D_1 and D_2 which satisfy these conditions (if there are, say D_1' and D_2', then we simply switch the discussion to them instead).

We know that D_1 and D_2 must be $k(d_1, \ldots d_n)$ and $k(d_1', \ldots d_n')$, since otherwise they would not unify. We have just argued that they cannot be identical, so there must be some d_i, d_i' such that $d_i \neq d_i'$. We need to show that $[[d_i \oplus d_i']]^M \neq [[d_i]]^M \cap [[d_i']]^M$, since if all the sub-descriptions of D_1 and D_2 fit the same items then D_1 and D_2 must do as well. We have to consider four cases:

(i) d_i is v and d_i' is v' for some variables v and v'. Then $\sigma(v)$ must be identical to $\sigma(v')$, since otherwise $\sigma(D_1)$ would not be the same as $\sigma(D_2)$, so $[[\sigma(v)]]^M = [[\sigma(v')]]^M$. But since $M \models \sigma$ this leads immediately to the conclusion that $[[v]]^M = [[v']]^M$.

(ii) d_i is v and d_i' is k where v is a variable and k is a constant. Then $\sigma(v)$ must be k, and so again $[[\sigma(v)]]^M = [[k]]^M$, from which the fact that $M \models \sigma$ leads us to $[[v]]^M = [[k]]^M$ (the same argument would apply if d_i was k and d_i' was v).

(iii) d_i is v and d_i' is $k(\delta_1, \ldots, \delta_n)$. We know that $\sigma(v)$ must be the same as $\sigma(k(\delta_1, \ldots, \delta_n))$, which in turn must be $k(\sigma(\delta_1), \ldots \sigma(\delta_n))$. But $\delta_i \oplus \sigma(\delta_i)$ is just $\sigma(\delta_i)$. From this we see that $[[\delta_i]]^M$ is the same as $[[\sigma(\delta_i)]]^M$, since we assumed that D_1 and D_2 were the smallest descriptions which unified but for which $[[D_1 \oplus D_2]]^M \neq [[D_1]]^M \cap [[D_2]]^M$. Thus $[[d'_i]]^M$ is the same as $[[\sigma(v)]]^M$, which is in turn the same as $[[v]]^M$ since $M \models \sigma$.

(iv) d_i and d'_i are $k(\delta_1, \ldots, \delta_n)$ and $k(\delta'_1, \ldots, \delta'_n)$. Then $[[d_i]]^M$ and $[[d'_i]]^M$ must be the same, since they are both smaller than D_1 and D_2 which were assumed to be the smallest descriptions for which $[[D_1]]^M$ and $[[D_2]]^M$ are different.

We thus see that in any case where $D_1 \oplus D_2$ is not the trivial description $\perp$, which does not fit anything, $D_1 \oplus D_2$ describes exactly the objects which are described by each of D_1 and D_2 separately. In other words, unification combines descriptions correctly when it applies. It can happen that D_1 and D_2 fail to unify even if $[[D_1]]^M \cap [[D_2]]^M \neq \emptyset$, so we cannot infer anything from the fact that two descriptions do not unify. In what follows we are interested in the fact that unification is correct as far as it goes. If we have two descriptions that fail to unify, we simply don't use them together.

We will often abuse the notation we have given above by writing descriptions like

$$item(feature_1(\ldots), \ldots, feature_2(\ldots))$$

where the ... stand for arbitrary sequences of unique variables. Such an arbitrary sequence will match any specific sequence of descriptions without adding any information to them. We will frequently use this rather sloppy notation when we know that some object has properties other than the ones we are interested in, but we do not want to list them explicitly. If required we could always explicitly complete the description with appropriate extra variables (and in any concrete implementation we will have to do exactly that).

The discussion above provided a semantics for L_D and showed that unification is an appropriate proof theory for L_D with respect to this semantics. We end this section by using L_D as the basis for a language L_G for talking about grammatical regularities.

We start by relating descriptions to texts. A **text** consists of a word or sequence of words. If w is a word and T is the text $\langle w_1, \ldots, w_n \rangle$ then $w + T$ is the text $\langle w, w_1, \ldots, w_n \rangle$. If T is the text $\langle w_1, \ldots, w_n \rangle$ and T' is the text $\langle w'_1, \ldots, w'_m \rangle$ then $T + T'$ is the text $\langle w_1, \ldots, w_n, w'_1, \ldots, w'_m \rangle$.

We now introduce the idea of a rule. If $D, D_1, \ldots, D_n$ are L_D descriptions then

$$D \longrightarrow D_1, \ldots, D_n$$

is a **rule** of L_G. D is the **goal** or the **left hand side** of this rule, the D_i are its **subgoals** which together make up its **right hand side**. We interpret the rule $D \longrightarrow D_1, \ldots D_n$ as follows. Suppose $T_1, \ldots, T_n$ are texts and σ is a substitution such that T_i is in $[\![\sigma(D_i)]\!]^M$ for each i. Then $D \longrightarrow D_1, \ldots, D_n$ says that the text $T_1 + \ldots + T_n$ is in $[\![\sigma(D)]\!]^M$.

We will need one further extension to L_G. It sometimes happens that we cannot express everything we need in terms of simple identity constraints between variables. This arises when we have a constraint that two features should have the same value, together with some extra information about what that value should be. It also arises where we know that the value of some feature should be drawn from some specified set of possibilities, but we do not know which member of the set is appropriate. In order to deal with these phenomena we add **constraints** to L_G:

(i) If D_1, D_2 are descriptions then $D_1 = D_2$ is an **equation**.

(ii) Any equation is a (simple) constraint. If C_1, C_2 are constraints then $C_1 \wedge C_2$ and $C_1 \vee C_2$ are (compound) constraints. We do not allow the other standard logical connectives to be used for combining constraints.

Suppose M is a model of L_D, i.e. M is an interpretation of the basic symbols of L_D, and consider a simple constraint such as $D_1 = D_2$. We will say that $M \models D_1 = D_2$ if D_1 and D_2 have an m.g.u., say σ, and $M \models \sigma$. This is a very minor extension of L_G. For compound descriptions, we simply say as usual that $M \models C_1 \wedge C_2$ if $M \models C_1$ and $M \models C_2$ and that $M \models C_1 \vee C_2$ if $M \models C_1$ or $M \models C_2$.

We now consider adding constraints to rules. Suppose $D, D_1, \ldots, D_n$ are descriptions, C is a constraint, and M is a model of L_D. Given M, the rule

$$D \longrightarrow D_1, \ldots, D_n$$
$$C$$

says that if $T_1, \ldots T_n$ are texts, σ is a substitution such that T_i is in $[\![\sigma(D_i)]\!]^M$ for each i, and $M \models \sigma(C)$, then $T_1 + \ldots + T_n$ is in $[\![\sigma(D)]\!]^M$. In other words, the constraint adds some information to the rule by imposing extra conditions on the substitution σ which is used to instantiate the general rule in any particular context.

We now have a precise analysis of the semantics of grammar rules, based on the notion that descriptions should be used for classifying sets of items. The grammar formalism we have developed is a subset of Pereira and Warren's [1980] **definite clause grammar** (DCG), which was presented initially as a way of encapsulating syntactic rules in PROLOG. The difference between L_G and DCG is that we have been very restrained in what we allow as constraints. In L_G, the only permitted constraints are equations and positive combinations of equations (i.e. conjunctions and disjunctions). DCG allows arbitrary PROLOG goals as constraints. A consequence of this is that the task of checking whether a text is describable by an unrestricted DCG is undecidable, whereas the same task for L_G is NP-complete [Rounds 88] — bad enough, but better.

If nothing else, our attempt to describe exactly what this formalism means should indicate that using a notation originally developed for one purpose (e.g. as a computationally tractable subset of predicate calculus) in some entirely new context (e.g. for describing syntactic regularities) is not always an entirely straightforward matter. The need for precise semantics for languages which are to be used for describing linguistic objects is highlighted by the problems that can arise if descriptions can make use of default rules. If the description language allows defaults then combination of descriptions may be non-monotonic, with all the problems that are known to be associated with non-monotonic logics [Ginsberg 87]. There have recently been numerous attempts to provide semantics for syntactic descriptions [Ramsay 1990, Gazdar et al. 1988, Rounds 1988]. None of them are any simpler than the analysis we have given above.

We end this section by remarking that various standard parsing algorithms, notably left-corner chart parsing, implement sound, complete, terminating theorem provers for L_G. We will say no more about parsing algorithms. In the remainder of this chapter we will describe a number of syntactic regularities, in order to be able to use them in Chapters 4 and 5 when we show how to construct descriptions of semantic content.

3.2   Common Framework

We assume that all syntactic structures are described in terms of a fixed set of basic classifications and classification structures. We start our presentation of a specific set of grammatical rules for English by setting out this common framework. The most basic division is into syntactic and semantic properties:

$$structure(syntax(\ldots), semantics(\ldots))$$

In other words, the description of a word or group of words contains information about purely syntactic properties and about meaning. We will not be looking at meaning in the current chapter, so the details of the second component of a structure description will always be left unspecified.

The *syntax* element of a descriptor is divided into groups of *major* and *minor* features:

$$structure(syntax(major(\ldots), minor(\ldots)),$$
$$semantics(\ldots))$$

The *major* features specify the structure's general type. We follow the conventions of **X-bar syntax** [Jackendoff 1977] in splitting the *major* features into a basic category and a bar-level. This facilitates making generalisations across categories such as verb, VP and sentence. We do not make extensive use of such generalisations, but they do occasionally make things clearer or more concise.

We illustrate this basic framework by presenting descriptions corresponding to a number of traditional syntactic categories. In particular we will examine descriptions corresponding to the categories *sentence, verb phrase, verb, noun phrase, nominal group* and *word*, starting with *sentences*.

(F1): Sentence
$$structure(syntax(major(cat(v), bar(two)), minor(\ldots))$$
$$semantics(\ldots))$$

This says that a sentence is a verb-like structure (specified by the basic category v) of level *two*. We will use abbreviations to keep our descriptors from getting too unwieldy. As an example, we define S as an abbreviation for $major(cat(v), bar(two))$ as follows:

$$S \stackrel{\text{def}}{=} major(cat(v), bar(two))$$

When we use abbreviations we explicitly mark them with $\#$, so that the description of a sentence using the abbreviation would be

$$structure(syntax(\#S, minor(\ldots)), semantics(\ldots))$$

Our general frame for verb phrases introduces an abbreviation for items whose basic category is v and whose bar level is *one*:

> **(F2): Verb phrase**
>
> $VP \stackrel{\text{def}}{=} major(cat(v), bar(one))$
>
> $structure(syntax(\#VP, minor(\ldots)), semantics(\ldots))$

We are deviating here from the normal X-bar analysis of VP's, under which both VP's and S's are of type $major(cat(v), bar(two))$, with the distinction between them marked in terms of whether or not they have a subject.

The description of verbs introduces an extension to L_G:

> **(F3): Verb**
> $structure(syntax(major(cat(v),$
> $\qquad\qquad\qquad [structure(syntax(\#VP, minor(\ldots)), semantics(\ldots))$
> $\qquad\qquad\qquad \longrightarrow$
> $\qquad\qquad\qquad \ldots]),$
> $\qquad\qquad minor(\ldots))$
> $\qquad semantics(\ldots))$

We have replaced the bar level by a grammatical rule, enclosed within square brackets $[\ldots]$ to help pick it out. The rule in this case says that a verb can be combined with some other structures to make a VP. Exactly what a given form of a given verb can combine with will vary from case to case, so we cannot specify the right hand side of the rule in general. This is information which will have to be derived from specific properties of the verb in question and its inflection. Nonetheless, we know that verbs are words which initiate VP's. We follow here the convention from GPSG that, at least in English, lexical items are always the initial elements of the structures they appear in. This looks as though it is an empirical claim about the nature of English. As far as we are concerned it is simply a technical device. If we found a case where a word appeared to be non-initial we could always explain it away by inventing a new type of structure for it to initialise, and then including this as a non-initial component of the larger structure.

The idea that information about the way words combine with other structures should be included in the description of word classes is familiar from categorial grammar and head-driven grammar. We will see later how specific information about words and their inflections can be combined to fill in the details on skeletal rules like the one in the general description of verbs above.

As far as the semantics of L_G are concerned, we note that a set of rules such as

$D \longrightarrow W, C_1, \ldots, C_n$ can be used to classify lexical items which fit the description W. Each partition of this classification will correspond to a particular **subcategorisation frame** — a particular set of items which can be combined with the given word. Incorporating classifications induced in this way by grammatical rules will require us to adapt our construction of a series of interpretations, since a rule may not initially coincide with a classification. Nonetheless, we can deal with this extension of L_G using much the same kind of fixed point construction as we used for descriptions of the form $k(d)$ where $f(k)$ was a classification but d was a compound description.

The rules that appear inside descriptions of lexical items always specify that the word being described can be combined with various other items to produce some more complex item. We thus have a description of a lexical item which contains a rule which refers to the lexical items itself. Rather than trying to find some way of embedding a description inside itself, we simply omit the first subgoal of the rule, assuming that it corresponds to the word being described. We refer to the lexical item as the *head* of the rule (the head of a rule is usually taken to be that subgoal which has the same basic category as the head and has lower bar level than any other subgoal which also has that basic category. If we assume that lexical items always share the basic category of the goal of their embedded rules, then they must always be the heads of those rules). We will often refer to the subgoals as the **complements** of the word; and we will say that the word **subcategorises** for these complements.

The frames corresponding to noun phrases and nominal groups are fairly simple:

(F4): Noun phrase	**(F5): Nominal group**
$NP \stackrel{\text{def}}{=} major(cat(n), bar(two))$	$NN \stackrel{\text{def}}{=} major(cat(n), bar(one))$
$structure(syntax(\#NP,$ $minor(\ldots)),$ $semantics(\ldots))$	$structure(syntax(\#NN,$ $minor(\ldots)),$ $semantics(\ldots))$

The *minor* features in all these descriptions are split into three groups, *head* features, *foot* features and *local* features. *Head* features are constrained by a convention that says that the goal of a rule must have the same *head* features as the head. This **head feature convention** (HFC) is embodied for lexical items in the following general specification of lexical items:

(F6): Lexical item
$structure(syntax(major(cat(C),$
$[structure(syntax(major(cat(C),\ldots),$
$minor(HEAD,\ldots)),$
$\longrightarrow$
$\ldots]),$
$minor(HEAD,\ldots)),$
$semantics(\ldots))$

This description uses the variables C and $HEAD$ as constraints. The two occurrences of C enforce the rule that the category of the goal is always the same as the category of the head, and the two occurrences of $HEAD$ enforce the HFC.

The behaviour of *foot* features is governed by a slightly more complex principle. The **foot feature principle** (FFP) essentially says that at most one subgoal is allowed to say anything non-trivial about a given *foot* feature. If a subgoal does say something non-trivial about a *foot* feature then the goal must say the same thing. Suppose for instance that we have a feature bundle wh, with two subfeatures qu and rel. wh is intended to indicate whether an NP or a PP contains a WH-word, and if so whether it is the kind of WH-word that marks a relative clause or the kind that marks a question. Thus the following NP's and PP's would have the values indicated for the feature wh:

the man: $wh(qu(-), rel(-))$
I: $wh(qu(-), rel(-))$
which: $wh(qu(+), rel(+))$
which man: $wh(qu(+), rel(-))$
what: $wh(qu(+), rel(-))$
under which: $wh(qu(-), rel(+))$
on which occasion: $wh(qu(+), rel(-))$
the man in which car: $wh(qu(+), rel(-))$
the owner of which: $wh(qu(-), rel(+))$
what owner of which car: ????

The FFP says that at most one subgoal can contribute a value of $+$ for either qu or rel. So in the examples where there is no WH-word the value of wh is $wh(qu(-), rel(-))$; in the examples where there is exactly one, the value of wh for the whole thing is the same as for the relevant word; and the example where there are two seems, at best, very ugly. We follow GPSG in assigning the features wh, *reflexive* and *slash* (which we use for describing **long distance dependencies**) to the bundle of *foot* features.

In terms of the semantics of L_G we read the FFP as another kind of constraint on substitutions. If *FOOT* is a variable denoting the *foot* features of the goal of some rule and $FOOT_1, \ldots, FOOT_n$ denote the *foot* features of n of its subgoals, then the equation $FOOT = FFP(FOOT_1, \ldots, FOOT_n)$ does two things. (i) It enforces the constraint that for each *foot* feature at most one of the $FOOT_i$ has a value other than $-$. (ii) It specifies that the value of each component of *FOOT* itself is $-$ if the value of that component for each of the $FOOT_i$ is $-$, and is the same as the unique value other than $-$ if there is one. These effects of the FFP can easily be accommodated within our semantics for L_G by making an appropriate extension to the semantics of constraints. As far as the proof theory of L_G is concerned, we cannot use the standard unification algorithm for checking the FFP. The necessary adaptation, however, adds nothing to the computational complexity of the process of matching descriptions — in particular we can check equations involving the constraint expressed by the FFP deterministically. We therefore use the FFP freely in descriptions from now on.

Local features are simply idiosyncratic features that obey neither the HFC nor the FFP. The HFC and FFP provide elegant descriptions of the properties of certain features, and we borrow them for dealing with those features. Where they do not fit so well, we simply ignore them and deal with the phenomena as best we can. *Local* features are defined as we need them, so it makes little sense to try to give an overall picture of them.

Head features are divided into three groups: *agr* specifies agreement features like number and person, *nform* specifies properties of the structure under consideration when it is viewed as a noun-like object, and *vform* specifies its properties when it is viewed as a verb-like object. We split *agr* into *first*, *second*, *third* and em count. *First*, *second* and *third* can each have the value *singular* or *plural*, or can be replaced by the null marker $-$. We separate them out since it seems to make it easier to account for the behaviour of the idiosyncratic verb *be*. *Count* distinguishes nouns which denote individuated entities from ones which denote amounts of stuff — *telephone*, for instance, would be specified as having *count*$(+)$, whereas *butter* would be specified as *count*$(-)$.

Nform covers four features. The first two deal with what is generally referred to as **case marking**: is the structure, when viewed as a noun-like object, suitable for use as a subject of a sentence, or as a complement of a verb or preposition or other complement-taking word, or is it marked as being possessive? The third *nform* feature specifies whether the structure is in fact based on a pronoun, and if so what sort of pronoun. The last one is a marker indicating whether or not the structure is suitable as a complement for copula verbs like *be* or *become*. This last marker is a rather *ad hoc* device to account for certain phenomena associated with these verbs, notably the fact that their complements can consist of coordinate groups of structures which seem to be of different types. We will return to this when we deal with the syntax of coordination. For the moment we will simply note that this device, which is again borrowed from GPSG, is difficult to motivate except as a way out of certain technical problems associated with these verbs.

Vform covers three features. The first deals with tense and aspect, dividing verbs into *tensed* and *nonfinite* forms, and dividing these into further sub-divisions. The second specifies the type of the verb's subject, so that we can distinguish between verbs whose subjects must be NP's and ones that accept other kinds of subject. The third distinguishes between active and passive forms.

We thus see that a description of a typical structure will contain a considerable amount of detail. Some of this is specified in terms of the properties of broad classes of structures, particularly lexical classes. Some is specified as idiosyncratic information associated with individual words or components of rules. Some is derived as a consequence of the information associated with particular forms of words, mainly changes to their endings. We consider next the interactions between descriptions of word classes, individual words, and the effects of various inflections.

3.3   Words and Word Classes

3.3.1   Closed class words

We start by considering **closed class** words like determiners and prepositions, since these do not undergo inflections and hence we can ignore the effects of inflections to start with. We start with determiners.

The general frame for determiners is as follows:

(F7): Determiner

$structure(syntax(major(\ldots,$
$\qquad [structure(syntax(\#NP,$
$\qquad\qquad\qquad minor(HEAD,$
$\qquad\qquad\qquad\qquad FOOT,$
$\qquad\qquad\qquad\qquad local(\ldots))),$
$\qquad\qquad semantics(\ldots))$
$\qquad\qquad \longrightarrow$
$\qquad\qquad structure(syntax(HEAD,$
$\qquad\qquad\qquad\qquad minor(\ldots, FOOT_1, \ldots)),$
$\qquad\qquad\qquad semantics(\ldots))]),$
$\qquad minor(\ldots, FOOT_2, local(\ldots))),$
$\qquad semantics(\ldots))$

$FOOT = FFP(FOOT_1, FOOT_2)$

In other words, a determiner is a word which will combine with something or other to make an NP. Since it is a word, we have not specified any information which is common to all words. In order to arrive at a description of any particular determiner, say *the*, we have to combine the properties it has by virtue of being a word, the properties it has by virtue of being a determiner, and any properties that are specific to it as itself. In particular, we do not need to constrain the *head* features of the word itself and the NP it leads to, since the HFC, which holds for all words, will do that (we do, however, have to force the *head* features of the goal — which by the HFC are the same as the *head* features of the determiner — to be the same as those of the single daughter of the rule. This explicit constraint does much the same work as the **control agreement principle** (CAP) in GPSG). Similarly we do not need to specify the *cat* of the word, since we know that what it leads to is an *NP*, i.e. something with $cat(n)$. From this we can infer that the word itself has $cat(n)$, since every word shares its basic type with the object that it leads to. We have, however, specified explicitly how the FFP combines the *foot* features of the determiner and its complement to produce the *foot* features of the NP.

We now consider a specific determiner, say the word *a*:

$structure(syntax(major(\ldots,$
$[\ldots$
$\longrightarrow$
$structure(syntax(\#NN,\ldots), semantics(\ldots))]),$
$minor(head(agr(first(-), second(-), third(singular),$
$count(+)),$
$nform(\ldots),$
$vform(\ldots)),$
$foot(slash(\ldots), wh(-,-), reflexive(\ldots)),$
$\ldots)),$
$semantics(\ldots))$

Combining the idiosyncracies of a with the general properties of determiners would produce:

$structure(syntax(major(cat(n),$
$[structure(syntax(\#NP$
$minor(HEAD, FOOT, local(\ldots))),$
$semantics(\ldots))$
$\longrightarrow$
$structure(syntax(\#NN,$
$minor(HEAD, FOOT_1, \ldots)),$
$semantics(\ldots))]),$
$minor(HEAD, FOOT_2, \ldots)),$
$semantics(\ldots))$

$HEAD = head(agr(first(-), second(-), third(singular), count(+)),$
$nform(\ldots), vform(\ldots)),$

$FOOT_2 = foot(slash(\ldots), wh(-,-), reflexive(\ldots)),$

$FOOT = FFP(FOOT_1, FOOT_2)$

We have had to use more constraints to describe the combination than were present in either of the individual descriptions. In order to accommodate the fact that we know some specific details of $HEAD$ and of $FOOT_2$ we have included constraints on these variables in the combination which are missing from the originals. These extra constraints simply reflect the properties of the m.g.u. of the basic descriptions, and would be implicit in the bindings that would be produced when the basic descriptions were unified.

We now consider a determiner which can occur with a range of complements. *One* can occur just like *a* with an ordinary nominal group, as in *one cat*. It can also occur with a PP whose main preposition is *of* and whose main NP is third person plural, as in *one of the cats*. We can represent this word as follows:

$$
\begin{aligned}
&structure(syntax(major(\dots, \\
&\qquad\qquad\qquad [\dots \longrightarrow COMPLEMENT]) \\
&\qquad\qquad minor(head(agr(first(-), second(-), third(singular), \\
&\qquad\qquad\qquad\qquad\qquad\qquad\qquad count(+)), \\
&\qquad\qquad\qquad nform(\dots), \\
&\qquad\qquad\qquad vform(\dots)), \\
&\qquad\qquad\qquad foot(slash(\dots), wh(-,-), reflexive(\dots)), \\
&\qquad\qquad\qquad local(\dots))), \\
&\qquad semantics(\dots)) \\[4pt]
&COMPLEMENT = structure(syntax(\#NN, \dots), semantics(\dots)) \\
&\vee \, (COMPLEMENT = structure(syntax(\#PP, M), semantics(\dots)) \\
&\quad \wedge \, M = minor(head(agr(\dots, third(plural), \dots), \dots), \dots), \\
&\qquad\qquad foot(\dots), \\
&\qquad\qquad local(ptype(of))
\end{aligned}
$$

We have used a disjunctive constraint here to cope with the ambiguity of the word *one*. We could have simply provided two entirely separate descriptions of the word, one for each of its senses. If we had done so, however, we would have failed to exploit their common elements. The disjunctive constraint enabled us to describe a lexical item with two minor local variants without having to introduce completely separate lexical entries. We will generally use disjunctive descriptions in situations like this, where there are two slightly different ways of looking at the same object and we do not want to repeat the information that is common to both viewpoints.

The above discussion of determiners introduced the notion that we can describe a word by combining a description of the properties it shares with other words of the same general type and a description of its own idiosyncracies. We saw that even for closed class words, the resulting description may be rather complex, and that we may need disjunctive descriptions for words with a range of slightly different senses. We end the discussion of closed class words by considering the other main group of such words, which are fortunately rather easier to describe.

(F8): Preposition

$$PP \overset{\text{def}}{=} major(cat(p), bar(two))$$

$$structure(syntax(major(\ldots,$$
$$[structure(syntax(\#PP,$$
$$minor(\ldots,$$
$$FOOT,$$
$$local(PTYPE))),$$
$$semantics(\ldots))$$
$$\longrightarrow$$
$$COMP]),$$
$$minor(\ldots, FOOT_1, local(PTYPE))),$$
$$semantics(\ldots))$$

$$COMP = structure(syntax(\#NP,$$
$$minor(\ldots, FOOT_2, \ldots)),$$
$$semantics(\ldots))$$

$$FOOT = FFP(FOOT_1, FOOT_2)$$

In other words, a preposition is a word which will combine with an object case NP to make a PP. The *local* features of the PP contain a description of the type of preposition involved. Just as with determiners, the HFC enforces identity between the *head* features of the preposition and the PP by virtue of the fact that the preposition is a word, and the fact that the preposition has $cat(p)$ comes from the general rule that words and the goals of their embedded rules have the same value for cat. And just as with determiners, we have explicitly recorded the way the FFP is to be used. These are common features of all our descriptions of general lexical classes, and we will not remark on them again except in cases where they do not in fact apply.

It is worth noting that the constraint that makes the *head* features of the PP the same as the *head* features of its NP daughter provides the information required by the disjunctive constraint in the lexical entry for *one*. When *one* combines with a PP headed by *of* to produce an NP, the NP embedded inside the PP must be plural — *one of the cats*, but not *one of the cat*. The relevant information is passed up from the NP to the PP via this explicit encoding of the CAP. This opens up the question of whether NP's like *the group* are singular or plural. Some English speakers will accept *one of the group* as an NP. Should they therefore regard

(93) *The first group have completed the course.*

or

(94) *The first group has completed the course.*

as more acceptable?

Specific prepositions then have descriptions like the following description of the word *in*:

$$structure(syntax(\ldots, minor(\ldots, local(ptype(in))), semantics(\ldots))$$

Most descriptions of specific prepositions simply mark the value of *ptype* in this way. We will return to consider the difference between the use of PP's as general modifiers, as in

(95) *There's a can of beer in the fridge.*

and the way they get used for providing subcategorised arguments, as in:

(96) *He made it for his niece.*

For the moment we just note that individual prepositions do not tend to be as idiosyncratic as determiners, so that most of the information is provided in the basic frame. The only thing that distinguishes different prepositions syntactically is the value of *ptype*.

3.3.2 Open class words and their suffixes

Closed class words, then, can be described by combining facts about the class in general with facts about the particular word. For open class words, like nouns, verbs and adjectives, we also have to consider the effects of inflections. Adding an *-s* to the end of a noun, for instance, will change its *agr* feature from singular to plural; adding *-er* to an adjective will change its meaning from a simple attribution to a comparison; adding endings to verbs can have quite substantial effects on their descriptions. We therefore need to combine three things for words that can take inflections — the general properties of the word class, the idiosyncracies of the individual words, and the significance of particular inflections. We will not discuss here the rules which affect the way that particular suffixes change their spelling in different contexts — the fact that adding the suffix *-s* to *tin* produces *tins*, adding it to *box* produces *boxes*, and adding it to *story* produces *stories*, and so on. For practical computer systems for dealing with natural language we need a description of how such spelling changes work, and in this context Koskiennemi's [1985] demonstration that they can be described concisely using **finite state automata** is of considerable interest. For our present purposes, however, the details of what happens to the appearance of a word when a suffix of a particular type is added to it are irrelevant. We will therefore simply assume that a word like *changing* can be seen as a combination of a root form *change* and a suffix *-ing*. What we are concerned with here is the effect of this combination on the syntactic properties of the word (and in Chapter 4, on its semantic properties), not with the appearance of the end result.

We will treat suffixes rather as though they were lexical items. We will describe them by specifying a frame which will contain an embedded rule. This rule will always have a single subgoal, which will be a description of the word the suffix is to be added to. The goal will be a description of the item that results from adding the suffix to the word.

3.3.3 Nouns

We start by considering the kinds of suffix that can be added to nouns. Nouns can have the suffix *-s* added to them, or they can be left unchanged. We will treat unchanged roots as though they had a null suffix -∅ added to them, so that we do not introduce an unhelpful asymmetry. The effect of the suffix -∅ on a noun is to specify its *agr* to be third singular, and the effect of *-s* is to fix this feature to be third plural. We therefore produce the following descriptions of -∅ and *-s* respectively:

(F9): $-\emptyset$ **as a noun suffix (singular)**
$structure(syntax(major(cat(suffix), [NOUN \longrightarrow NOUN]),$
$\qquad\qquad\qquad ...),$
$\qquad\qquad semantics(...))$

$NOUN = structure(syntax(major(cat(n), [... \longrightarrow ...]),$
$\qquad\qquad\qquad\qquad\qquad minor(head(agr(first(-),$
$\qquad\qquad\qquad\qquad\qquad\qquad\qquad\qquad second(-),$
$\qquad\qquad\qquad\qquad\qquad\qquad\qquad\qquad third(singular),$
$\qquad\qquad\qquad\qquad\qquad\qquad\qquad\qquad count(...)),$
$\qquad\qquad\qquad\qquad\qquad\qquad ...), ...)),$
$\qquad\qquad\qquad semantics(...))$

(F10): -*s* as noun suffix (plural, +count)
structure(*syntax*(*major*(*cat*(*suffix*), [*NOUN* —→ *NOUN*]),
                ...),
        semantics(...))

NOUN = *structure*(*syntax*(*major*(*cat*(*n*), [... —→ ...]),
                        minor(*head*(*agr*(*first*(−), *second*(−), *third*(*plural*),
                                count(+)),
                            ...), ...)),
                semantics(...))

The embedded rules specify that we are talking about nouns. The first description specifies that the noun it is describing must be third person singular, and not first or second person, but that nothing else is known about it. The second describes an item which is third person plural, and also notes that the item must be a count noun. In the embedded rules in (F9) and (F10), the goal and subgoal have identical descriptions, with the equation specifying extra detail which is not provided by the description of the root form. The frame for -∅, for instance says that if you combine the suffix -∅ with the root form of a noun you will obtain a noun which has all the properties of the root together with specific agreement features. Most of the suffixes we will look at in this chapter simply add information to the root in this way, but it is not always as simple as this. If it were, we would not need quite such a complex representation for suffixes.

We now introduce the general framework for nouns:

(F11): Noun
structure(*syntax*(*major*(*cat*(*n*),
                    [*structure*(*syntax*(#*NN*, ...), *semantics*(...))
                    —→
                    ...]),
                minor(...)),
            semantics(...))

We have left the right-hand side of the embedded rule unspecified, since some nouns do subcategorise for particular complements (*conversation*, for instance, subcategorises for a PP headed by *with* and another headed by *about*, as in *John's argument with Paddy about the vacant position*). We now consider a couple of specific nouns, *pig* and *pork*. The frame for *pig* is:

$$structure(syntax(major(cat(n),$$
$$[\ldots \longrightarrow \emptyset]),$$
$$minor(head(agr(\ldots, count(+), \ldots), \ldots)),$$
$$semantics(\ldots))$$

The $\emptyset$ on the right-hand side of the embedded rule indicates that *pig* does not require any complements in order to make up an NN. This description can be combined with the general frame for lexical items and the frame for nouns simply by unifying them all together to get a detailed description of the lexical item *pig*:

$$structure(syntax(major(cat(n),$$
$$[structure(\#NN, minor(HEAD, FOOT, \ldots)),$$
$$semantics(\ldots))$$

$$\longrightarrow$$
$$\emptyset]),$$
$$minor(HEAD, FOOT_1, \ldots)),$$
$$semantics(\ldots))$$

$$FOOT = FFP(FOOT_1)$$

We can then combine this with the subgoal of the embedded rule for the suffix -$\emptyset$ to obtain the following description of the goal of this rule, which is what we use as our description of the actual lexical item *pig*-$\emptyset$:

$structure(syntax(major(cat(n),$
$\qquad\qquad\qquad [structure(\#NN, minor(HEAD, FOOT, \ldots)),$
$\qquad\qquad\qquad\qquad\qquad semantics(\ldots))$
$\qquad\qquad\qquad \longrightarrow$
$\qquad\qquad\qquad \emptyset]),$
$\qquad\qquad minor(HEAD, FOOT_1, \ldots)),$
$\qquad semantics(\ldots))$

$HEAD = head(agr(first(-), second(-), third(singular), count(+)), \ldots),$
$FOOT = FFP(FOOT_1)$

Similarly it can be combined with the basic lexical frame, the frame for nouns and the frame for -s to produce the following description of *pig-s*:

$structure(syntax(major(cat(n),$
$\qquad\qquad\qquad [structure(syntax(\#NN, minor(HEAD, FOOT, \ldots)),$
$\qquad\qquad\qquad\qquad\qquad semantics(\ldots))$
$\qquad\qquad\qquad \longrightarrow$
$\qquad\qquad\qquad \emptyset]),$
$\qquad\qquad minor(HEAD, FOOT_1, \ldots)),$
$\qquad semantics(\ldots))$

$HEAD = head(agr(first(-), second(-), third(plural), count(+)), \ldots),$
$FOOT = FFP(FOOT_1)$

The frame for *pork* is:

$structure(syntax(major(cat(n), [\ldots \longrightarrow \emptyset]),$
$\qquad\qquad\qquad minor(head(agr(\ldots, count(-)), \ldots)),$
$\qquad\qquad semantics(\ldots))$

This will combine with the frames for lexical items, nouns and the null suffix to produce:

$$structure(syntax(major(cat(n),$$
$$[structure(\#NN, minor(HEAD, FOOT, \ldots)),$$
$$semantics(\ldots))$$
$$\longrightarrow$$
$$\emptyset]),$$
$$minor(HEAD, FOOT_1, \ldots)),$$
$$semantics(\ldots))$$

$$HEAD = head(agr(first(-), second(-), third(singular), count(-)), \ldots),$$
$$FOOT = FFP(FOOT_1)$$

The presence of $count(-)$ in its agr feature, however, rules out the possibility of combining it with the suffix -s — you can't say *the porks* or *some porks*.

The only other suffix that can be added to a noun is the possessive marker -'s (or just -' if the word being added to has had a plural-marking -s added already, as in *your friends' friends*, or if it is a proper name of Greek or Semitic origin, as in *Moses' beliefs*). The information provided by this suffix is captured in the following frame:

(F12): Possessive marked noun
$$structure(syntax(major(cat(suffix), [NOUN \longrightarrow NOUN]),$$
$$\ldots),$$
$$semantics(\ldots))$$

$$NOUN = structure(syntax(major(cat(n), [\ldots \longrightarrow \ldots]),$$
$$minor(head(\ldots,$$
$$nform(ntype(\ldots), poss(+), \ldots), \ldots),$$
$$\ldots))$$
$$semantics(\ldots))$$

This frame specifies that nouns with a possessive marker have the feature $poss(+)$. We can now extend our simple description of prepositions to rule out NP's with this feature as possible complements:

(F13): Preposition

$PP \overset{\text{def}}{=} major(cat(p), bar(two))$

$structure(syntax(major(\ldots,$
$\qquad\qquad\qquad [structure(syntax(\#PP,$
$\qquad\qquad\qquad\qquad\qquad\qquad minor(HEAD,$
$\qquad\qquad\qquad\qquad\qquad\qquad\qquad FOOT,$
$\qquad\qquad\qquad\qquad\qquad\qquad\qquad local(PTYPE))),$
$\qquad\qquad\qquad\qquad\qquad semantics(\ldots))$
$\qquad\qquad\qquad\qquad \longrightarrow$
$\qquad\qquad\qquad\qquad COMP]),$
$\qquad\qquad\qquad minor(\ldots, FOOT, local(PTYPE))),$
$\qquad\qquad semantics(\ldots))$

$COMP = structure(syntax(\#NP,$
$\qquad\qquad\qquad\qquad minor(HEAD)),$
$\qquad\qquad\qquad\qquad \ldots)),$
$\qquad\qquad semantics(\ldots))$

$HEAD = head(\ldots, nform(\ldots, poss(-), \ldots), \ldots)$

This frame disallows PP's like *in your friend's* where the main NP has a possessive marker, though cases where the possessive NP is functioning as a determiner, such as *in your friend's garden*, are still acceptable.

3.3.4 Adjectives and adverbs

The discussion above indicates that the syntactic effects of adding a suffix to a noun can be dealt with by adding extra frames to be superimposed on the basic form. When we consider other types of word that can have suffixes added to them, we see that the syntactic properties of adjectives and adverbs are unchanged by their standard suffixes *-er* and *-est*. We can therefore deal with their syntactic properties just by combining a basic frame for the class with a frame containing the details of each individual word. We need two frames for adjectives, one for dealing with their usual role as modifier for NN's and one for the kind of NP that can occur as the complement of a copula verb (as in *The sky is blue* or *He got angry*):

(F14): Adjective₁
$structure(syntax(major(\ldots,$
$\qquad\qquad\qquad [structure(syntax(\#NN, MINOR), semantics(\ldots))$
$\qquad\qquad\qquad \longrightarrow$
$\qquad\qquad\qquad structure(syntax(\#NN, MINOR), semantics(\ldots))]),$
$\qquad\qquad \ldots),$
$\qquad\quad semantics(\ldots))$

(F15): Adjective₂
$structure(syntax(major(\ldots,$
$\qquad\qquad\qquad [structure(syntax(\#NP,$
$\qquad\qquad\qquad\qquad\qquad minor(head(agr(\ldots),$
$\qquad\qquad\qquad\qquad\qquad\qquad nform(\ldots, pred(+)),$
$\qquad\qquad\qquad\qquad\qquad\qquad vform(\ldots)),$
$\qquad\qquad\qquad\qquad\qquad\qquad \ldots)),$
$\qquad\qquad\qquad\qquad semantics(\ldots))$
$\qquad\qquad\quad \longrightarrow$
$\qquad\qquad\quad \emptyset]),$
$\qquad\qquad \ldots),$
$\qquad\quad semantics(\ldots))$

Adverbs can occur either before or after almost any verb-based construction:

(97) *Quickly, he removed the pan from the cooker.*
(98) *He quickly removed the pan from the cooker.*
(99) *He removed the pan quickly from the cooker.*
(100) *He removed the pan from the cooker quickly.*

We will provide grammatical rules for dealing with these in Section 5.6. For now we simply provide a lexical frame that wraps adverbs up inside the kind of structure required by the rules in Section 5.6:

> **(F16): Adverb**
> $structure(syntax(major(cat(adv)),$
> $\qquad\qquad\qquad [structure(syntax(major(cat(adv), bar(two)),$
> $\qquad\qquad\qquad\qquad\qquad MINOR),$
> $\qquad\qquad\qquad\qquad semantics(\ldots))$
>
> $\qquad\qquad\qquad \longrightarrow$
>
> $\qquad\qquad\qquad \emptyset]),$
> $\qquad\qquad MINOR),$
> $\qquad semantics(\ldots))$

This frame keeps us within our convention that lexical items always occur as the initial elements of any structures that contain them. It does so rather degenerately, by producing a type of structure whose distribution will exactly coincide with the distribution of adverbs. The existence of frames like this one rather undermines the convention, since it indicates that it has very little real force. The current example is our worst, and is a reflection of the somewhat anomalous behaviour of adverbs. We will see later that the rules that really describe their behaviour are very similar to the rules that describe the behaviour of PP's: it is, indeed, fairly tempting to suggest that adverbs are essentially prepositions with empty complement sets.

3.3.5 Verbs

Adding a suffix to a noun changes its syntax in ways which can be dealt with by superimposing a frame with some extra detail. Adding a suffix to an adjective or an adverb has no effect on the word's syntactic properties. Adding a suffix to a verb, however, is a rather more complicated matter. Consider the forms of the word *walk* in the following sentences:

(101) *She walks to work.*
(102) *She is walking to work.*
(103) *She walked to work.*
(104) *She has walked to work.*

In each of these cases, the form of the verb *walk* says something about when the action happened, and something about the way it is being reported — is it a habitual activity, is it a single completed action, is it a partially completed action, and so on. The details of these facets of the verb's meaning are not fully specified by the appearance of the verb itself. Extra information may be provided by auxiliary verbs, so that *is walking* describes a current incomplete action whereas *was walking* describes a past one. Temporal modifiers can also affect the interpretation, so that

(105) *She walked to work every day for a year.*

uses the form *walked* to refer to a past habitual action, whereas

(106) *She walked to work on Thursday.*

uses the same form to refer to a specific completed action in the past. We thus see that the semantic changes induced by these suffixes may be rather difficult to describe. Their syntactic effects, however, are fairly easy to deal with. We distinguish between *tensed* and *nonfinite* forms; within *tensed* verbs we distinguish between *present* and *past*, within *nonfinite* we distinguish *infinitive, to, participle(present), participle(past)* and *participle(passive)*. These labels provide us with enough information to describe the contexts in which particular forms are acceptable — that

(107) *She is walking.*
(108) *She has walked.*

are acceptable, for instance, while

*(109) *She has walking.*

is not. *Tensed* and *nonfinite* are possible values for *vform*, which is itself a *head* feature. We thus see that VP's and S's will have the same *vform* as their main verb, so that we can use the same information for distinguishing between, say, a verb like *see* which subcategorises for an NP and a VP, where the VP can be either *vform(nonfinite(infinitive))* or *vform(nonfinite(participle(present)))*, and one like *like* which also subcategorises for an NP and a VP, but this time only accepts the VP if it is *vform(nonfinite(participle(present)))* or *vform(nonfinite(to))*.

(110) *I saw her fixing her bike.*
(111) *I saw her fix her bike.*
*(112) *I saw her to fix her bike.*
(113) *I like people scratching my back.*
*(114) *I like people scratch my back.*
(115) *I like people to scratch my back.*

We can associate frames with particular verb suffixes to impose these values of *vform* just as we did for agreement in the case of nouns (and indeed, as we have to for agreement for verbs as well). We will just look at the details of the frames for *-s* and *-ing* — the others are all very similar, and we will leave them to the reader's imagination:

(F17): -s as verb suffix (Third person singular, present tense)
$structure(syntax(major(cat(suffix), [VERB \longrightarrow VERB]),$
$\qquad \ldots),$

$\qquad semantics(\ldots)),$
$VERB = structure(syntax(major(cat(v), [\ldots \longrightarrow \ldots]),$
$\qquad minor(head(agr(first(-), second(-),$
$\qquad third(singular), \ldots),$
$\qquad nform(\ldots),$
$\qquad vform(tensed(present), \ldots),$
$\qquad \ldots),$
$\qquad semantics(\ldots))$

(F18): -ing as verb suffix (Present participle)
$structure(syntax(major(cat(suffix), [VERB \longrightarrow VERB]),$
$\qquad \ldots),$
$\qquad semantics(\ldots)),$

$VERB = structure(syntax(major(cat(v), [\ldots \longrightarrow \ldots]),$
$\qquad minor(head(agr(\ldots),$
$\qquad nform(\ldots),$
$\qquad vform(nonfinite(participle(present))),$
$\qquad \ldots),$
$\qquad \ldots),$
$\qquad semantics(\ldots))$

It is clear that we can combine these with frames which say nothing about *agr* and *vform* in order to obtain the effect generated by adding a suffix to a verb, just as we did for nouns. Unfortunately, the addition of a suffix to a verb can have a rather more dramatic effect on the verb's syntactic properties than we have acknowledged so far. Consider the following:

(116) *He eats the peach.*
(117) *He is eating the peach.*
(118) *He has eaten the peach.*
(119) *He ate the peach.*

In each case there is a subject *He* and an NP complement *the peach*. This is as we would expect from our treatment of lexical items, since we have assumed that somewhere in the description of any lexical item there will be information about its expected complements. This assumption leads us into trouble as soon as we see:

(120) *The peach was eaten.*
(121) *The peach was eaten by him.*

It seems that the addition of the suffix *-en* to *eat* can change it into a verb which subcategorises for a completely different set of complements, either an empty set or a set containing a PP headed by the preposition *by*.

This seems to be a regular pattern for verbs. Almost any verb which has an NP complement has a **passive** form, marked by the addition of either *-ed* or *-en*, which omits the NP and optionally adds a PP. There are verbs which do not passivise in this way:

(122) *He had a new bike.*
(123) *Everyone had a good time.*
*(124) *A new bike was had.*
??? (125) *A good time was had by all.*

Furthermore, the change can affect the form of other subcategorised items:

(111) *I saw her fix her bike.*
(126) *She was seen to fix her bike.*

Nonetheless, there does seem to be a regular pattern, even if it is not quite as regular as it might initially appear. There are a number of other similar phenomena. **Dative movement**, for instance, refers to the fact that verbs which subcategorise for a PP and an NP also generally have a form in which they subcategorise for two NP's:

(127) *John gave a book to Mary.*
(128) *John gave Mary a book.*
(129) *He made a toy boat for his niece.*
(130) *He made his niece a toy boat.*

Verbs which normally subcategorise for an NP and a VP can often drop the NP. The exact details of how this works can vary from verb to verb. We will concentrate on the behaviour of verbs like *want*:

(131) *I want you to mow the lawn.*
(132) *I want to mow the lawn.*

This phenomenon is much more idiosyncratic than the others. *Like*, for instance, exhibits it but *see* does not:

(133) *I like people scratching my back.*
(134) *I like scratching other people's backs.*
(135) *I saw her fixing her bike.*
*(136) *I saw fixing her bike.*

It is also closely connected with the acceptability of reflexive pronouns:

(137) *I saw myself fixing her bike.*
*(138) *I like myself scratching other people's backs.*

Phenomena of this kind have, of course, been at the centre of grammatical debate since Chomsky (1957) first introduced the idea of transformations. All existing treatments, from **transformations** to **metarules**, depend on the notion that a given verb has a "normal" subcategorisation frame, which can be changed under certain circumstances. It is hard, indeed, to see how else to explain these phenomena. We use the fact that suffixes can generate new descriptions of lexical items on the basis of the description of their root, and these new descriptions will contain embedded rules, to deal with them. We will illustrate this with a description of the word *prove* and with two alternative frames for the suffix *-ed*:

(F19): Lexical entry for *prove*
$structure(syntax(major(\ldots, [\ldots \longrightarrow COMP]),$
$\qquad\qquad\quad minor(head(\ldots,$
$\qquad\qquad\qquad\qquad\qquad vform(\ldots, subject(SUBJ), \ldots),$
$\qquad\qquad\qquad\quad foot(\ldots),$
$\qquad\qquad\qquad\quad local(\ldots))),$
$\qquad\quad semantics(\ldots))$

$COMP = structure(syntax(\#NP, minor(\ldots)), semantics(\ldots))$
$SUBJ = structure(syntax(\#NP, minor(\ldots)), semantics(\ldots))$

(F20): *-ed* **as verb suffix (past tense)**
$structure(syntax(major(cat(suffix), [VERB \longrightarrow VERB]),$
$\qquad\qquad ...),$
$\qquad\qquad semantics(...))$

$VERB = structure(syntax(major(cat(v),$
$\qquad\qquad\qquad\qquad\qquad\qquad [... \longrightarrow COMP]),$
$\qquad\qquad\qquad\qquad\quad minor(head(agr(...),$
$\qquad\qquad\qquad\qquad\qquad\qquad\quad nform(...),$
$\qquad\qquad\qquad\qquad\qquad\qquad\quad vform(tensed(past),$
$\qquad\qquad\qquad\qquad\qquad\qquad\qquad\qquad subject(SUBJ), ...)),$
$\qquad\qquad\qquad\qquad\qquad\quad foot(...),$
$\qquad\qquad\qquad\qquad\qquad\quad local(...))),$
$\qquad\qquad\qquad semantics(...))$

(F21): *-ed* **as verb suffix (passive, without PP)**
$structure(syntax(major(cat(suffix), [VERB_1 \longrightarrow VERB_2]),$
$\qquad\qquad ...),$
$\qquad\qquad semantics(...))$

$VERB_1 = structure(syntax(major(cat(v),$
$\qquad\qquad\qquad\qquad\qquad\qquad\quad [... \longrightarrow COMP]),$
$\qquad\qquad\qquad\qquad MINOR),$
$\qquad\qquad\qquad\quad semantics(...))$
$VERB_2 = structure(syntax(major(cat(v),$
$\qquad\qquad\qquad\qquad\qquad\qquad\quad [... \longrightarrow ARG_1, COMP]),$
$\qquad\qquad\qquad\qquad MINOR),$
$\qquad\qquad\qquad\quad semantics(...))$
$MINOR = minor(head(agr(...),$
$\qquad\qquad\qquad\quad nform(...),$
$\qquad\qquad\qquad\quad vform(nonfinite(participle(passive))), ...),$
$\qquad\qquad\quad foot(...),$
$\qquad\qquad\quad local(...))$

The embedded rule for *prove* specifies that it normally requires an NP as its subject, and that its normal complement consists of an NP followed by nothing. The past tense frame says that the subject and complement of a past tense form are exactly as given for the root form. The passive frame says that a verb which specifies locally that it requires a complement consisting of an NP and something else will have a passive form whose subject is the initial NP from the local complement, and whose complement is whatever is left. If we combine the entry for *prove*, the general frame for lexical items, the general frame for verbs and the passive frame we will get:

$$
\begin{aligned}
&structure(syntax(major(cat(v), \\
&\qquad\qquad\qquad [structure(syntax(\#VP, minor(HEAD, FOOT, \ldots)) \\
&\qquad\qquad\qquad\qquad semantics(\ldots)) \\
&\qquad\qquad\qquad \longrightarrow \\
&\qquad\qquad\qquad \emptyset]), \\
&\qquad\qquad minor(HEAD, FOOT_1, local(\ldots)))), \\
&\qquad semantics(\ldots)) \\
\\
&NP = structure(syntax(\#NP, \ldots), semantics(\ldots)) \\
&HEAD = head(agr(\ldots), \\
&\qquad\qquad nform(\ldots), \\
&\qquad\qquad vform(nonfinite(participle(passive)), subject(NP), \ldots)) \\
&FOOT = FFP(FOOT_1)
\end{aligned}
$$

In other words, *proved* can be seen as a passive participle which has an empty set of complements, and whose subject is expected to be an NP.

The passive frame given above only deals with cases where the initial element of the local complement is taken as the subject, and the local subject is ignored. We can extend this frame so that it deals with cases where the local subject is dealt with by adding a PP headed by *by* to the complement as follows:

(F22): *-ed* **as verb suffix (passive, with PP)**

$structure(syntax(major(cat(suffix), [VERB_1 \longrightarrow VERB_2]),$
$\qquad \ldots),$
$\qquad\qquad semantics(\ldots))$

$VERB_1 = structure(syntax(major(cat(v),$
$\qquad\qquad\qquad\qquad\qquad\qquad [\ldots \longrightarrow COMP, PP]),$
$\qquad\qquad\qquad\qquad MINOR),$
$\qquad\qquad\qquad\qquad semantics(\ldots))$
$VERB_2 = structure(syntax(major(cat(v),$
$\qquad\qquad\qquad\qquad\qquad\qquad [\ldots \longrightarrow ARG_1, COMP]),$
$\qquad\qquad\qquad\qquad MINOR),$
$\qquad\qquad\qquad\qquad semantics(\ldots))$
$MINOR = minor(head(agr(\ldots),$
$\qquad\qquad\qquad nform(\ldots),$
$\qquad\qquad\qquad vform(nonfinite(participle(passive))), \ldots),$
$\qquad\qquad foot(\ldots),$
$\qquad\qquad local(\ldots))$
$PP = structure(syntax(\#PP,$
$\qquad\qquad\qquad minor(\ldots, local(ptype(by)))),$
$\qquad\qquad semantics(\ldots))$

We will not elaborate the further refinements that are required to develop a frame which will account for examples like (126). The two remaining points we want to make about these examples concern the *subject* component of the *vform* group of features, and the relation between passive forms and other alternative subcategorisation phenomena we have mentioned.

We note that some verbs accept S's and VP's as subjects whereas others do not:

(139) *That all the students passed their exam surprised the teacher.*
(140) *Eating bread before it is cool gives you tummy ache.*
*(141) *Being happy sleeps well.*

This seems to be local information about particular verbs. Its consequences, however, only show up when an NP is proposed as the subject of a VP. By specifying that it should be a *head* feature we can ensure that VP's have the correct value for *subject*, so that everything will work out right.

Or will it? Consider auxiliary and modal verbs like *is, have* and *will.* In many ways these behave just like ordinary verbs. In particular they subcategorise for specific complements — *is*, for instance, subcategorises for a VP with *vform* specified as either *nonfinite(participle(present)), ...)* or *nonfinite(participle(passive)), ...)*. However they do not impose particular constraints on their subjects. Instead they impose whatever constraint the main verb of their complement imposes, so that we get:

(142) *Eating bread before it is cool will give you tummy ache.*
*(143) *Being happy will sleep well.*

We therefore need frames like the following:

(F23): Auxiliary and modal
$structure(syntax(major(cat(v), [... \longrightarrow COMP])$
$\qquad\qquad minor(head(..., vform(..., subject(SUBJ), inv(+), ...)),$
$\qquad\qquad\qquad foot(...),$
$\qquad\qquad\qquad local(...))),$
$\qquad\quad semantics(...))$

$COMP = structure(syntax(\# VP,$
$\qquad\qquad\qquad minor(head(...,$
$\qquad\qquad\qquad\qquad\qquad vform(..., subject(SUBJ), inv(+),$
$\qquad\qquad\qquad\qquad\qquad\qquad\qquad ...)),$
$\qquad\qquad\qquad\qquad foot(...),$
$\qquad\qquad\qquad\qquad local(...))),$
$\qquad\qquad semantics(...))$

This says that for these verbs the local specification of the subject is the same as that for the subject of the complement, which is required to be a VP. We can add this to specific descriptions of individual words, which will specify for instance that the main verb of the complement of *be* must be either a present participle or a passive one, and combine the result of doing this with the usual frames for lexical items, verbs, and specific endings to get complete descriptions of the syntactic properties of auxilary and modal verbs.

We end our discussion of verb subcategorisations by considering the relation between the forms induced by specific endings and the general alternative forms allowed for particular types of words. Consider the verb *given*, for instance. This can be either a past participle or a passive participle. When we consider it as a past participle, we see that it can appear with either two NP's or an NP and a PP(*to*):

(144) *He has given everything he owns to the dogs' home.*

(145) *He has given the dogs' home everything he owns.*

Each of these has an NP as its first complement. Should they both have passive forms?

(146) *Everything he owns was given to the dogs' home.*
(147) *The dogs' home was given everything he owns.*

These are both acceptable. It seems as though you can combine the extra subcategorisations permitted for verbs with (NP, PP) complements with the ones induced by passive forms. This has consequences for the way we think about the frames we have introduced for these phenomena. Our analysis of passives depends on our having two descriptions of the complement of any given verb: a local one and one which is derived from it by the passive frame and which appears in the embedded rule for the word. If we were to try to use the same mechanism for dealing with datives we would need three such descriptions — a local one, one to embody the effect of the dative frame on this one, and another to embody the effect of the passivising suffix. We prefer to suggest that words may have systematically related sets of local subcategorisation frames, using specifications like the following:

(F24): Ditransitive verb (*give, tell, ...*)

$ditransitive(FRAME, PREP) \overset{\text{def}}{=}$
$\quad\quad (FRAME = (structure(syntax(\#NP, minor(\ldots)),$
$\quad\quad\quad\quad\quad\quad\quad\quad\quad semantics(\ldots)),$
$\quad\quad\quad\quad\quad\quad structure(syntax(\#PP,$
$\quad\quad\quad\quad\quad\quad\quad\quad\quad minor(\ldots,$
$\quad\quad\quad\quad\quad\quad\quad\quad\quad\quad\quad local(ptype(PREP))),$
$\quad\quad\quad\quad\quad\quad\quad\quad semantics(\ldots)))$
$\quad\quad \lor (FRAME = (structure(syntax(\#NP, minor(\ldots)),$
$\quad\quad\quad\quad\quad\quad\quad\quad\quad semantics(\ldots)),$
$\quad\quad\quad\quad\quad\quad structure(syntax(\#NP, minor(\ldots)),$
$\quad\quad\quad\quad\quad\quad\quad\quad semantics(\ldots)))$

$structure(syntax(major(cat(v)), [\ldots \longrightarrow COMP]),$
$\quad\quad\quad\quad minor(\ldots)),$
$\quad\quad\quad semantics(\ldots))$

$\#ditransitive(COMP, to)$

This frame captures the syntactic properties of a word like *give*. It says that the local specification of the expected arguments provides a choice of either an NP plus a PP headed by *to*, or two NP's. This is a very common pattern, and numerous other verbs will have specifications which employ the abbreviation *ditransitive*, with a variety of different prepositions (the frame for *make*, for instance, would specify that the required preposition was *for*). We can provide similar disjunctive descriptions for other phenomena of this kind:

(F25): "Subject control"

$$scontrol(FRAME, VFORM) \overset{\text{def}}{=}$$
$$(FRAME = structure(syntax(\#NP,$$
$$minor(\ldots),$$
$$foot(\ldots, reflexive(-)),$$
$$local(\ldots))),$$
$$semantics(\ldots)),$$
$$structure(syntax(\#VP,$$
$$minor(head(\ldots, VFORM, \ldots), \ldots)),$$
$$semantics(\ldots)))$$
$$\lor (FRAME = structure(syntax(\#VP,$$
$$minor(head(\ldots, VFORM, \ldots), \ldots)),$$
$$semantics(\ldots)))$$

$$structure(syntax(major(cat(v), [\ldots \longrightarrow COMP]),$$
$$minor(\ldots)),$$
$$semantics(\ldots))$$

$$\#scontrol(COMP, vform(nonfinite(NF), \ldots))$$
$$\land (NF = to \lor NF = participle(present))$$

The definition of *scontrol* specifies that the complement of any verb to which it applies must be either an NP followed by a VP, in which the NP must not have a reflexive marker, or just a VP. The detailed structure which follows would then describe the syntactic properties of *like*, which has exactly this subcategorisation frame where the main verb of the VP must be either a *to*-form or a present participle. The presence of the restriction that the NP, if it is present, must not have a reflexive marker, rules out cases like:

*(148) *I like myself scratching other people's backs.*

We have described families of verbs which have the same disjunctive characterisations of their local embedded rules, and we have specified the effects that verb suffixes have on the embedded rule for a word. There is a clear distinction between the two types of phenomenon. One deals with properties of groups of verbs, the other with the effects of suffixes. In making this distinction we have followed a line of argument proposed within **lexical functional grammar** [Bresnan & Kaplan 1982]. It is worth noting that this treatment does not commit us to a specific order for applying frames. In particular, the combination of the disjunction in the definition of *ditransitive* and the disjunction in our second frame for passives will permit each of the following:

(149) *Everything he had owned was given to the dog's home.*
(150) *The dog's home was given everything he had owned.*
(151) *Everything he had owned was given to the dog's home by his executors.*
(152) *The dog's home was given everything he had owned by his executors.*

We note one final lexical frame. We have dealt with auxiliaries and modal verbs on the assumption that they are just like ordinary verbs, apart from the fact that the constraints they impose on their subjects are derived from their complement VP's. They do, however, also have an entirely different subcategorisation frame:

(153) *Is John writing a book?*
(154) *Have you finished using that terminal?*
(155) *Will she be in the office this afternoon?*

We suggest that the frames for suffixes which produce tensed versions of such verbs should include options which will unify with the following:

(F26): ∅ **as suffix for modal or auxiliary ("aux-inversion")**

$structure(syntax(major(cat(suffix), [VERB_1 \longrightarrow VERB_2]),$
$minor(\ldots)),$
$semantics(\ldots))$

$VERB_1 = structure(syntax(major(cat(v),$
$[structure(syntax(\#S, MINOR),$
$semantics(\ldots))$

$\longrightarrow$

$SUBJ,$
$COMP])),$
$minor(\ldots))),$
$semantics(\ldots))$

$VERB_2 = structure(syntax(major(cat(v),$
$[structure(syntax(\#VP, MINOR),$
$semantics(\ldots))$

$\longrightarrow$

$COMP])),$
$minor(head(\ldots, vform(\ldots, subject(SUBJ), \ldots)),$
$FOOT_1,$
$local(\ldots))),$
$semantics(\ldots))$

$MINOR = minor(HEAD, FOOT, local(mood(query(polar))))),$
$HEAD = head(\ldots, vform(tensed(\ldots), \ldots, inv(+), \ldots))$
$SUBJ = structure(syntax(\ldots,$
$minor(head(\ldots, nform(ntype(nom), \ldots), \ldots),$
$FOOT_2,$
$\ldots))$
$semantics(\ldots))$
$COMP = structure(syntax(\ldots, minor(\ldots, FOOT_3, \ldots)$
$semantics(\ldots))$
$FOOT = FFP(FOOT_1, FOOT_2, FOOT_3)$

This frame requires the verb to be tensed, so that we do not allow:

*(156) *Be John writing a book?*

The verb also must have the value $vform(\ldots, inv(+), \ldots)$, thus ruling out:

*(157) *Writes John a book?*

It is interesting to note here that the verbs *be* and *have*, which can be either auxiliaries or transitive verbs, are invertible in both cases; but that *do*, which can also
have a transitive-like reading, can only be inverted when functioning as a modal:

(158) *Is John writing a book?*
(159) *Is John an author?*
(160) *Have you made any croissants today?*
(161) *Have you any croissants?*
(162) *Did John write a book?*
*(163) *Did John it?*

A very similar frame would also allow us to describe the structure of imperative
sentences, where the subject is omitted and the verb is required to be of the form
vform(nonfinite(infinitive), ...). We will not present this frame here, since it can
easily be obtained by adapting (F26).

There are a number of other lexical frames, mainly for words like proper names and
pronouns which can constitute entire NP's by themselves. The syntactic properties
of these words are comparatively uninteresting, and we leave them to Chapter 4
where we will consider their syntactic properties at the same time as their semantic
ones.

The frames we have developed so far enable us to describe the properties of individual words in considerable detail. Since they include embedded rules, they contain
much of the information we require in order to explain how words get grouped together to form larger structures. We cannot, however, easily describe the whole of
English grammar using these very local rules. In addition to the local rules embedded within the descriptions of individual words we need global grammar rules.

3.4   Grammar Rules

The main difference between global rules and the embedded rules that occur inside
lexical frames is that global rules do not have an implicit head as the first subgoal.
Indeed the notion of head becomes somewhat obscure when we come to the rules
describing coordination, since in these rules there is no unique subgoal which has the
same category as the goal of the rule and lower bar level than any other subgoal with
this category. We therefore no longer rely on the general HFC to enforce identity
between head features on the goal and the head. Instead we mark it explicitly, via a
place holder. Most of the time the effect is the same as the effect of the HFC would
have been, but we avoid the problems that are introduced if we try to apply the
HFC throughout the grammar, at the cost of making fewer empirical claims about
the nature of natural language syntax.

3.4.1 Sentences

We start with a rule for sentences. This rule says that a sentence is made up of a VP preceded by whatever kind of structure the main verb of the VP accepts as its subject.

(R1): Sentence
$[structure(syntax(\#S, minor(HEAD, FOOT, local(mood(declarative), \ldots)))),$
$\qquad semantics(\ldots))$

$\longrightarrow$

$SUBJECT,$
$structure(syntax(\#VP, minor(HEAD, FOOT_1, \ldots)), semantics(\ldots))]$

$HEAD = head(agr(AGREE),$
$\qquad\qquad \ldots,$
$\qquad\qquad\quad vform(tensed(\ldots), \ldots, subject(SUBJECT), \ldots))$
$SUBJECT = structure(syntax(\ldots,$
$\qquad\qquad\qquad\qquad minor(head(agr(AGREE),$
$\qquad\qquad\qquad\qquad\qquad\qquad nform(ntype(nom), \ldots), \ldots),$
$\qquad\qquad\qquad\qquad\quad FOOT_2,$
$\qquad\qquad\qquad\qquad\quad \ldots))$
$\qquad\qquad\qquad semantics(\ldots))$
$FOOT = FFP(FOOT_1, FOOT_2)$

Most of this rule is fairly self-explanatory. It is worth noting the extra information within the specification of *HEAD* which is used for enforcing agreement between the subject and the main verb of the VP. The fact that we also use the specification of the *subject* within *HEAD* in order to enforce the VP's requirements is also of interest.

The main new feature of this rule, however, is buried in the requirement that the subject have the feature *nform(ntype(nom), ...)*. This looks very uncontroversial. We want to ensure that

(164) *I am tired.*

is accepted by our grammar, but

*(165) *Me am tired.*

is ruled out, and the only way we can do this is via some sort of case marker. We also, however, need to permit

(166) *The exercise made me tired.*

while ruling out:

*(167) *The exercise made I tired.*

It turns out that the only place where NP's are expected to have the feature *nform(ntype(nom), ...)* is when they appear as subjects. In all other contexts they must have *nform(ntype(acc), ...)* instead. Rather than specify this everywhere that it is required, we introduce a **default**:

$$
\begin{aligned}
&default(structure(syntax(\ldots, \\
&\qquad\qquad\qquad minor(head(\ldots, nform(ntype(acc),\ldots),\ldots),\ldots), \\
&\qquad\qquad\qquad\ldots)), \\
&\qquad\quad semantics(\ldots))
\end{aligned}
$$

The use of defaults in grammatical formalisms has led to a great deal of debate and controversy. We recognise that the use of defaults in general leads to the need for a semantics for non-monotonic inference, and thereby to a great deal of confusion. We therefore interpret defaults in the simplest way possible. We view defaults as ways of adding information to the items on the right hand sides of grammatical rules (this applies to the embedded rules that occur within descriptions of lexical items as well as to the rules of the current section). The default given above, for instance, says that structures should be required to fit the given pattern if this requirement does not clash with any non-default requirements. In our rule for sentences, the requirement embodied in the default does clash with the concrete information that the subject is required to have the feature *nform(ntype(nom),...)*. In this case, then, the default is overruled. This and the frame given above for polar questions are the only places where we say anything about this feature. The default is therefore compatible with the descriptions of all the subgoals in other rules in our grammar, so the requirement that it embodies is always added to all other specifications of subgoals.

Our interpretation of defaults, then, is that they add information to subgoals so long as they are compatible with them. They are essentially a means of expanding underspecified rules, in order to save us the effort of repeating some very common constraint or set of constraints. They are not claims about general properties of English grammar, nor are they inference rules which can be used during syntactic processing in order to fill in missing detail. We could eliminate them completely by inspecting our rules to see if the information embodied in the defaults is compatible with their subgoals, and adding it if it is. We therefore avoid the problems normally associated with defaults in their role as "common sense". Nonetheless, even with our simple view of them we will see that there are problems, in particular when we come to consider coordination.

3.4.2 Complex NP's

We have seen that determiners initiate NP's. There are a number of other ways for NP's to be built. In particular, it is not always essential to have a determiner, and it may happen that the NP includes some kind of modifier such as a relative clause or a PP. We consider first some rules for building NP's either with no determiners or with possessive NP's as determiners:

(R2): NP without determiner
$[structure(syntax(\#NP, MINOR)$
$\qquad semantics(\ldots))$
$\longrightarrow$
$structure(syntax(\#NN, MINOR),$
$\qquad semantics(\ldots))]$

$(MINOR = minor(head(agr(\ldots, THIRD, COUNT), \ldots), \ldots)$
$\qquad \wedge (THIRD = third(plural) \vee COUNT = count(-)))$

This rule legitimates NP's like *figs* and *music* in

(168) *My father used to try to grow figs.*
(169) *I always listen to music when I need to unwind.*

without allowing *fig* by itself as one:

*(170) *His tree never produced fig in all the time he tried.*

(R3): NP with possessive NP as determiner
$[structure(syntax(\#NP, MINOR), semantics(\ldots))$
$\longrightarrow$
$structure(syntax(\#NP, minor(head(\ldots, nform(\ldots, poss(+)), \ldots), \ldots), \ldots)),$
$\qquad semantics(\ldots)),$
$structure(syntax(\#NP, MINOR), semantics(\ldots))]$

The feature *poss*(+) corresponds to the presence of the possessive marker -'*s*, so that this rule allows in NP's like *a girl's best friend*, where *a girl's* is the possessive NP functioning as a determiner for the NN *best friend*:

(171) *Diamonds are a girl's best friend.*

The next group of rules is concerned with relative clauses. We need two sets of rules here, one to specify what relative clauses are and another to explain what to do with them. We start with the rules which say what they are.

There are numerous kinds of relative clause. We will consider five. We start with clauses like *who hate cats*, where the subject is an NP consisting of one of the **relative pronouns** *who, which, that*. These are exemplified in the following examples:

(172) *Your friend who likes cats is looking after Tibbles for us.*
(173) *Frank has solved the problem which caused us so much trouble.*
(174) *The law that led to this anomaly has recently been repealed.*

We do not actually need an additional rule for describing this kind of relative clause. The lexical entries for *who, which*, ... specify that they have the foot feature *wh*(*rel*(+),...) when they function as pronouns. The FFP then says that any sentence which has one of these as its subject will also have *wh*(*rel*(+),...). We therefore use this feature as the way to determine whether a simple sentence is a relative clause.

The next kind of relative clause also starts with an NP consisting of a relative pronoun, this time one of the ones we have already seen or *whom, when* or *where* (some dialects of English may not allow *who* in this context). This NP is then followed by a clause which has an NP (or temporal or locative PP) "missing" from it. This item can be missing from any arbitrarily deeply embedded structure. We have included a marker in the following examples to show where the NP is "missing" from:

(175) *The unripe peach which John ate ⌣ made him ill.*
(176) *The woman who I was talking to ⌣ left with her husband.*
(177) *The man who I wanted you to meet ⌣ hasn't arrived yet.*
(178) *The man who I told you I wanted you to meet ⌣ hasn't arrived yet.*
(179) *I left my bag on the seat where we were sitting ⌣.*
(180) *... about the time when the door knob broke ⌣.*

There seems to be no restriction on how deeply embedded the missing item may be, beyond the sheer difficulty of comprehending very complex sentences. There is some debate over whether there are any restrictions on the role it can play. It can seem very ugly, for instance, for the NP complement of a subject-control verb to be missing:

??? (181) *Have you seen the boy who I wanted ⌣ to eat the last chocolate?*

It is difficult to tell whether this violates some grammatical constraint, or whether it is just hard to parse. The fact that

(182) *The man who I said ⌣ wanted to meet you hasn't arrived yet.*

seems much more acceptable suggests that the problem with (181) may be some kind of processing/performance difficulty, akin to the difference in acceptability between

(183) *The donkey beaten by its owner had to be put down.*

and:

*(184) *The horse raced past the barn fell.*

The appropriate readings of *beaten by its owner* and *raced past the barn* in these examples involve very similar syntactic analyses. The problem with (184) is that there is an alternative analysis which is at first sight more probable, and which leads you up a **garden path** [Milne 1986]. We are agnostic as to whether (181) is actually ungrammatical or whether the problem with it stems from some kind of garden path.

Whatever we decide to say about (181), our analysis of these cases requires us to be able to talk about "missing" items. We follow the convention that the feature *slash* should be used to carry this kind of information. The value of *slash* can be either −, indicating that nothing is missing, or a description of some structure. Since *slash* is a *foot* feature, the FFP will ensure that at most one subgoal of a rule will have a structure as the value of *slash*. If any subgoal has a structure as the value of *slash* then the goal will have that structure as its value, otherwise it will have −.

If we decide to make *slash* a *foot* feature like this, we get nearly all the behaviour of missing items for free. At most one subgoal of a rule can have something missing, and if anything is missing from a subgoal then it will be missing from the goal. We have not, however, said anything about how missing items are detected. For this we need the following rule:

(R4): Slash elimination
$[structure(syntax(MAJOR,$
$\qquad\qquad minor(\ldots,$
$\qquad\qquad\qquad\qquad foot(slash(structure(syntax(MAJOR,\ldots),$
$\qquad\qquad\qquad\qquad\qquad\qquad semantics(\ldots))),\ldots),$
$\qquad\qquad\qquad\ldots)),$
$\qquad\qquad semantics(\ldots))$

$\longrightarrow$

$\emptyset]$

This rule says you can hallucinate an X which has an X missing any time you want to. There is no restriction here on the kind of thing that can be missing. The only restrictions come from the fact that there must be some other rule which expects some specific kind of object to be missing, since otherwise the entire utterance will be seen as incomplete. The following rule, for instance, introduces the idea that a sentence can have something extraposed for emphasis, leaving a gap in the position it was extraposed from.

(R5): Topicalisation
$[structure(syntax(\#S,$
$\qquad\qquad\qquad minor(HEAD, foot(slash(-),\ldots), LOCAL)),$
$\qquad\qquad semantics(\ldots))$

$\longrightarrow$

$X,$
$structure(syntax(\#S,$
$\qquad\qquad\qquad minor(HEAD, foot(slash(X),\ldots), LOCAL)),$
$\qquad\qquad semantics(\ldots))$

$LOCAL = local(mood(declarative))$

We have placed no restrictions on the kind of structure that can be topicalised by this rule. Different dialects of English permit different ranges of topicalisation:

(185) *A kick in the teeth I don't need $\smile$ at this point.*

? (186) *If dig we must $\smile$ then dig we shall $\smile$.*

??? (187) *Getting too hot I don't enjoy $\smile$.*

We can restrict (R5) as required by putting constraints on the allowable forms for X.

We can also use *slash* to characterise our second type of relative clause:

(R6): Relative clauses$_1$
$[structure(syntax(\#S,$
$\qquad\qquad minor(HEAD,$
$\qquad\qquad\qquad\quad foot(slash(-), WH, \ldots),$
$\qquad\qquad\qquad LOCAL)),$
$\qquad\quad semantics(\ldots))$
$\longrightarrow$
$structure(syntax(X, minor(\ldots, foot(\ldots, WH, \ldots), \ldots)),$
$\qquad\qquad semantics(\ldots)),$
$structure(syntax(\#S,$
$\qquad\qquad minor(HEAD,$
$\qquad\qquad\qquad\quad foot(slash(structure(syntax(X, \ldots), semantics(\ldots))),$
$\qquad\qquad\qquad\qquad\ldots),$
$\qquad\qquad\qquad LOCAL)),$
$\qquad\quad semantics(\ldots))]$

$HEAD = head(\ldots, vform(tensed(\ldots), \ldots))$
$(WH = wh(qu(+), \ldots) \vee WH = wh(\ldots, rel(+)))$

This rule describes the configurations of items required for our second kind of relative clause, where we have a relative NP or PP followed by a sentence missing an NP or PP:

(188) *The man who you wanted to see* ⌣ ...
(189) *The man to whom you wanted to talk* ⌣ ...
(190) *The bench where I left my coat* ⌣ ...

With a different kind of NP, however, it also describes the configurations of items required for questions like

(191) *What are you eating* ⌣ *?*

and:

(192) *Where do you think you're going* ⌣ *?*

We have not provided enough detail in (R6) to rule out cases like:

*(193) *The man what you wanted to see* ‿ ...

The extra constraints needed for this can be provided by replacing the final disjunction in (R6) by:

$$((WH = wh(qu(+), \ldots) \wedge LOCAL = local(mood(query(polar)))) $$
$$\vee \ (WH = wh(\ldots, rel(+)) \wedge LOCAL = local(mood(declarative))))$$

(R6) captures the essential properties of the second type of relative clause, and of WH-questions, very neatly. Unfortunately, the relations between the *foot* features on the various items mentioned in this rule are not what the FFP would lead us to expect. In particular, the goal has *slash*$(-)$ even though one of the subgoals is required to have a structure as the value of *slash*. If we are simply using the FFP as a convenient way of describing some fairly common pattern of relations between features this may not matter too much. If we regard it as a universal property of the way these features behave, however, this instance of a *foot* feature is a major problem. Since we are only developing our grammatical rules in order to provide a foundation for the compositional rules of Chapters 4 and 5, we choose to take the weaker of these positions, that the FFP is a useful way of talking about a common pattern rather than a universal of English grammar.

The next kind of relative clause undermines the notion that the FFP is a universal even further. It turns out that the initial NP preceding a clause with a missing NP can frequently be omitted:

(194) *The unripe peach John ate made him ill.*
(195) *The woman I was talking to left with her husband.*
. . .

(196) ... *about the time the door knob broke* ...

We can easily adapt (R6) to deal with these cases, just by dropping the initial NP:

(R7): Relative clauses$_2$
$[structure(syntax(\#S,$
$\qquad\qquad minor(HEAD,$
$\qquad\qquad\qquad foot(slash(-), wh(qu(-), rel(+)), \ldots),$
$\qquad\qquad\qquad LOCAL)),$
$\qquad\quad semantics(\ldots))$

$\longrightarrow$

$structure(syntax(\#S,$
$\qquad\qquad minor(HEAD,$
$\qquad\qquad\qquad foot(slash(structure(syntax(\ldots), semantics(\ldots))),$
$\qquad\qquad\qquad \ldots),$
$\qquad\qquad\qquad LOCAL)),$
$\qquad\quad semantics(\ldots))]$

$HEAD = head(\ldots, vform(tensed(\ldots), \ldots))$
$LOCAL = local(mood(declarative))$

This version of the rule is constrained to apply to relative clauses but not questions. Again we have a subgoal with a structure as the value of *slash* when the goal has $slash(-)$. This time we also have the goal with $wh(qu(-), rel(+))$ even though the only subgoal has $wh(qu(-), rel(-))$. Thus although (R7) provides a convenient description of the kinds of relative clause in (194) to (196), the relations between the *foot* features of the goal and those of the sole subgoal again fail to fit the pattern predicted by the FFP.

The next kind of relative clause concerns cases where the sentence the relative clause is based on has some version of the auxiliary *be* as its main verb:

(197) *The man beating the donkey will kill it.*
$\qquad$ (*The man who is beating the donkey will kill it.*)
(198) *The donkey beaten by its owner looks very sad.*
$\qquad$ (*The donkey which was beaten by its owner looks very sad.*)

These are clearly reduced forms of the basic type of relative clause, with the relative NP and the initial auxiliary omitted. We propose the following rule for them:

(R8): Relative clauses (*whiz*-deletion)
$[structure(syntax(\#S,$
$\qquad\qquad minor(head(\ldots),$
$\qquad\qquad\qquad foot(slash(-), wh(qu(-), rel(+)), \ldots),$
$\qquad\qquad\qquad local(mood(declarative))))),$
$\qquad\qquad semantics(\ldots))$

$\longrightarrow$

$\quad structure(syntax(\#VP,$
$\qquad\qquad minor(head(\ldots,$
$\qquad\qquad\qquad\qquad vform(nonfinite(participle(PART)), \ldots),$
$\qquad\qquad\qquad\qquad \ldots)),$
$\qquad\qquad semantics(\ldots))]$

$(PART = present \vee PART = passive)$

The name "*whiz*-deletion" reflects the intuition that a WH-word and an instance of the word *be*, such as *is*, have been deleted. The rule as we have given it fails to express the generalisation that *PART* should be the sort of participle that the auxiliary *be* requires. We could have expressed this by introducing a new feature into the bundle of features grouped under *vform* to indicate whether the item in question was the sort of thing that is required by *be*. Doing so would have emphasised the fact that this construction is associated with this particular auxiliary, but it would not really have explained very much. We have therefore just left the disjunction between *present* and *passive* participles.

There are several other English constructions which resemble relative clauses. We note in particular the use of **appositive** NP's, and of *to*-form VP's:

(199) *Bobby Robson, the England manager, announced an unchanged team.*
    (*Bobby Robson, who is the England manager, ...*)
(200) *We need someone to teach us PROLOG.*
    (*We need someone who can/will teach us PROLOG.*)
(201) *He needs someone to look up to.*
    (*He needs someone who he can/will look up to ⌣.*)

(199) is very similar to (197) and (198), in that it seems to be some kind of abbreviated form of a relative clause starting with *who is* .... We can either introduce a new rule, saying that a relative clause consists of nothing but an NP, or we can make use of the notion of a marker for "suitable object to be the complement of *be*" to extend (R8). For simplicity we take the first of these options:

(R9): Relative clause (appositive NP)
$[structure(syntax(\#\S,$
$\qquad\qquad minor(head(\ldots),$
$\qquad\qquad\qquad foot(slash(-), wh(qu(-), rel(+)), \ldots),$
$\qquad\qquad\qquad local(mood(declarative))))),$
$\qquad\quad semantics(\ldots))$
$\longrightarrow$
$structure(syntax(\#NP,$
$\qquad\qquad minor(head(\ldots, nform(ntype(acc)), \ldots, pred(+)), \ldots),$
$\qquad\qquad\qquad \ldots)),$
$\qquad\quad semantics(\ldots))]$

(200) and (201) are more problematic. We can describe the syntactic structure of relative clauses of this kind with the following rule:

(R10): Relative clause (*to*-form VP)
$[structure(syntax(\#S,$
$\qquad\qquad minor(head(\ldots),$
$\qquad\qquad\qquad foot(slash(-), wh(qu(-), rel(+)), \ldots),$
$\qquad\qquad\qquad local(mood(declarative))))),$
$\qquad\quad semantics(\ldots))$
$\longrightarrow$
$structure(syntax(\#VP,$
$\qquad\qquad minor(head(\ldots,$
$\qquad\qquad\qquad\qquad vform(nonfinite(to)), \ldots),$
$\qquad\qquad\qquad foot(slash(SLASH), \ldots),$
$\qquad\qquad\qquad \ldots),$
$\qquad\quad semantics(\ldots))]$

$(SLASH = - \lor SLASH = structure(syntax(\#NP, \ldots), \ldots)))$

The main syntactic peculiarity of this rule is that the value of *slash* may be either $-$ or a structure description. As far as the purely syntactic properties of this rule are concerned we can dismiss this as a minor oddity. It will cause us rather more trouble when we come to try to include a semantic element in this rule, as will our inability to decide whether (200), for instance, means *We need someone who can teach us*

PROLOG or *We need someone who will teach us PROLOG*, or indeed something else entirely.

3.4.3   Coordination

We end this preliminary discussion of our set of syntactic rules by considering probably the most awkward of all grammatical constructions, namely **coordination**. It seems as though almost any English grammatical structure may be joined with another structure of the same type by a **conjunction** to produce a coordinated structure:

> (202) *John cooked a cake and Mary ate it.*
> (203) *I sold it to either Bill or Peter.*
> (204) *I sold it to Bill or Peter.*
> (205) *The French flag is red, white and blue.*

There seem to be no restrictions on the kinds of object that may be coordinated — any kinds of lexical items, NN's, NP's, VP's, S's and so on (though not conjunctions themselves):

> (206) *Each and every one of you will regret this.* (Determiners)
> (207) *I cycle to and from Enniskerry every day.* (Prepositions)
> (208) *He buys and sells used articles of clothing.* (Verbs)
> (209) *She ate some raspberries and strawberries.* (NN's)
> (210) *The old man and his son talked for a long time.* (NP's)
> (211) *He both bought a new suit and actually wore it to the wedding.* (VP's)
> (212) *Either she likes him or she's good at pretending.* (S's)

It looks as though the simplest way of describing this phenomenon is as follows. We start with lexical frames for prefix and infix conjunctions (prefix conjunctions are words like *both* and *either*, which can be used to mark the start of a coordinated structure, and infix ones are words like *and* and *or* which appear in between the two constituents):

$$CONJ \overset{\text{def}}{=} major(cat(conj), bar(two))$$

(F27): Prefix conjunction (*either, both, ...*)
$structure(syntax(major(cat(conj),$
$\qquad\qquad [structure(SYNTAX, semantics(...))$
$\qquad\qquad \longrightarrow$
$\qquad\qquad\qquad structure(SYNTAX, semantics(...)),$
$\qquad\qquad\qquad structure(syntax(\#CONJ,$
$\qquad\qquad\qquad\qquad\qquad minor(...,$
$\qquad\qquad\qquad\qquad\qquad\qquad local(conjtype(CTYPE),$
$\qquad\qquad\qquad\qquad\qquad\qquad\quad structure(SYNTAX,$
$\qquad\qquad\qquad\qquad\qquad\qquad\qquad\qquad semantics(...))]),$
$\qquad\qquad\quad minor(..., local(conjtype(CTYPE))))),$
$\qquad\quad semantics(...))$

(F28): Infix conjunction (*and, or ...*)
$structure(syntax(major(cat(conj),$
$\qquad\qquad [structure(syntax(\#CONJ),$
$\qquad\qquad\qquad\qquad minor(...,$
$\qquad\qquad\qquad\qquad\qquad local(conjtype(CTYPE),$
$\qquad\qquad\qquad\qquad\qquad\quad structure(SYNTAX,$
$\qquad\qquad\qquad\qquad\qquad\qquad\quad semantics(...))))),$
$\qquad\qquad\quad semantics(...))$
$\qquad\qquad \longrightarrow$
$\qquad\qquad\qquad structure(SYNTAX, semantics(...))]),$
$\qquad\qquad\quad minor(..., local(conjtype(CTYPE))))),$
$\qquad\quad semantics(...))$

The frame for prefix conjunctions specifies that they subcategorise for an arbitrary item and a *CONJ* which contains another item of the same basic category. The *conjtype* is used to ensure that conjunctions appear in matching pairs, i.e. to rule out things like *either John and Mary* or *both John but Mary*.

The frame for infix conjunctions just wraps up whatever follows the conjunction inside a structure of the right kind to be part of a coordination.

The lexical frames for prefix- and infix-conjunctions deal with cases like *Both eats and drinks, Either he or I*, and so on. For cases where there is no prefix-conjunction we need the following rule:

> **(R11): Coordination (infix-form)**
> $[structure(SYNTAX, semantics(\ldots))$
> $\longrightarrow$
> $structure(SYNTAX, semantics(\ldots)),$
> $structure(syntax(\#CONJ,$
> $minor(\ldots, local(SYNTAX)),$
> $semantics(\ldots)))]$

This rule simply says you can combine any kind of structure with a *CONJ* containing something of the same kind, as required by (206) to (210).

The lexical frames (F27) and (F28) and the rule (R11) provide a very neat description of most of what happens in coordination. Unfortunately it is very hard to extend them to describe all of what happens rather than just most of it. Although the general picture is that coordinated structures contain constituents which have the same syntactic properties, there are numerous minor differences between them. Furthermore, although it is roughly true to say that coordinated structures are made up of pairs of structures linked by conjunctions, it turns out that there are situations which do not really fit this description. We will consider the minor details first.

From the frame (F28) and the rule (R11) we would expect to find that we can join two NP's together with *and* if they agree on all their syntactic properties, and that the result of this would be an NP with the same syntactic properties as each constituent. Consider, however, the following:

(213) *Joe and Martha are going back to work.*
(214) *Peter and his friends have already left.*

In (213) the constituents are both singular NP's, but the coordination of the two is plural, i.e. it has different syntactic properties from its constituents. In (214) one constituent is singular and the other is plural, so they do not have the same syntactic properties and yet they can be joined together.

This effect is an idiosyncracy of the way *and* conjoins NP's. Conjunctions of verbs or VP's do not change the syntactic characteristics of the constituents. Disjunctions of NP's seem to have the same agreement features as their second disjunct (different people judge this differently):

(215) *Either Peter or Bill has already left.*
? (216) *Either Peter or his friends have already left.*

It therefore looks as though we need a lot of case-by-case specifications of exactly what features are constrained to be shared by the constituents of the coordination and the coordination itself. This can be done, though it is rather messy and tedious.

If we look closely, however, we discover a set of phenomena which are almost impossible to account for using our simple frames and rule. These are cases where the coordinated items do not appear to be well-defined syntactic structures at all, or where at the very best they seem to share hardly any syntactic properties. We note three instances of this kind. We can have **non-constituent** coordinations where the items being coordinated seem to be groups of structures:

(217) *John gave Mary a book and Susan a record.*
(218) *He stole a TV from the first house he entered but nothing from the second.*

The coordinated structures *Mary a book* and *Susan a record* each contain two NP's. The structures *a TV from the first house he entered* and *nothing from the second* each contain an NP and a PP. It seems as though we are doing roughly what our treatment says we should be doing except that we are doing it with groups of items rather than just items.

The next case we consider concerns coordination of structures with **gaps** in them:

(219) *John gave Mary a book, and Peter, Susan a record.*
(220) *Mr. X stole a TV from the first house, but Mr. Y nothing from the second.*

These examples are fairly ugly, but they do make sense. They are even harder to deal with, since they involve combining a well-defined structure (*John gave Mary a book*, *Mr. X stole a TV from the first house*) with a group of structures (three NP's in *Peter, Susan a record*, two NP's and a PP in *Mr. Y nothing from the second*).

Finally there are cases where the coordinated structures are simply of different types (the following examples are from [Gazdar et al. 1985]):

(221) *His father was well-known to the police and a devout catholic.*
(222) *She walked slowly and with great care.*

In these cases each of the coordinated items is something which could legitimately appear by itself in the position where the coordination actually appears:

(223) *His father was well-known to the police.*
(224) *His father was a devout catholic.*
(225) *She walked slowly.*
(226) *She walked with great care.*

It is possible to contort the analysis embodied in (F27) and (F28) and (R11) to fit these examples. The contortions that are required, however, destroy the claim that this analysis is neat or intuitively appealing. It is easier to describe what is going on in these examples if we talk about syntactic processing, rather than about static descriptions of permissible structures. Suppose we consider parsing (221), for instance, using some kind of top-down left-to-right parser. After we have inspected the word *was* we will have a range of expectations — the next structure might be an NP, or an AP, or passive VP, or ... If we applied our analysis of coordination to expectations, rather than to perceived structures, then we would be able to argue that in a context where either an NP or an AP would be acceptable in isolation, a combination of the two would also be acceptable.

We could put much the same argument for the kind of non-constituent coordination in (217) and (218). Encountering the verb would lead to the prediction that either two NP's or an NP and a PP should follow. If predictions can be coordinated, rather than just structures, then a pair of occurrences of two NP's or of an NP and a PP would be exactly the kind of thing you would expect.

We will not follow this suggestion up any further here. It seems unlikely that it can be developed in any detail without a considerable amount of argument about the precise parsing/generation processes that underly human language processing. We do not wish to propose any specific psychologically plausible processing mechanisms here, and hence cannot specify the kinds of expectation that would be available for coordination. We will simply note that if we did have an account which dealt with the complex phenomena we have been considering it is clear that it would also deal with the basic cases (though the idiosyncracies of words like *and* would still need to be spelt out in detail). For our purposes in the next chapter we will assume that the account embodied in (F27), (F28) and (R11) is accurate enough to describe at least some cases, and we will ignore the others. It will turn out that we have quite enough difficulty with the semantics associated with even the basic cases.

The rules and lexical frames described above cover the syntactic structure of a substantial fragment of English — a variety of subcategorisation frames for verbs and determiners, various "transformational" phenomena such as passivisation, dative movement and subject-control, a range of forms of relative clause, a number of coordination schemes. We will present a few more grammatical rules at points when we are ready to deal with their semantics. The syntactic treatment in the present chapter, and the rules that we will present later, are fairly orthodox. We are, further, presenting them entirely as a description of the phenomena we are interested in: they embody no empirical claims about, for instance, the range of phenomena which could have been included in English but for historical accidents, or about linguistic universals. The most we want to say is that the notation we have used has allowed us to write down certain well-known facts about English grammar in a clear, concise manner. The important thing is that we now have enough grammatical machinery to be able to start developing our description of English semantics.

4 BASIC MEANING

In Chapter 2 we described a language for specifying semantic content. In Chapter 3 we described a language for specifying syntactic structures, and also developed a grammar for a fragment of English. Our task now is to combine the two, using the language for semantic content to add a semantic treatment to the rules of the grammar. We will do this in two stages. In the present chapter we will assume that English sentences express facts about events and states involving individuals. We will use the freedom provided by property theory to blur the distinction between events and states on the one hand and individuals on the other. We will, however, still take it that the main verb of an English sentence denotes a state or an event, and that the other elements say either something about the individuals that participate in that state or event or something about its manner — its time, or its place, or the way it was performed, or ... In Chapter 5 we will consider the internal structure of states and events in more detail. For the moment we will simply assume that any English main verb denotes either a state or an event, and leave it at that.

4.1 Simple Sentences

We start by considering certain very simple sentences, namely present tense propositions about named individuals:

(225) *John hates Michael.*

What can we say about someone who sincerely utters this to us? They must think we know who they mean when they refer to John and Michael, they must believe that John hates Michael, and they must want us to know they believe this. In terms of our decision to talk in terms of the presupposition and content of an utterance, the speaker must presuppose that we know who John and Michael are, and the content of their utterance is the proposition that John hates Michael:

$$Presupposition :$$
$$\{(\exists!X : salient(X))(name(X, [\![John]\!]),$$
$$(\exists!Y : salient(Y))(name(Y, [\![Michael]\!]))\}$$
$$Content : (\exists I : interval(I))(CONTAIN(I, now)$$
$$\wedge\ DURING(I, \bullet[[\![hate]\!](X, Y)]))$$

We will use the convention that $[\![<word>]\!]$ is a constant of PT with the same interpretation as the English word $<word>$, so that $[\![hate]\!]$, for instance, is a constant which denotes the relation of hatred.

The presupposition part of the above commitment says that there is exactly one salient individual called John and exactly one salient individual called Michael. We will not say any more about when an individual is **salient**. It clearly depends on a great many factors — physical proximity, recency of mention, expected utility for problem solving, ... We need to refer to this notion in order to explain the significance of various linguistic constructions, such as the use of proper names in (225). Characterising the circumstances in which some item is indeed salient, however, is outside the scope of the present work. We will simply use the notion, without any further analysis.

The content of this commitment says that John currently hates Michael. There is very little more to be said about it, since we have already introduced $DURING$ as a relation between intervals and propositions, and $CONTAIN$ as a relation between intervals and instants, and refused to say anything about the properties of instants and intervals. Now is just a name for the time at which the sentence is uttered.

We need to see how the meanings of the individual words in (225) combine to produce this commitment. Before we attempt to do this for (225) we will look at an even simpler sentence:

(226) *I sleep.*

$$Presupposition : \{\exists!X(speaker(X)\}$$
$$Content : (\exists I : interval(I))(CONTAIN(I, now)$$
$$\wedge\ DURING(I, \bullet[[\![sleep]\!](X)]))$$

We allow I to introduce the presupposition that there is a unique individual who is the speaker. We need this in order to account for Barwise and Perry's [1983] example of someone at a fancy dress party who utters the sentence *There's my wife* in order to provide information about who they are themselves. (226) consists of an

NP *I* and a VP *sleep*. In order to see how its commitment can be as given above, then, we need to see what the commitment of each of these is, and how they are combined together. For the NP we need to introduce a general frame for pronouns, and a specific entry for *I*:

$structure(syntax(major(\dots,$
$$[structure(syntax(\#NP, MINOR),$$
$$semantics(pre(PRE),$$
$$content(CONTENT)))$$
$$\longrightarrow$$
$$\emptyset]),$$
$$MINOR),$$
$$semantics(pre(PRE), content(CONTENT)))$$

(F29): Pronoun

In other words, a pronoun produces an NP with the same *minor* features as the pronoun itself and the same *semantics*, which is split into *pre* and *content* components. The detailed frame for *I* is then as follows:

$structure(syntax(major(\dots),$
$$minor(head(agr(first(singular), second(-), third(-),$$
$$count(+)),$$
$$foot(slash(-), wh(-,-), reflexive(-)),$$
$$local(-))),$$
$$semantics(pre(\{\exists! X(speaker(X))\}),$$
$$content(\bullet[P, X \in P])))$$

The syntactic details in this frame are very straightforward, and we will not comment further on them.

The presupposition contains a single element, namely a proposition which specifies that there is a unique individual who is uttering the given sentence. We will return to the significance of this presupposition in Chapter 6 when we consider the effects of language. For the moment we will simply accept that a personal pronoun such as *I* or *you* may introduce a presupposition of this kind.

The content, which denotes the property of being something which is true of the speaker, may be more surprising. We will follow common practice in model theoretic semantics in assuming that NP's denote properties of this kind, rather than pointing directly to individuals. We might be able to interpret pronouns, proper names and NP's with definite articles in terms of specified individuals, and NP's with indefinite articles in terms of particular but unspecified individuals. We might also be able to think of definite plural NP's in terms of sets of individuals — *All students sleep* could specify a property of the set of all students. *Most students sleep*, however, cannot be interpreted as a statement about any set of students. There is not a well-defined set of *most students*. *Most students sleep* is a statement about a relation between the property of being a student and the property of sleeping.

Since we are forced to conclude that *sleep* denotes a relation between the property of sleeping and some other property in at least one situation, we assume for the sake of uniformity that it always denotes a relation between things of this kind. This in turn forces us to assume that all NP's denote properties. In the case of **indexical** pronouns like *I* the relevant property is as we have given it, the property of being something which is true of the indexed entity. We will consider the interpretations of more complex kinds of NP later.

The VP, *sleep*, contributes two kinds of information to the content of (226). It specifies that the speaker is asleep at some time; and it specifies that the time is in fact now. The first of these comes from the meaning of the lexical item *sleep*, and the second from the fact that this occurrence of this item has the suffix -∅, denoting the present tense form. These two are combined to produce a description of the property of being asleep now. This is done by requiring all suffixes to fit the following pattern:

(F30): Semantics of suffix attachment

$structure(syntax(major(cat(suffix), [WORD_1 \longrightarrow WORD_2]),$
$\qquad\qquad minor(\ldots)),$
$\qquad semantics(\ldots, content(S)))$

$WORD_1 = structure(syntax(major(\ldots,$
$\qquad\qquad\qquad\qquad [structure(\ldots,$
$\qquad\qquad\qquad\qquad\qquad\qquad semantics(pre(PRE),$
$\qquad\qquad\qquad\qquad\qquad\qquad\qquad content(LEX \in S)))$
$\qquad\qquad\qquad\qquad \longrightarrow \ldots]),$
$\qquad\qquad\qquad \ldots),$
$\qquad\qquad semantics(\ldots))$
$WORD_2 = structure(syntax(major(\ldots,$
$\qquad\qquad\qquad\qquad [structure(\ldots,$
$\qquad\qquad\qquad\qquad\qquad\qquad semantics(pre(PRE),$
$\qquad\qquad\qquad\qquad\qquad\qquad\qquad content(LEX)))$
$\qquad\qquad\qquad\qquad \longrightarrow \ldots]),$
$\qquad\qquad\qquad \ldots),$
$\qquad\qquad semantics(\ldots))$

What we are really interested in when we consider the semantics of an open class word is the semantics of the structure that can be built from it. We therefore combine the semantics of the goal of the embedded rule with the semantics of the suffix. (F30) says that when a suffix is added to a root form of an open class word, the presupposition of the goal of the embedded rule is unchanged. Its content is obtained by instantiating the content of the suffix with the content of the goal of the embedded rule of the root. We will see the effect of this shortly.

We now need the descriptions of the root form of *sleep* and the present tense suffix -$\emptyset$. We will ignore the syntactic components of these descriptions here, since we have already seen them in Chapter 3. We will generally omit syntactic detail from frames and rules in the current chapter if we have already seen it in Chapter 3. The semantic details of the present tense suffix are given by the following:

(F31): Present tense (semantics)
$structure(\ldots,$
$\qquad semantics(pre(\ldots), content(\bullet[R, PRESTENSE \in R])))$

$PRESTENSE = \bullet[P, (\exists I : interval(I))((I \in PRESENT)$
$\qquad\qquad\qquad\qquad\qquad\qquad \wedge (I \in (P \in TENSED))))]])))$
$PRESENT = \bullet[J, CONTAIN(J, now)]$
$TENSED = \bullet[J', \bullet[Q, DURING(J', \bullet[Q])]]$

This says that the present tense suffix indicates that whatever the VP says is true at the time the utterance is produced. Note that since $DURING$ is a relation between intervals and propositions, we have had to objectify the expression which denotes the meaning of the VP, changing it from Q to $\bullet[Q]$.

The verb *sleep* is typical of the class of intransitive verbs. When we combine such a verb with the kind of temporal information provided by suffixes and auxiliaries, and with the information provided by an NP, we will obtain a description of a temporally located proposition. The semantic structure of such a verb before it is combined with this extra information, then, must be that it is a relation between temporal specifications and properties of properties of individuals (i.e. the sort of thing denoted by NP's). We therefore specify the general semantic pattern for intransitive verbs as follows:

(F32): Intransitive verb (semantics)
$structure(syntax(major(\ldots,$
$\qquad\qquad\qquad\qquad [structure(syntax(\#VP, \ldots),$
$\qquad\qquad\qquad\qquad\qquad\qquad semantics(pre(\emptyset),$
$\qquad\qquad\qquad\qquad\qquad\qquad\qquad\qquad content(CONTENT)))$

$\qquad\qquad\qquad\qquad\qquad \longrightarrow$

$\qquad\qquad\qquad\qquad\qquad \ldots]),$
$\qquad\qquad\qquad \ldots)),$
$\qquad\qquad semantics(pre(\emptyset), content(VERB)))$

$CONTENT = \bullet[T, \bullet[A, (\bullet[u, (u \in VERB) \in T]) \in A]]$

Sleep is then a particular intransitive verb, with its semantics given by the following frame:

(F33): *sleep* **(semantics)**
$structure(\ldots,$
$$semantics(pre(\ldots), content(\bullet[x, [\![sleep]\!](x)])))$$

We will consider what happens as we combine the general frame for intransitive verbs with the particular one for *sleep*, and then add the present tense frame associated with the suffix -$\emptyset$. We start by unifying the frame for intransitive verbs and the one for *sleep*:

$structure(syntax(major(\ldots,$
$\qquad\qquad\qquad [structure(syntax(\# VP, \ldots),$
$\qquad\qquad\qquad\qquad\qquad semantics(pre(\emptyset),$
$\qquad\qquad\qquad\qquad\qquad\qquad\qquad content(CONTENT))))$
$\qquad\qquad\qquad \longrightarrow$
$\qquad\qquad\qquad \ldots]),$
$\qquad\qquad \ldots)),$
$\qquad semantics(pre(\emptyset), content(\bullet[x, [\![sleep]\!](x)])))$

$CONTENT = \bullet[T, \bullet[A, (\bullet[u, (u \in \bullet[x, [\![sleep]\!](x)]) \in T]) \in A]]$

We then use (F30) to obtain:

$structure(syntax(major(cat(v),$
$\qquad\qquad\qquad [structure(syntax(\# VP, \ldots),$
$\qquad\qquad\qquad\qquad\qquad semantics(pre(\emptyset),$
$\qquad\qquad\qquad\qquad\qquad\qquad\qquad content(CONTENT)))$
$\qquad\qquad\qquad \longrightarrow$
$\qquad\qquad\qquad \ldots]),$
$\qquad\qquad \ldots)),$
$\qquad semantics(pre(\emptyset), content(\bullet[u, (u \in \bullet[x, [\![sleep]\!](x)])])))$

$CONTENT = \bullet[T, \bullet[A, (\bullet[u, (u \in \bullet[x, [\![sleep]\!](x)]) \in T]) \in A]]$
$\qquad\qquad \in \bullet[R, \bullet[P, ((\exists I : interval(I))$
$\qquad\qquad\qquad\qquad\qquad\qquad ((I \in \bullet[J, CONTAIN(J, now)])$
$\qquad\qquad\qquad\qquad\qquad\qquad \wedge (I \in \bullet[J', DURING(J', \bullet[P])]))] \in R]$

The *content* looks extremely complicated. If we look closely at it, however, it turns out that it consists of expressions which can be simplified by using the Tarski biconditional TB, which we restate here in the relevant form:

(TB) $\quad (t \in \bullet[x, A]) \equiv A_{t/x}$

We recall that (TB) holds so long as the defence of $A_{t/x}$ does not require us to claim $\neg A_{t/x}$. This will always be the case if A is negation free, as it is in the *content* above. We can therefore use (TB) repeatedly to simplify this *content*, as follows:

(i) $\bullet[T, \bullet[A, (\bullet[u, (u \in \bullet[x, [\![sleep]\!](x)]) \in T]) \in A]]$
$\qquad \in \bullet[R, \bullet[P, ((\exists I : interval(I))((I \in \bullet[J, CONTAIN(J, now)])$
$\qquad\qquad\qquad\qquad \wedge (I \in \bullet[J', DURING(J', \bullet[P])]))] \in R]$

(ii) $\bullet[P, (\exists I : interval(I))(I \in \bullet[J, CONTAIN(J, now)]$
$\qquad\qquad\qquad \wedge I \in \bullet[J', DURING(J', \bullet[P])])]$
$\qquad\qquad \in \bullet[T, \bullet[A, (\bullet[u, (u \in \bullet[x, [\![sleep]\!](x)]) \in T]) \in A]]$

(iii) $\bullet[P, (\exists I : interval(I))(CONTAIN(I, now) \wedge DURING(I, \bullet[P]))]$
$\qquad\qquad \in \bullet[T, \bullet[A, (\bullet[u, (u \in \bullet[x, [\![sleep]\!](x)]) \in T]) \in A]]$

(iv) $\bullet[A, (\bullet[u, (u \in \bullet[x, [\![sleep]\!](x)])$
$\qquad\qquad \in \bullet[P, (\exists I : interval(I))(CONTAIN(I, now)$
$\qquad\qquad\qquad\qquad \wedge DURING(I, \bullet[P]))]]) \in A]$

(v) $\bullet[A, (\bullet[u, ([\![sleep]\!](u) \in \bullet[P, (\exists I : interval(I))(CONTAIN(I, now)$
$\qquad\qquad\qquad\qquad \wedge DURING(I, \bullet[P]))]]) \in A]$

(vi) $\bullet[A, (\bullet[u, (\exists I : interval(I))(CONTAIN(I, now)$
$\qquad\qquad \wedge DURING(I, \bullet[[\![sleep]\!](u)]))]) \in A]$

We need to be able to combine this, the *content* of the VP *sleep*, with the *content* we derived earlier for the NP *I* to obtain the *content* of the sentence *I sleep*. We therefore add a semantic component to our rule for S's:

(R12): Sentence (semantics)
$[structure(syntax(\#S, \ldots),$
$\qquad\qquad semantics(pre(PRE_{subj} \cup PRE_{pred}),$
$\qquad\qquad\qquad content(CONTENT_{subj} \in CONTENT_{pred}))$
$\longrightarrow$
$structure(syntax(\#NP, \ldots),$
$\qquad\qquad semantics(pre(PRE_{subj}), content(CONTENT_{subj}))),$
$structure(syntax(\#VP, \ldots),$
$\qquad\qquad semantics(pre(PRE_{pred}), content(CONTENT_{pred})))]$

This rule shows how to construct the interpretation of an S by simple combinations of the interpretations of its constituent NP and VP. The presuppositions are simply added together, and the content of the VP is instantiated with the content of the NP. In the current instance, the VP has $\emptyset$ as its presupposition, so the presupposition of the entire sentence is identical to the presupposition of the NP, i.e. $\{\exists!X(speaker(X))\}$.

The content of the sentence is

$$\bullet[P, X \in P] \in \bullet[A, (\bullet[u, (\exists : interval(I))(CONTAIN(I, now)$$
$$\wedge\ DURING(I, \bullet[[[sleep]](u)])])]$$
$$\in A].$$

We can continue our simplifying reductions on this:

(vii) $\bullet[P, X \in P] \in \bullet[A, (\bullet[u, (\exists I : interval(I))(CONTAIN(I, now)$
$$\wedge\ DURING(I, \bullet[[[sleep]](u)])])])$$
$$\in A]$$

(viii) $(\bullet[u, (\exists I : interval(I))(CONTAIN(I, now) \wedge DURING(I, \bullet[[[sleep]](u)])])])$
$$\in \bullet[P, X \in P]]$$

(ix) $X \in \bullet[u, (\exists I : interval(I))(CONTAIN(I, now)$
$$\wedge\ DURING(I, [[sleep]](u)))]$$

(x) $(\exists I : interval(I))(CONTAIN(I, now) \wedge DURING(I, \bullet[[[sleep]](X))])$

It might seem that we have had to work terribly hard to derive a fairly simple representation of the meaning of (226). The important point about the way we have dealt with (226) is that the semantic descriptions, and the operations for combining semantic descriptions, were all very simple. The most complex description was the general one for intransitive verbs, which had to combine appropriately with the representations of the content of the temporal element and the subject. The other descriptions were about as simple as they could be, and the operations for combining semantic descriptions each simply conjoined two expressions or instantiated one with another — again, just about as simple as they could be.

The analysis did involve the construction of rather opaque looking expressions. The application of (TB), which is itself an extremely simple rule, showed that this opacity could easily be removed. It might, therefore, have *seemed* that we had to work terribly hard to obtain the representation of the meaning of (226); but in fact it was rather easy, once we had the right representations of the meanings of the lexical items involved.

We will not in general explicitly show the way that (TB) is used to simplify complex expressions. We will simply rely on the fact that it is available, except in certain pathological cases involving negated self-reference which will not occur in any of our examples, and easy. We now return to the analysis of (225).

For (225) we will need a frame for proper names, and one for transitive verbs. We want to say that when a speaker uses a proper name they are assuming that the hearer can pick out a unique object which bears that name — that when someone says *I love Paris in the spring* their hearer will think of the Paris that is the capital of France, not of Paris, Texas, or Paris who fell in love with Helen of Troy. The frame for proper names will thus contain a presupposition which refers to the property of being the name of something:

(F34): Proper name
$structure(syntax(major(\ldots,$
$$[structure(syntax(\#NP, MINOR),$$
$$semantics(pre(PRE),$$
$$content(\bullet[A, X \in A])))$$

$$\longrightarrow$$

$$\emptyset]),$$
$$MINOR),$$
$$semantics(\ldots, content(NAME)))$$

$PRE = \{(\exists! X : salient(X))(name(X, NAME))\}$

We are ignoring the possibility of compound proper names here — *Paris, Texas*, or *Martin Luther King*. Individual proper names such as *John* have frames like:

$structure(syntax(\ldots,$
$$minor(head(agr(first(-), second(-), third(singular),$$
$$count(+)),$$
$$\ldots),$$
$$\ldots)),$$
$$semantics(\ldots, content([[John]]))))$$

If we combine this with the general frame for proper names we will get

$structure(syntax(major(\dots,$
$\qquad\qquad\qquad [structure(syntax(\#NP, MINOR),$
$\qquad\qquad\qquad\qquad\qquad semantics(pre(PRE),$
$\qquad\qquad\qquad\qquad\qquad\qquad content(\bullet[A, X \in A])))$

$\qquad\qquad\qquad\longrightarrow$
$\qquad\qquad\qquad\emptyset]),$
$\qquad\qquad MINOR),$
$\qquad\qquad semantics(\dots, content(NAME)))$

$MINOR = minor(head(agr(first(-), second(-), third(singular),$
$\qquad\qquad\qquad\qquad\qquad\qquad\qquad count(+)),$
$\qquad\qquad\qquad\dots),$
$\qquad\qquad\dots)$
$NAME = [\![John]\!]$
$PRE = \{(\exists!X : salient(X))(name(X, NAME))\}$

The NP consisting of the word *John*, then, is described by the following structure:

$structure(syntax(\#NP,$
$\qquad\qquad minor(head(agr(first(-), second(-), third(singular),$
$\qquad\qquad\qquad\qquad\qquad\qquad count(+)),$
$\qquad\qquad\qquad\dots),$
$\qquad\qquad\dots)),$
$\qquad\qquad semantics(pre(PRE), content(\bullet[A, X \in A])))$

$NAME = [\![John]\!]$
$PRE = \{(\exists!X : salient(X))(name(X, NAME)\}$

We do not equate the use of names in English with the use of constants in PT. The fact that John's name is *John* is just one of John's properties. It is one that we will often choose when we need to construct an identifying expression to pick him out, but it is basically just the same as any of his other properties. The interpretation of the word *John* that appears in the above description is the string itself. $[\![John]\!]$ is just the word *John*. The interpretation of the NP consisting of this word contains a presupposition that there is exactly one salient person whose name is this string.

The frame for transitive verbs is very similar to the one for intransitive ones, except that it needs to be able use up the information provided by two NP's (the subject and the complement) rather than just one:

(F35): Transitive verb (semantics)

$structure(syntax(major(\ldots,$
$[structure(syntax(\#VP,\ldots),$
$semantics(pre(PRE),$
$content(CONTENT_{vp})))$

$\longrightarrow$

$structure(\ldots,$
$semantics(pre(PRE),$
$content(CONTENT_{comp})))]),$
$\ldots)),$
$semantics(pre(\emptyset),content(VERB)))$

$CONTENT_{vp} = \bullet[T,$
$\quad CONTENT_{comp}$
$\qquad \in \bullet[A', \bullet[A, (\bullet[v, \bullet[u, (u \in (v \in VERB))$
$\qquad\qquad \in T]]) \in A] \in A']]$

The identification of the presupposition of the VP and the presupposition of its complement reflects that the fact that anything which is required before you can understand the complement will also be required before you can understand the VP. The structure of the content is similar to the structure of the content for intransitive verbs. The changes reflect the expectation that two NP's will be supplied rather than one, together with the realisation that one of these NP's has already been described inside the embedded rule.

The specific description of *hate* is:

(F36): *hate* semantics

$structure(\ldots,$
$\quad semantics(pre(\ldots), content(\bullet[x, \bullet[y, [[hate]](x, y)]])))$

We now have everything we need in order to interpret (225), if we assume that the present tense third person singular frame for -*s* as a verb suffix has the same semantics as the present tense interpretation of -$\emptyset$ that we have already seen. With these frames and rules, the description of (225) is:

$structure(syntax(\#S, \ldots),$
$\qquad semantics(pre(PRE), content(CONTENT)))$

$PRE = \{(\exists!X : salient(X))(name(X, [\![John]\!]),$
$\qquad\qquad (\exists!Y : salient(Y))(name(Y, [\![Michael]\!]))\}$
$CONTENT = \bullet[U', X \in U']$
$\qquad\qquad \in (\bullet[P, \exists(I : interval(I))(CONTAIN(I, now)$
$\qquad\qquad\qquad\qquad\qquad\qquad\qquad \wedge DURING(I, \bullet[P])]$
$\qquad\qquad \in \bullet[T,$
$\qquad\qquad\qquad \bullet[U, Y \in U]$
$\qquad\qquad\qquad\quad \in \bullet[A',$
$\qquad\qquad\qquad\qquad \bullet[A,$
$\qquad\qquad\qquad\qquad\quad (\bullet[v, \bullet[u, (u \in (v \in \bullet[x, \bullet[y, [\![hate]\!](x, y)]\!]))$
$\qquad\qquad\qquad\qquad\qquad\qquad\qquad \in T) \in A) \in A']]]]$

The content here looks outrageously complicated. In fact after a few applications of (TB) it reduces to

$$(\exists I : interval(I))(CONTAIN(I, now) \wedge DURING(I, \bullet[[\![hate]\!](X, Y)]))$$

as required.

We now consider a sentence with a slightly more complex NP in it:

(227) *Mary owns a farm.*

Owns here is a transitive verb which we will treat exactly as we treated *hates* above. We need frames for determiners and nouns in general, and for *a* and *farm* in particular:

(F37): Determiner (semantics)

$structure(syntax(major(ldots,$

$[structure(\ldots,$

$semantics(pre((CONT_{comp} \in PRE_{det})$

$\cup PRE_{comp}),$

$content(CONT_{comp}$

$\in CONT_{det})))$

$\longrightarrow$

$structure(\ldots, semantics(pre(PRE_{comp}),$

$content(CONT_{comp})))]),$

$\ldots),$

$semantics(pre(PRE_{det}), content(CONT_{comp})))$

Some determiners contribute something to the presupposition, some contribute to the content. In either case, what they add is combined with the content of the complement. We will see the difference when we consider the difference between (227) and:

(228) *Mary owns the farm.*

The specific frame for *a* is then:

(F38): Semantics for *a*

$structure(\ldots,$

$semantics(pre(\bullet[A, \emptyset]),$

$content(\bullet[B, \bullet[B', (\exists x : x \in B)(x \in B')]])))$

For ordinary nouns (i.e. ones which do not require a complement) the frame is:

> **(F39): Noun (semantics)**
> $structure(syntax(major(n,$
> $\qquad\qquad\qquad [structure(\ldots,$
> $\qquad\qquad\qquad\qquad\qquad semantics(PRE, CONTENT))$
> $\qquad\qquad\qquad \rightarrow$
> $\qquad\qquad\qquad \ldots]),$
> $\qquad\quad \ldots),$
> $\qquad semantics(PRE, CONTENT))$

The frame for a particular noun like *farm* is:

> $structure(\ldots,$
> $\qquad\qquad semantics(\ldots, content(\bullet[w, [\![farm]\!](w)])))$

From these frames we see that the structure corresponding to the NP *a farm* is:

> $structure(syntax(\ldots),$
> $\qquad\qquad semantics(pre(\bullet[w, [\![farm]\!](w)] \in \bullet[A, \emptyset]),$
> $\qquad\qquad\qquad content(\bullet[w, [\![farm]\!](w)]$
> $\qquad\qquad\qquad\qquad\qquad \in \bullet[B, \bullet[B', (\exists x : x \in B)(x \in B')]])))$

Appropriate applications of (TB) will simplify this to:

> $structure(syntax(\ldots),$
> $\qquad\qquad semantics(pre(\emptyset),$
> $\qquad\qquad\qquad content(\bullet[B', (\exists x : [\![farm]\!](x))(x \in B')])))$

In other words, *a farm* denotes the property of being true of some object which is a farm. The presupposition here is empty, since the phrase is being used to introduce an entity into the discussion rather than drawing on one that is already salient. The presupposition of the determiner *a* is a vacuous abstraction over the empty set — however it is instantiated it comes out as $\emptyset$.

This description of *a farm* leads to the following description of (227):

$$structure(syntax(\#S, \ldots),$$
$$semantics(pre(\{(\exists!X : salient(X))(name(X, [\![Mary]\!])\}),$$
$$content((\exists I : interval(I))(CONTAIN(I, now)$$
$$\wedge\ DURING(I, \bullet[(\exists Z : [\![farm]\!](Z))$$
$$([\![own]\!](X, Z))])))))$$

Suppose we consider (228) instead. Anyone saying this must assume that their hearer will have some particular farm in mind, in much the same way that they will have a particular person called Mary in mind. The description of *the* must therefore contain a skeleton presupposition to support this kind of treatment:

(F40): Semantic frame for *the*
$$structure(syntax(\ldots),$$
$$semantics(pre(\bullet[A, \{(\exists!X : salient(X)(X \in A)\}]),$$
$$content(\bullet[A, \bullet[A', X \in A']])))$$

Here it is the content that has a vacuous abstraction with respect to A. We need it for uniformity, since we assume that the contents of determiners are always objectified with respect to two arguments, but in the case of *the* we do not actually do anything with it.

With this description of the semantics of *the* we would obtain

$$structure(syntax(\ldots),$$
$$semantics(pre(\{(\exists!X : salient(X)([\![farm]\!](X)\}),$$
$$content(\bullet[A', X \in A'])))$$

as the representation of *the farm*. This in turn would lead to

$$structure(syntax(\#S, \ldots),$$
$$semantics(pre(\{(\exists!X : salient(X))(name(X, [\![Mary]\!]),$$
$$(\exists!Y : salient(Y))([\![farm]\!](Y))\}),$$
$$content((\exists I : interval(I))$$
$$(CONTAIN(I, now)$$
$$\wedge\ DURING(I, \bullet[([\![own]\!](X, Y))])))))$$

as the representation of (228). The presupposition indicates that the speaker assumes the hearer knows which person called Mary and which farm are being talked about. The content says that the person owns the farm, using the convention that presuppositions need to be verified, and that this verification may provide interpretations for variables, in order to fix the reference of X and Y.

4.2 Auxiliaries and Temporal Specification

We have looked so far at sentences made up of a VP with a simple tensed main verb, and with simple NP's as subject and complement. We need to consider more complex VP's and more complex NP's. We start with complex VP's where the complexity comes from the presence of auxiliary sequences.

We assumed above that a tensed verb carries the message that the state or event denoted by the verb took place over an interval, and that for present tense verbs the relevant interval included the time when the sentence was uttered. This analysis may well be over-simple, but it is at least a good starting place. We will not attempt to develop this treatment so that it will deal with all the subtleties of sentences involving tensed verbs. Our goal here is to show where the elements of the message are encoded, and how they are to be combined together, rather than to describe their every nuance. We will therefore assume that our treatment of tensed verbs is roughly correct, and show how to contrast them with various non-finite forms.

Consider the following pair of sentences:

(229) *John built a house.*
(230) *John was building a house.*

We are assuming that (229) implies that John started to build a house at some time t_0, and that at some later time t_1 he finished building it. We do not wish to get involved in debates about whether he spent all the time between t_0 and t_1 building it (even at weekends, or when he was at home asleep), or about whether the instant when he finished should be included in the period t_0 to t_1, or any other detailed questions of this nature. We simply assume (229) refers to an interval over which John performed this action, without worrying further about what it means to perform an action over an interval.

(230), on the other hand, seems to refer to an instantaneous state of affairs. We can develop the contrast between (229) and (230) by adding temporal modifiers to them:

(229′) *John built a house at 3:30 on Thursday.*
(230′) *John was building a house at 3:30 on Thursday.*
(229″) *John built a house last year.*

(230″) *John was building a house last year.*

(229′) and (230″) sound slightly more awkward than (230′) and (229″). The difference is not sufficient to make (229′) and (230″) sound unacceptable, but they are at the very least less fluent than (230′) and (229″). We suggest that the problem with them is that (229′) combines a temporal modifier that refers to an instant (*at 3:30 on Thursday*) with a relation between an interval and a proposition; and that (230″) combines a temporal modifier that refers to an interval (*last year*) with a relation between an instant and a proposition. The fact that they are both acceptable indicates that the distinction between instants and intervals is not very clear-cut. Nonetheless, it does seem to provide some sort of description of what is going on.

We can deal with (229) simply by adapting the frame for present tense verbs so it refers to a past interval rather than one including *now*:

(F41): Past tense (semantics)
$structure(\ldots,$
$\qquad semantics(pre(\ldots), content(\bullet[R, PASTTENSE \in R])))$

$PASTTENSE = \bullet[P, (\exists I : interval(I))((I \in PAST)$
$\qquad\qquad\qquad\qquad\qquad \wedge\, (I \in (P \in TENSED)))]))))$
$PAST = \bullet[J, (\forall T : instant(T))(CONTAIN(J,T) \to BEFORE(T, now))]$
$TENSED = \bullet[J', \bullet[Q, DURING(J', \bullet[Q])]]$

This refers to a proposition which was true during some interval I, where every instant which is contained in I was before the time of the utterance. Note that we can use this analysis of the meaning of the past tense suffix no matter how we feel about intervals, beyond the assumption that they can *CONTAIN* instants. We can, for instance, use (F41) with either dense or non-dense intervals.

This description of the semantics of the past tense suffix will lead to the following description of (229):

$structure(syntax(\ldots),$
$\qquad semantics(pre(\{(\exists!X : salient(X))(name(X, \llbracket John \rrbracket))\}),$
$\qquad\qquad content((\exists I : interval(I))$
$\qquad\qquad\qquad (\forall T : instant(T))$
$\qquad\qquad\qquad\qquad (CONTAIN(I, T)$
$\qquad\qquad\qquad\qquad\quad \rightarrow BEFORE(I, now))$
$\qquad\qquad\qquad\qquad \wedge DURING(I, \bullet[(\exists Z : \llbracket house \rrbracket(Z))$
$\qquad\qquad\qquad\qquad\qquad\qquad (\llbracket build \rrbracket(X, Z))]))))$

The temporal content of (229) is contained entirely in the past tense suffix. In (230), both the suffix and the auxiliary make a contribution. The auxiliary places the reported event with respect to the time of the utterance, and the suffix indicates that it is being considered in terms of the instantaneous truth of some proposition. We therefore require a frame for present participles, one for tensed forms of auxiliaries, and one for what the verb *be* contributes when it combines with a present participle form. The present participle indicates that we are considering an instantaneous state of affairs:

(F42): Present participle (semantics)
$structure(syntax(\ldots,$
$\qquad\qquad minor(head(\ldots, vform(nonfinite(participle(present)))), \ldots),$
$\qquad\qquad\qquad \ldots)),$
$\qquad semantics(pre(\ldots),$
$\qquad\qquad content(\bullet[B, \bullet[t, \bullet[C, AT(t, \bullet[C])] \in B]])))$

The present tense form for auxiliaries indicates that the state or event denoted by the complement is happening at the time of utterance:

(F43): Present tense (auxiliary, semantics)
$structure(syntax(\ldots),$
$\qquad semantics(\ldots,$
$\qquad\qquad content(\bullet[R, \bullet[F, now \in F] \in R])))$

Finally, the root frame for *be* as an auxiliary taking a VP with a present participle main verb just converts the content of the complement so that it is ready for
temporal information to be added:

(F44): Semantic frame for *be* **(Present participle complement)**

$structure(syntax(major(\dots,$

$[structure(\dots,$

$semantics(pre(PRE),$

$content(\bullet[Q, Q \in VP])))$

$\longrightarrow$

$structure(\dots,$

$semantics(pre(PRE),$

$content(VP)))])$

$\dots),$

$semantics(\dots, \dots))$

If we use (F30) to combine (F44) and (F43) we obtain

$structure(syntax(major(\dots,$

$[structure(\dots,$

$semantics(pre(PRE),$

$content(CONTENT_{main})))$

$\longrightarrow$

$structure(\dots,$

$semantics(pre(PRE),$

$content(CONTENT_{comp})))])$

$\dots),$

$semantics(\dots, \dots))$

$CONTENT_{main} = \bullet[Q, Q \in CONTENT_{pred}] \in \bullet[R, \bullet[F, now \in F] \in R]$

---

as the representation of the present tense form of the verb *be*. (TB) reduces
$CONTENT_{main}$ here to $\bullet[F, now \in F] \in CONTENT_{pred}$. From (F42) we see that a
typical VP with a present participle main verb, such as *sleeping*, can be described
by a structure like:

$$structure(syntax(\ldots),$$
$$semantics(, pre(\emptyset),$$
$$content(CONTENT)))$$

$$CONTENT = \bullet[T, \bullet[A, (\bullet[u, ([\![sleep(u)]\!] \in T]) \in A]]$$
$$\in \bullet[B, \bullet[t, \bullet[C, AT(t, \bullet[C])] \in B]]$$

If we use the content from this structure as the value for $CONTENT_{pred}$, our description of the content of *is sleeping* becomes:

$$\bullet[F, now \in F] \in (\bullet[T, \bullet[A, (\bullet[u, ([\![sleep(u)]\!] \in T)]) \in A]]$$
$$\in \bullet[B, \bullet[t, \bullet[C, AT(t, \bullet[C])] \in B]])$$

This in turn reduces to $\bullet[A, \bullet[u, AT(now, \bullet[[\![sleep]\!](u))]]]]$, which would lead to an interpretation of

(231) *John is sleeping.*

as:

$$structure(syntax(\ldots),$$
$$semantics(pre(\{(\exists!X : salient(X))(name(X, [\![john]\!])\}),$$
$$content(AT(now, \bullet[[\![sleep]\!](X)]))))$$

This approach would lead us to analyse

(232) *He is irritably tapping his fingers on his desk.*

as though it referred to an instantaneous state of affairs. This seems to contradict our intuitions about (232), since "tapping his fingers on his desk" requires several contacts between the fingers and the desk. We take refuge here in the fact that we have not so far attempted to say anything about the internal structure of events. In particular, the event corresponding to $[\![tap]\!]$ might well have an internal structure which involves repeated contact. This would not be inconsistent with instantaneously being in the middle of such an extended event.

We can easily adapt our analysis for other forms of the auxiliary. For

(233) *John was sleeping.*

we simply need a description of the effect of the past tense modifier on auxiliary verbs. This introduces a past instant, and indicates that the state or event being talked about happened at that instant:

(F45): Past tense (auxiliary, semantics)
$structure(syntax(\ldots),$
$\qquad semantics(pre(\ldots),$
$\qquad\qquad content(\bullet[R, \bullet[F, (\exists T : instant(T) \wedge BEFORE(T, now))$
$\qquad\qquad\qquad\qquad (T \in F))] \in R])))$

The description of (233) is now:

$structure(syntax(\ldots),$
$\qquad semantics(pre(\{(\exists!X : salient(X))(name(X, [\![john]\!]))\}),$
$\qquad\qquad content((\exists T : instant(T) \wedge BEFORE(T, now))$
$\qquad\qquad\qquad AT(T, \bullet[[\![sleep]\!](X)])))))$

We use the same framework to deal with sentences involving other auxiliaries. For sentences using *have* as an auxiliary, such as

(234) *John has slept.*

we need descriptions of the effect of the past participle suffix and one of the root form of *have*. We will interpret (234) as saying that it is currently true that over some past interval John was asleep. This interpretation may well fail to capture some of the differences between (234) and:

(235) *John slept.*

The differences between these two are very subtle, and may even be too subtle to be captured within a framework that ignores matters such as emphasis and emotional overtones. Our interpretation of (234) does at least produce most of the right entailments. More importantly, though, it shows that we can use much the same machinery for *have* + past participle as we used for *be* + present participle.

The frame for the past participle suffix places the report in the past:

(F46): Past participle (semantics)
$structure(syntax(\ldots,$
$\qquad minor(head(\ldots, vform(nonfinite(participle(past))))),$
$\qquad\qquad \ldots)),$
$\qquad semantics(pre(\ldots),$
$\qquad\qquad content(\bullet[B, \bullet[t, \bullet[C, PASTPART] \in B]])))$

$PASTPART = (\exists I : interval(I)$
$\qquad\qquad \wedge (\forall t' : instant(t') \wedge CONTAIN(I, t')) BEFORE(t', t))$
$\qquad (DURING(I, \bullet[C]))] \in B]])))$

The frame for *have*, just like the one for *be*, simply converts the content of the complement so that it is ready for the temporal information:

(F47): Semantic frame for *have* (past participle complement)
$structure(syntax(major(\ldots),$
$\qquad\qquad [structure(syntax(\ldots),$
$\qquad\qquad\qquad semantics(pre(PRE),$
$\qquad\qquad\qquad\qquad content(\bullet[Q, Q \in VP])))$

$\qquad\qquad \longrightarrow$

$\qquad\qquad structure(\ldots,$
$\qquad\qquad\qquad semantics(pre(PRE),$
$\qquad\qquad\qquad\qquad content(VP)))]],$
$\qquad \ldots),$
$\qquad semantics(\ldots))$

From these we could derive the following description of (234):

$structure(syntax(\ldots),$
$\qquad semantics(pre(\{(\exists X : salient(X))(name(X, [\![john]\!]))\}),$
$\qquad\qquad content(CONTENT)))$

$CONTENT = (\exists I : interval(I)$
$\qquad\qquad \wedge (\forall t' : instant(t') \wedge CONTAIN(I, t')) BEFORE(t', now))$
$\qquad\qquad\qquad DURING(I, \bullet[[\![sleep]\!](X)]])))$

Furthermore, we can use the description of the effect of the past tense suffix on auxiliaries to analyse

(236) *John had slept.*

as:

$structure(syntax(\ldots),$
$\qquad semantics(pre(\{\{(\exists X : salient(X))(name(X, [\![john]\!]))\}\}),$
$\qquad\qquad content(CONTENT)))$

$CONTENT = (\exists I : interval(I) \wedge PAST)DURING(I, \bullet[[\![sleep]\!](X)])$
$PAST = (\exists t : instant(t))(\forall t' : instant(t') \wedge CONTAIN(I, t'))BEFORE(t', t)))$

We can use exactly the same approach for modal verbs like *do, can, will,* ... These all require a complement consisting of a VP with an infinitive main verb, and they each do something different with it. We therefore want the infinitive form to produce a structure which says very little about time or context, whilst the modal verbs say quite a lot. We will illustrate with:

(237) *Mary does own a farm.*

We need frames for the interpretation of the null suffix as an infinitive form and for the modal verb *do*. The infinitive form has no effect on the semantics:

(F48): Infinitive (semantics)
$structure(syntax(\ldots,$
$\qquad\qquad minor(head(\ldots, vform(nonfinite(infinitive))),$
$\qquad\qquad\qquad \ldots)),$
$\qquad semantics(pre(\ldots), content(\bullet[P, P])))$

Do says that the state or event denoted by the complement occurred over some extended interval:

(F49): Semantic frame for *do*

$structure(syntax(major(\ldots),$
$\qquad\qquad [structure(syntax(\ldots),$
$\qquad\qquad\qquad semantics(pre(PRE),$
$\qquad\qquad\qquad\qquad content(CONTENT_{do})))$

$\qquad\qquad \longrightarrow$

$\qquad\qquad structure(\ldots,$
$\qquad\qquad\qquad semantics(pre(PRE),$
$\qquad\qquad\qquad\qquad content(CONTENT_{pred})))]),$

$\qquad \ldots),$
$\qquad semantics(\ldots))$

$CONTENT_{do} = \bullet[B, (\bullet[T, \bullet[C, (\exists I : interval(I) \wedge CONTAIN(I,T))$
$\qquad\qquad\qquad\qquad DURING(I, \bullet[C])] \in B] \in CONTENT_{pred})]$

If we combine this with the suffix for present tense auxiliaries we will obtain a description with an embedded rule whose goal has the following content:

$\bullet[B, (\bullet[T, \bullet[C, (\exists I : interval(I) \wedge CONTAIN(I,T))$
$\qquad\qquad DURING(I, \bullet[C])] \in B] \in CONTENT_{pred})]$
$\qquad\qquad\qquad \in \bullet[R, \bullet[F, now \in F]]$

This reduces to

$\bullet[C, (\exists I : interval(I) \wedge CONTAIN(I, now)) DURING(I, \bullet[C])] \in CONTENT_{pred}$

If we substitute the content of *own a farm* for $CONTENT_{pred}$ and continue to simplify with (TB) we get

$\bullet[A, \bullet[u, (\exists I : interval(I) \wedge CONTAIN(I, now))$
$\qquad\qquad DURING(I, \bullet[(\exists Z : [[farm]](Z))([[own]](u, Z))])] \in A]$

as the interpretation of *does own a farm*. From this and the usual analysis of *Mary* we get the following description of (237):

$$
\begin{aligned}
&structure(syntax(\#S, \ldots),\\
&\qquad semantics(pre(\{\{(\exists!X : salient(X))(name(X, [\![Mary]\!])\}\}),\\
&\qquad\qquad content((\exists I : interval(I))(CONTAIN(I, now)\\
&\qquad\qquad\qquad \wedge\ DURING(I, \bullet[(\exists Z : [\![farm]\!](Z))\\
&\qquad\qquad\qquad\qquad ([\![own]\!](X, Z))])))))
\end{aligned}
$$

This is identical to the analysis of (227) (*Mary owns a farm*). As happened with (234) and (235), we have a description of (237) which produces roughly the right entailments, but we have failed to explain the differences between this and (227). Again it seems that our descriptive framework, which fails to consider the goals of the speaker and hence to explain the role of things like emphasis, is inadequate.

We will not consider the other modal verbs in detail. The pattern is identical to what we have just done for *do*, but with different specific effects produced by each such verb. The important point is that we have shown how to combine the kind of temporal and contextual information provided by auxiliaries and modals with the information provided by VP's with nonfinite main verbs. Furthermore, we have done this completely uniformly by combining (fairly) simple descriptions of the meanings of the components by instantiation. In other words, we have done it compositionally.

The auxiliary *be* also occurs with passive participles, as in:

(238) *This house was built by John and Mary.*

We could deal with these in very much the same way as we dealt with the temporal effects of *be* when it occurs with present participles. Passivisation, however, is very similar to a number of other syntactic forms whose semantic effects cannot easily be described until we have a theory of the structure of states and events. We therefore leave this use of *be* to Chapter 5, where we will look in more detail at the components of states and events, and in particular at **thematic roles**. For the moment we will return to the question of complex NP's.

4.3   Complex NP's

4.3.1   Adjectives

Our first extra complication is hardly a complication at all. We simply want to be able to consider NP's which contain adjectives. For this we need to add a semantic element to our frame for adjectives. We start by trying the following:

(F50): Adjective (semantics, additive)
$structure(syntax(major(\ldots,$
$\qquad [structure(syntax(\#NN,\ldots)),$
$\qquad\qquad semantics(pre(PRE),$
$\qquad\qquad\qquad content(\bullet[X, X \in C_{adj}$
$\qquad\qquad\qquad\qquad \wedge\ X \in C_{NN}])))$
$\qquad\qquad \longrightarrow$
$\qquad\qquad structure(syntax(\#NN,\ldots)),$
$\qquad\qquad\qquad semantics(pre(PRE, content(C_{NN})))]),$
$\qquad \ldots),$
$\qquad semantics(pre(\ldots), content(C_{adj})))$

Suppose we have the following specific description of the word *white*:

(F51): Semantic frame for *white* (additive)
$structure(syntax(\ldots),$
$\qquad semantics(pre(\ldots),$
$\qquad\qquad content(\bullet[v, [\![white]\!](v)])))$

Consider the NP *a white elephant*. The determiner *a* combines with the NN *white elephant*, which is in turn composed of the adjective *white* and the NN *elephant*. The content of the NN *elephant* is, by the rules we already have for simple NN's, $\bullet[w, [\![elephant]\!](w)]$. The frame above for adjectives then leads to

$\quad \bullet[X, X \in \bullet[u, [\![white]\!](u)] \wedge X \in \bullet[w, [\![elephant]\!](w)]]$

as the content of the frame for *white elephant*. (TB) reduces this to $\bullet[X, [\![white]\!](X) \wedge [\![elephant]\!](X)]$ — the property of being something which is white and is an elephant. Combining this with the frame for *a* we get the following description of the NP *a white elephant*:

$structure(syntax(\ldots),$
$\qquad semantics(pre(\emptyset),$
$\qquad\qquad content(\bullet[B, (\exists x : [\![white]\!](x) \wedge [\![elephant]\!](x))(x \in B)])))$

This is fine for adjectives whose meanings do not depend on the nature of the object they are applied to. Suppose we had the following description of *a big elephant*:

$$structure(syntax(\ldots),$$
$$semantics(pre(\emptyset),$$
$$content(\bullet[B, (\exists x : [[big]](x) \wedge [[elephant]](x))(x \in B)])))$$

What is $[[big]]$? It seems to shift, depending on the view being taken of the item under consideration. Suppose for instance there was a rat the size of an alsation living at the bottom of the garden. We would certainly want to describe it as "a big rat". Someone who happened to be passing by, and who simply caught a glimpse of it, however, might not realise it was a rat. They would refer to it as "an animal", but they would probably not call it "a big animal". Our willingness to call something *big* seems to depend on how we view it: the same thing can be both big (when viewed as a rat) and not big (when viewed as an animal).

This strongly suggests that our additive analysis of the semantics of adjectives is inadequate, at least for some adjectives. We suggest that it is better to think of adjectives like *big* as relations between individuals and properties. The relation $[[big]]$ holds between an individual X and a property such as $\bullet[x, [[rat]](x)]$ if the individual is "big when viewed as a rat". This does not, of course, help us decide whether something actually is big for a rat, but at least it gives us a formal framework to work in. We therefore propose the following alternative frame for adjectives:

(F52): Adjective (semantics, applicative)
$$structure(syntax(major(\ldots,$$
$$[structure(syntax(\#NN,\ldots)),$$
$$semantics(pre(PRE),$$
$$content(\bullet[X,$$
$$X \in (C_{NN} \in C_{adj})])))$$
$$\longrightarrow$$
$$structure(syntax(\#NN,\ldots)),$$
$$semantics(pre(PRE, content(C_{NN})))]),$$
$$\ldots),$$
$$semantics(pre(\ldots), content(C_{adj})))$$

We can recapture the behaviour of seemingly additive adjectives such as *white* by providing them with frames like the following:

> **(F53): Semantic frame for** *white* **(applicative)**
> $structure(syntax(\ldots),$
> $\qquad semantics(pre(\ldots),$
> $\qquad\qquad content(\bullet[P, \bullet[X, [\![white]\!](X) \wedge (X \in P)]])))$

The content here is something which will generate a property if it is itself instantiated with a property. Thus we can still treat adjectives as though they were additive if that seems appropriate — (F53) will lead to exactly the same analysis of *a white elephant* as the one we obtained above. For cases like *big*, however, we can simply leave the adjective unanalysed. The frame for *big* is now:

> **(F54): Semantic frame for** *big*
> $structure(syntax(\ldots),$
> $\qquad semantics(pre(\ldots),$
> $\qquad\qquad content(\bullet[P, \bullet[X, [\![big]\!](X, P)]])))$

This would lead to a description of the NP *a big rat* as:

> $structure(syntax(\ldots),$
> $\qquad semantics(pre(\emptyset),$
> $\qquad\qquad content(\bullet[B, (\exists x : [\![big]\!](x, \bullet[u, [\![rat]\!](u)]))(x \in B)]])))$

$[\![big]\!]$ here is a relation between individuals and properties — $[\![big]\!](x, \bullet[u, [\![rat]\!](u)])$ says that x is "big for a rat".

4.3.2 Relative clauses

We turn now to **relative clauses**. At first sight relative clauses are rather like additive adjectives. They provide extra information which constrains the property denoted by the basic NN. In

(239) *A woman who owns a farm.*

the property of being someone who owns a farm is added to the property of being a woman to obtain the interpretation of the NN. We therefore need the following rule for combining this kind of **restrictive** relative clause with an NN.

(R13): NN + relative clause
$[structure(syntax(\#NN, minor(\ldots)),$
$\quad\quad semantics(pre(PRE_{NN} \cup PRE_{rclause}),$
$\quad\quad\quad\quad content(\bullet[X, X \in CONT_{NN} \wedge X \in CONT_{rclause}])))$

$\longrightarrow$

$structure(syntax(\#NN, minor(\ldots)),$
$\quad\quad semantics(pre(PRE_{NN}),$
$\quad\quad\quad\quad content(CONT_{NN})))$
$structure(syntax(\#S,$
$\quad\quad\quad\quad minor(\ldots, foot(slash(-)), wh(\ldots + rel(+)), \ldots)),$
$\quad\quad semantics(pre(PRE_{rclause}),$
$\quad\quad\quad\quad content(CONT_{rclause})))]$

What is the content of the relative clause? For the relative clause *who owns a farm* from (239), it is clearly:

$[\![who]\!] \in \bullet[A, \bullet[u, (\exists I : interval(I) \wedge CONTAIN(I, now))$
$\quad\quad\quad\quad DURING(I, \bullet[(\exists x : [\![farm]\!](x))[\![own]\!](u, x)])] \in A]$

What is $[\![who]\!]$, the content of the NP *who*, in this expression? If we take it to be the identity $\bullet[R, R]$, then the content of *who owns a farm* simplifies to

$\bullet[u, (\exists I : interval(I) \wedge CONTAIN(I, now))$
$\quad\quad\quad DURING(I, \bullet[(\exists x : [\![farm]\!](x))[\![own]\!](u, x)])]$

(R13) would combine this with the content of *woman* to obtain an NN with the following content:

$\bullet[Y, [\![woman]\!](Y)$
$\quad\quad \wedge (\exists I : interval(I) \wedge CONTAIN(I, now))$
$\quad\quad\quad\quad DURING(I, \bullet[(\exists x : [\![farm]\!](x))[\![own]\!](Y, x)])]$

This leads to the following description for the NP in (239):

$$structure(syntax(\#NP, \ldots),$$
$$semantics(pre(\emptyset),$$
$$content(CONTENT)))$$

$$CONTENT = \bullet[B, (\exists y : ([\![woman]\!](y) \land FARMOWNER))(y \in B)]$$
$$FARMOWNER = (\exists I : interval(I) \land CONTAIN(I, now))$$
$$DURING(I, \bullet[(\exists x : [\![farm]\!](x))[\![own]\!](y, x)])$$

This is just like the description of *a woman*, except that the constraint on the existential quantifier for y is rather more complicated here.

We would like to use (R13) to deal with relative clauses with gaps, as in:

(240) *A farm which Mary owns* ...

To deal with this we need to add a semantic component to our syntactic rule for this kind of relative clause:

(R14): Relative clause with gap, semantics
$$[structure(syntax(\#S,$$
$$minor(\ldots, foot(slash(-), wh(\ldots + rel(+)), \ldots), \ldots)),$$
$$semantics(pre(PRE),$$
$$content(\bullet[A, \bullet[T, (\bullet[X, X] \in CONT_S)] \in A])))$$

$$\longrightarrow$$

$$structure(syntax(SLASH, minor(\ldots, foot(\ldots, wh(\ldots + rel(+)), \ldots), \ldots)),$$
$$semantics(\ldots))$$
$$structure(syntax(\#S,$$
$$minor(\ldots,$$
$$foot(slash(structure(syntax(SLASH, \ldots),$$
$$semantics(pre(\ldots),$$
$$content(\bullet[Z,$$
$$Z \in T])))),$$
$$\ldots),$$
$$\ldots)),$$
$$semantics(pre(PRE),$$
$$content(CONT_S)))]$$

This is undeniably complex. This is perhaps inevitable, since the phenomenon we are trying to deal with is complex. Unfortunately, it is also not strictly compositional according to our criteria for compositionality. The problem is that the content for the goal of this rule contains an objectification with respect to T, where T appears free in the content of the slashed structure (the "missing item"). The semantics of the missing item is thus not well-defined, at least if the missing item is considered as a free-standing constituent of the relative clause. It is not entirely clear, however, that the missing item is a "constituent", since there is not actually anything there. We leave this as a problem. The above rule provides as simple an analysis of the semantics of relative clauses with missing items as we can manage. It may fail to be quite as compositional as we would like, or it may suggest that we should not regard missing items as constituents. What it does do is enable us to describe (240) as:

$$structure(syntax(\#NP, \ldots),$$
$$semantics(pre(\{(\exists!X : salient(X))(name(X, [\![Mary]\!]))\}),$$
$$content(CONTENT)))$$

$$CONTENT = \bullet[B, (\exists Y : ([\![farm]\!](Y)$$
$$\wedge (\exists I : interval(I) \wedge CONTAIN(I, now))$$
$$DURING(I, \bullet[\![own]\!](X, Y))(Y \in B)])]$$

We can easily adapt (R14) to deal with cases where the WH-pronoun is missing, since we do not actually do anything with its semantics in (R14). We can also deal with *whiz*–deleted forms and appositive NP's, since these are simply contractions of the kind of relative clause starting with *who is/which is*. All we need to do in order to deal with them, then, is to project the effects of the missing words onto the meaning of what we do have. We can thus derive the semantic effects of nearly all the kinds of relative clause we discussed in Chapter 3. The only ones we do not have a treatment for are *to*-relative clauses, as in *a sight to behold*. We do not provide an analysis of the meaning of these cases since we simply do not know what they mean.

The discussion above dealt with relative clauses as though they were like adjectives, adding some extra information to help constrain our specifications of individuals. This is not their only function. In

(241) *Mary, who owns a farm, loves John.*

the relative clause *who owns a farm* is not there to help distinguish the Mary who owns a farm from the one who lives in the centre of Bradford. Its function is to provide some extra new information about Mary. We could paraphrase (241) as

(242) *Mary owns a farm and loves John.*

without distorting its meaning all that much. We therefore need the following alternative rule for such **attributive** uses of relative clauses:

(R15): NP + relative clause
$[structure(syntax(\#NP, \ldots),$
$\quad\quad semantics(pre(PRE_{NP} \cup PRE_{rclause}),$
$\quad\quad\quad content(\bullet[A, \bullet[X, ((X \in A)$
$\quad\quad\quad\quad\quad\quad \wedge (X \in (\bullet[Y, Y] \in CONT_{rclause})))]$
$\quad\quad\quad\quad\quad\quad\quad\quad \in CONT_{NP}])))$

$\longrightarrow$

$structure(syntax(\#NP, \ldots),$
$\quad\quad semantics(pre(PRE_{NP}),$
$\quad\quad\quad content(CONT_{NP})))$
$structure(syntax(\#S, \ldots),$
$\quad\quad semantics(pre(PRE_{rclause}),$
$\quad\quad\quad content(CONT_{rclause})))]$

Using this rule we can describe (241) as:

$structure(syntax(\#S, \ldots),$
$\quad\quad semantics(pre(\{(\exists!X : salient(X))(name(X, [\![Mary]\!])),$
$\quad\quad\quad\quad\quad\quad (\exists!Y : salient(Y))(name(Y, [\![John]\!]))\}),$
$\quad\quad\quad content(CONTENT)))$

$CONTENT = ((\exists I : interval(I) \wedge CONTAIN(I, now))$
$\quad\quad\quad DURING(I, \bullet[(\exists W : [\![farm]\!](W))[\![own]\!](X, W)$
$\quad\quad \wedge (\exists I' : interval(I') \wedge CONTAIN(I', now))$
$\quad\quad\quad\quad DURING(I', \bullet[[\![love]\!](X, Y)]))$

The statement that Mary owns a farm is part of the content of the sentence, rather than being a component of the description of Mary. We have managed to distinguish the semantic effects of the two types of relative clause on the basis of different syntactic analyses. Restrictive relative clauses are combined with NN's to obtain more complex constraints on quantifiers. Attributive relative clauses are combined with NP's to obtain more complex overall statements about the world.

4.3.3   Plural NP's

We finish our discussion of NP's for the moment by considering **plurals**. We start with definite plurals NP's, as in

(243) *Mary sold the cows.*

We read this as saying that Mary sold each member of some salient group of cows, so that our target description would be:

$$
\begin{aligned}
&structure(syntax(\#S,\ldots),\\
&\qquad semantics(pre(\{(\exists!X:salient(X))(name(X,[\![Mary]\!])),\\
&\qquad\qquad\qquad (\exists!Y:salient(Y))(Y\subseteq[\![cow]\!]))\}),\\
&\qquad\qquad content(CONTENT)))
\end{aligned}
$$

$$
\begin{aligned}
CONTENT=&(\exists I:interval(I))\\
&(\forall T:instant(T)\wedge CONTAIN(I,T))(BEFORE(T,now))\\
&\wedge DURING(I,\bullet[(\forall W:W\in Y)[\![sell]\!](X,W)])
\end{aligned}
$$

The expression $P\subseteq P'$ here is an abbreviation for $(\forall x:x\in P)(x\in P')$. $t\in t'$ was introduced as an abbreviation for $\pi_1(t,t')$, in order to emphasise the similarity between t satisfying the property t' and the more classical notion of t being a member of t'. Given this similarity, it seems only reasonable to use $P\subseteq P'$ as an abbreviation if everything that satisfies P also satisfies P'.

In order to obtain this description for (243), we need a frame for *the* when its complement is a plural NN:

(F55): **Semantic frame for *the* (plural)**
$$
\begin{aligned}
&structure(syntax(\ldots),\\
&\qquad semantics(pre(\bullet[A,\{(\exists!X:salient(X))(X\subseteq A)\}]),\\
&\qquad\qquad content(\bullet[A,\bullet[A',X\subseteq A']])))
\end{aligned}
$$

This is very similar to our frame for *the* as a determiner for singular NP's. The only difference is that in the plural case we talk in terms of $\subseteq$ where we used $\in$ for the singular one. We could make them even more similar by using identical frames for *the*, and assuming that the property corresponding to a singular NN is guaranteed to be a singleton. It makes little difference. What does matter is that our treatments of singular and plural definite NP's are very similar.

We can adapt the frame for *a* in the same way to obtain the semantics of *some*:

(F56): Semantic frame for *some*
$structure(syntax \ldots),$
$\qquad semantics(pre((\bullet[A, \emptyset]),$
$\qquad\qquad content(\bullet[A, \bullet[A', (\exists x : x \subseteq A)(x \subseteq A')]])))$

It seems as though we can deal with most plural NP's very much as we dealt with singular ones. It turns out that there are a number of cases where the analysis of plural NP's cannot easily be made to parallel the treatment we have given for singular ones. The first of these concerns complex determiner sequences, as illustrated by:

(244) *One of the students is asleep.*

It seems here as though *of the students* is playing the role of an NN. (244) looks very like:

(245) *One student is asleep.*

We would expect to treat *one* in (245) almost exactly as we would treat *a* in:

(246) *A student is asleep.*

We would therefore like to treat *one* in (244) in much the same way as well, in which case we need an analysis of *of the students* which treats it just like an NN. For this we need the following description of the word *of*:

(F57): Semantic frame for *of* **(in complex determiner sequence)**
$structure(syntax(major(\ldots,$

$$[structure(syntax(\#NN,\ldots),$$
$$semantics(pre(PRE),$$
$$content(C_{NN})))$$

$$\longrightarrow$$

$$structure(syntax(\#NP,\ldots),$$
$$semantics(pre(PRE),$$
$$content(C_{NP})))]),$$

$$\ldots),$$
$$semantics(pre(\ldots),content(\ldots)))$$

$C_{NN} = \bullet[C \bullet [Y, (\forall B : Y \in B)(B \in C)]]$

With this, and using the normal description of *a* as our description of *one*, we can obtain the following description of:

(247) *Mary sold one of the cows.*

$structure(syntax(\#S,\ldots),$
$$semantics(pre(\{(\exists!X : salient(X))(name(X,[\![Mary]\!])),$$
$$(\exists!Y : salient(Y))(Y' \subseteq [\![cow]\!])\}),$$
$$content(CONTENT)))$$

$CONTENT = (\exists I : interval(I))$
$$(\forall T : instant(T) \wedge CONTAIN(I,T))(BEFORE(T,now))$$
$$\wedge \; DURING(I,$$
$$\bullet[(\exists W : (\forall B : W \in B)(B \subseteq Y))[\![sell]\!](X,W)])$$

Note, however, that $Y \subseteq Y$. Hence if $(\exists W : (\forall B : W \in B)(B \subseteq Y))[\![sell]\!](X,W))$ then $(\exists W : W \in Y)[\![sell]\!](X,W)$. In other words, there is a W which is a member of Y, the salient group of cows, and Mary (X) sold it.

We can deal with

(248) *Mary sold some of the cows.*
(249) *Mary sold all of the cows.*

in exactly the same way. This analysis breaks down, however, when we come to consider:

(250) *Mary sold most of the cows.*

(250) seems to lie somewhere between (248) and (249). Given (249) we can infer for any cow in the relevant group that Mary sold it. Given (248) there is nothing we can say about any particular cow. And from (250) we would expect to be able to infer for any particular cow that Mary probably sold it. Any treatment of (250), then, is going to require us to include probabilities in our description language. There are currently two broad approaches to the task of including probabilities in a formal language such as PT. We could incorporate the mechanisms of classical statistics, or we could turn to recent work in **non-monotonic logic**. Classical statistics, unfortunately, requires independence assumptions which are unrealistic in the present context; and non-monotonic logic is not yet settled enough for us to want to make a choice from among the competing theories. We therefore leave quantifiers like *most*, along with modifiers like *probably*, as a problem we cannot yet tackle.

The final problem with plural NP's is still more intractable. Consider the following:

(251) *Henry is eating peaches.*
(252) *Henry eats peaches.*

We might try to deal with (251) as though it were really:

(253) *Henry is eating some peaches.*

(253), however, seems to refer to some particular, though unspecified, collection of peaches. There is a pile of peaches which Henry is eating. (251) seems to make less reference to such a pile, and (252) could certainly be true in the absence of any particular pile of peaches that Henry eats. We will attempt to deal with such **generic** uses of **bare plural NP's** by treating them as though they were:

(251') *Henry is peach-eating.*
(252') *Henry peach-eats.*

Peach-eat may not be a common English expression, but this kind of construction does occur:

(254) *People often go house-hunting in the spring.*

We will not be able to deal with this kind of construction until we have made some assumptions about the structure of actions like eating and hunting. We therefore leave the rest of this discussion of NP's until Chapter 5, where we will investigate such assumptions.

4.4   Coordination

We end this chapter with a look at coordination. Our treatment of the syntax of coordination dealt with it using frames and rules that combined items of any type whatever, so long as they were of the same type. In order to add a semantic component to this analysis, we have to have semantic operators which can also be applied to objects of any type whatsoever. The syntactic analysis will, for instance, deal with all of the following:

(255) *He ate an apple and a peach.*
(256) *She left her husband and moved to France.*
(257) *John baked a cake and Mary ate it.*

The phrases which are conjoined in (255) – (257) are of different types — two NP's in (255), two VP's in (256) and two S's in (257). The frames and rule we presented in Chapter 3 for coordination allow for this. When we come to add a semantic component to this treatment, we have a problem. It seems at first sight that we are going to want to use the standard logical connectives $\land, \lor, \rightarrow$ as the basis of our semantic analysis. Unfortunately, these connectives are used only for joining formulae — things whose meaning is taken to be a truth value. This will not cause us any trouble with examples like (257), where the conjoined items are indeed the sort of thing whose meaning corresponds to some extent to a truth value, but it will be awkward when we try to deal with the other examples.

We start then by considering (257), since it is fairly easy to see how we can translate this using the logical connective $\land$. (257) consists of two sentences joined together by *and*. The obvious way to construct the commitment for (257) is to say that its presupposition consists of the union of the presuppositions for the constituent sentences, and its content consists of the conjunction of their contents. In general, if we have a coordination of two sentences then the presupposition consists of the union of their individual presuppositions and the content consists of the appropriate combination of their contents. To achieve this, we need to add semantic components to the frame for infix coordinators and the rule for coordination as follows:

(F58): Infix conjunction (*and, or* ...)
structure(syntax(major(conj,
                  [structure(syntax(#CONJ),
                             minor(...,
                                   local(conjtype(CTYPE),
                                         structure(SYNTAX,
                                                   semantics(...))))))),
                  semantics(pre(PRE),
                            content(•[X, X CONJ X'])))

$\longrightarrow$

structure(SYNTAX,
          semantics(pre(PRE), content(X')))]),
minor(..., local(conjtype(CTYPE)))),
semantics(pre(...), content(CONJ)))

(R16): Coordination (infix-form)
[structure(SYNTAX,
           semantics(pre(PRE_1 ∪ PRE_2),
                     content(X ∈ CONTENT_CONJ)))

$\longrightarrow$

structure(SYNTAX,
          semantics(pre(PRE_1), content(X))),
structure(syntax(#CONJ,
                 minor(..., local(SYNTAX)),
          semantics(pre(PRE_1), content(CONTENT_CONJ))))]

With this frame and rule, we can analyse (257) as required. The semantics of the lexical frame will produce the following content for *and Mary ate it* (with U and V constrained appropriately in the presupposition so that they correspond to *Mary* and *it*):

$$\bullet[X,X$$
$$\wedge\ (\exists I : interval(I) \wedge (\forall t : instant(t))(CONTAIN(I,t) \rightarrow BEFORE(t,now))$$
$$DURING(I, \bullet[[[(eat)]](U,V)])]$$

Combining this with the content of *John baked a cake* would then lead directly to:

$$(\exists I' : interval(I') \wedge (\forall t' : instant(t'))(CONTAIN(I',t') \rightarrow BEFORE(t',now))$$
$$DURING(I', \bullet[[[(bake)]](U',V')])]$$
$$\wedge\ (\exists I : interval(I) \wedge (\forall t : instant(t))(CONTAIN(I,t) \rightarrow BEFORE(t,now))$$
$$DURING(I, \bullet[[[(eat)]](U,V)])]$$

This looks perfectly reasonable. If we try to deal with, say, (255) the same way we run into trouble. The content for (255) would be $\bullet[A, (\exists x : apple(x))(x \in A)] \wedge \bullet[A', (\exists y : peach(y))(y \in A')]$. This expression is simply not well-formed according to the presentation of PT in Chapter 2. The syntactic rules for PT we presented there allow logical connectives such as $\wedge$ to be used for combining formulae, whereas $\bullet[A, (\exists x : apple(x))(x \in A)]$ and $\bullet[A', (\exists y : peach(y))(y \in A')]$ are just terms. We need to allow these connectives to construct terms from terms, as well as formulae from formulae. We also need to supplement our proof theory with distribution rules for eliminating such complex terms:

$$\frac{\Delta \vdash_V (T \wedge T') \in P}{\Delta \vdash_V (T \in P) \wedge (T' \in P)} \text{ (Left } \wedge \text{ dist.)} \qquad \frac{\Delta \vdash_V T \in (P \wedge P')}{\Delta \vdash_V (T \in P) \wedge (T \in P')} \text{ (Right } \wedge \text{ dist.)}$$

$$\frac{\Delta \vdash_V (T \vee T') \in P}{\Delta \vdash_V (T \in P) \vee (T' \in P)} \text{ (Left } \vee \text{ dist.)} \qquad \frac{\Delta \vdash_V T \in (P \vee P')}{\Delta \vdash_V (T \in P) \vee (T \in P')} \text{ (Right } \vee \text{ dist.)}$$

If we follow our standard treatment of transitive verbs, using the above content for *an apple and a peach*, we find that the content of (255) is:

$$(\exists I : interval(I) \wedge (\forall t : instant(t))(CONTAIN(I,t) \rightarrow BEFORE(t,now))$$
$$DURING(I, \bullet[\bullet[u, [[(eat)]](X,u)] \in (\bullet[A, (\exists x : apple(x))(x \in A)]$$
$$\wedge\ \bullet[A', (\exists y : peach(y))(y \in A')]])]$$

Using Right $\wedge$ distribution and simplifying, this becomes

$$(\exists I : interval(I) \wedge (\forall t : instant(t))(CONTAIN(I,t) \rightarrow BEFORE(t,now))$$
$$DURING(I, \bullet[(\exists x : apple(x))[[(eat)(X,x)]]$$
$$\wedge(\exists y : peach(y))[[eat]](X,y)])$$

This is very similar to what we would have obtained if we had started with

(258) *He ate an apple and he ate a peach.*

except that in that case we would have had a conjunction of two statements about past intervals, with X eating x during one of them and y during the other. Are they equivalent? It all depends on the properties we ascribe to intervals. They are, however, definitely very similar.

Very much the same happens with (256), and also with:

(259) *John and Mary built a house.*

The content for (259) turns out to be:

$$(\exists I : interval(I) \wedge (\forall t : instant(t))(CONTAIN(I,t) \rightarrow BEFORE(t,now))$$
$$DURING(I, \bullet[(\exists x : house(x))(build(X,x) \wedge build(Y,x))])$$

This again looks fine. If we analyse

(260) *John or Mary built a house.*

the same way, however, the analysis looks less convincing. The content

$$(\exists I : interval(I) \wedge (\forall t : instant(t))(CONTAIN(I,t) \rightarrow BEFORE(t,now))$$
$$DURING(I, \bullet[(\exists x : house(x))(build(X,x) \vee build(Y,x))])$$

seems to correspond to

(261) *There is a house which either John built or Mary built.*

whereas (260) looks more like:

(262) *Either there is a house which John built or there is one which Mary built.*

For disjunctions, the distinction turns out not to matter all that much. It is hard to see anything which is entailed by one of (260) and (261) and not by the other, so we seem to have the right analysis of (260) after all. For conjunctions it is much more important. It looks as though

(263) *John and Mary built a house each.*

means something quite different from what (259) means. Words like *each* and *respectively* introduce considerable extra complexity into both the syntax and the semantics. We leave the analysis of sentences like (263) for another occasion.

We have now developed analyses of a range of English constructions. We have done this whilst assuming that states and events are indivisible unstructured wholes. To make any further progress we need to abandon this assumption and investigate the structure imposed on states and events by the way we talk about them. We therefore turn in the next chapter to the structure which our perception of the world must impose on states, events and particularly actions if the organisation of our language is indeed a reflection of our view of the world.

5 ROLES AND STRUCTURES

There are numerous phenomena which cannot be captured within the framework of Chapter 4. In particular, we may need to consider the internal structure of states and events, rather than just taking them to be atomic unanalysable objects. In the present chapter we will try to see exactly how much we have to assume about this internal structure in order to deal with a range of linguistic phenomena. We do not want to assume too much, since the more we assume the more likely we are to be wrong. Nonetheless, anything we do find ourselves forced to assume will be of interest, since it will correspond to a claim about the structure our perceptions impose on the world. To put it very simply, if we find ourselves forced to make a distinction between, say, verbs that correspond to states and verbs that correspond to actions then our view of the world must also include a distinction between states and actions.

We start by considering the notion of **thematic role**. This is a term which has been used in a wide variety of ways, to deal with a wide variety of problems. We will not provide a survey of everything that has been said about thematic roles over the past twenty years. Our intention is rather to take one specific view of the idea, and see what we can do with it.

Suppose we applied the mechanisms of Chapter 4 to the following sentences (from Fillmore [1968]):

(264) *John opened the door.*
(265) *The key opened the door.*
(266) *The door opened.*

The contents in the descriptions we would obtain for (264) and (265) would each contain mention of a proposition like $\bullet[[[open]](X, Y)]$, where X would denote John in (264) and the key in (265). The content in the description of (266) would mention a proposition like $\bullet[[[open]](X)]$, where X denotes the door. There is clearly something wrong here. First, we have introduced two predicates for a single kind of event. We have a 2-place predicate $[[open]]$, as required for (264) and (265), and a 1-place predicate $[[open]]$ as required for (266); and we have no understanding of the relation between them. Second, the 2-place predicate itself seems to denote two different kinds of event. If we were to start to develop a general theory of actions and events, we would expect to include assumptions such as the following:

$$(\forall X : (\exists Y [\![open]\!] (X, Y))) animate(X)$$

In other words, only animate beings can open things. This assumption would clearly be contradicted if we interpreted (265) using $\bullet [\![[open]\!] (X, Y)]$ with X denoting the key. There is, however, no alternative within the framework of Chapter 4.

Fillmore was interested in sentences like (264) – (266), and their relationship with things like

(267) *John opened the door with the key.*

as examples of a subtle syntactic phenomenon. His proposed answer introduced some rather "semantic" seeming ideas into syntactic theory. Consider the following sets of sentences and non-sentences:

(268) *John was cooking.*
(269) *Mary was cooking.*
(270) *John and Mary were cooking.*

(268) *John was cooking.*
(271) *The cake was cooking*
*(272) *John and the cake were cooking.*

(268), (269) and (271) all seem to have very similar syntactic structures, yet we can conjoin (268) and (269) but not (268) and (271). Why not?

Fillmore's suggestion is that the surface position of an NP within a sentence is just an indication of its **thematic role** with respect to the state or event denoted by the main verb. *John*, *Mary* and *The cake* are all **surface subjects** in (268) – (271). In (268) and (269), however, the surface subject is in fact the **agent** of the action of cooking, whereas in (271) it is the **semantic object**.

If thematic roles are marked distinctly at some level of **deep structure** then (268) and (271) will in fact have different syntactic structures, and hence it will be no surprise that they cannot be conjoined to form (272). These markings are not, however, visible in the surface forms. The only way that we can tell that *John* must be an agent appearing in surface subject position while *The cake* must be a semantic object is that people are the sort of things that can do cooking and cakes are the sort of things that can be cooked. The sort of information that is required for this kind of distinction can be quite subtle:

(273) *The cannibal was cooking carefully.*
(274) *The missionary was cooking nicely.*
? (275) *The cannibal and the missionary were cooking.*

(275) may not actually be ungrammatical, in the way that (272) seemed to be. Nonetheless it does not combine the obvious interpretations of (273) and (274).

5.1 Structured Meanings

We will take part of Fillmore's analysis, but not all of it. We accept the suggestion that there is a restricted set of relationships between objects and states or events. In any particular case, the relevant relationships are indicated by specific syntactic forms — agents can be syntactic subjects, semantic objects can be syntactic subjects or syntactic objects, and so on. The range of relationships for any particular verb, however, is not a purely syntactic property, nor is the eligibility of any particular NP for a given role. Our descriptions of individual words provide some information about their surrounding syntactic context — that *kill*, for instance, subcategorises for an NP as syntactic object whereas *die* requires an empty complement. They also, however, provide information about their semantics. It is the combination of these two kinds of information that leads to the phenomena we are interested in here. We will illustrate what is going on by comparing *kill* and *die*. We start with rather general frames for these kinds of verb:

(F59): Simple agentive verb (e.g. *kill*)

$structure(syntax(major(\ldots,$

$$[structure(syntax(\#VP,\ldots)$$
$$semantics(pre(PRE),$$
$$content(CONTENT_{VP})))$$

$$\longrightarrow$$

$$structure(syntax(\#NP,\ldots),$$
$$semantics(pre(PRE),$$
$$content(CONTENT_{NP})))]],$$

$$\ldots),$$
$$semantics(pre(\ldots),content(VERB)))$$

$AG = \bullet[EVENT, \bullet[A, \bullet[A', (\exists E : event(E) \wedge type(E, EVENT))$
$$((\bullet[u, agent(E, u)] \in A')$$
$$\wedge (\bullet[v, object(E, v)] \in A))]]]$$
$CONTENT_{VP} = \bullet[T, (CONTENT_{NP} \in (VERB \in AG)) \in T]$

(F60): Simple agentless verb (e.g. *die***)**
$structure(syntax(major(\ldots,$

$\qquad\qquad [structure(syntax(\#VP,\ldots)$

$\qquad\qquad\qquad\qquad semantics(pre(PRE),$

$\qquad\qquad\qquad\qquad\qquad content(CONTENT)))$

$\qquad\qquad\qquad\xrightarrow{\qquad}$

$\qquad\qquad \emptyset]),$

$\qquad\quad \ldots),$

$\qquad semantics(pre(\ldots), content(VERB)))$

$CONTENT = \bullet[T, (VERB \in \bullet[EVENT,$

$\qquad\qquad\qquad\qquad \bullet[A, (\exists E : event(E) \wedge type(E, EVENT))$

$\qquad\qquad\qquad\qquad\qquad (\bullet[u, object(E, u)] \in A))) \in T]$

These frames are slightly simpler than the frames we presented in Chapter 4 for transitive and intransitive verbs. In Chapter 4, we had no access to the internal structure of events. As a consequence, we had to describe how the information supplied by the NP's was to be combined with the property corresponding to the verb. To do this we effectively had to **type-raise** [Hendriks 1987, Moortgat 1987] this property. Now that we have separated out the roles of the various subcategorised NP's, we can incorporate their contributions rather more directly. This not only simplifies the presentation of frames for verbs; it will also enable us to provide, in Section 5.3, a very neat characterisation of the meaning of "bare plural" NP's.

The specific frames for *kill* and *die* are:

(F61): Frame for *kill*
$structure(syntax(\ldots),$

$\qquad\qquad semantics(pre(\ldots), content(die)))$

(F62): Frame for *die*
$structure(syntax(\ldots),$

$\qquad\qquad semantics(pre(\ldots), content(die)))$

These are identical. The only difference between the words *kill* and *die* is that *kill* is an agentive verb, so its frame should be unified with (F59), whereas *die* is agentless so its description should be unified with (F60).

The description of *kill* that we obtain by unifying (F59) and (F61) tells us two things. It tells us the (syntactic) fact that *kill* requires an NP complement; and it tells us that it denotes an event in which someone or something dies, and that both the person or thing that dies and some person or thing that brought this about are going to be described.

We can compare the combination of (F59) and (F61) with the frame we would have provided for it in Chapter 4, where the content would have been something like $\bullet[X, \bullet[Y, [\![kill]\!](X,Y)]]$. If we use (TB) to simplify the combination of (F59) and (F61), we see that the **internal structure** of $[\![kill]\!]$ is given by the following equivalence:

$$\forall X (\forall Y ([\![kill]\!](X,Y) \equiv (\exists A : event(A) \wedge type(A, die))(object(A,Y) \wedge agent(A, X))$$

The frames for agentive and agentless verbs replace the less specific frames we had in Chapter 4 for intransitive and transitive verbs. These more precise descriptions enable us to characterise classes of verbs in terms of their semantic structures. We will make more use of this below.

The frames for *kill* and *die* seem to contain redundant information. The content of the frame for *kill*, for instance, objectifies the formula $(\exists A : event(A) \wedge type(A, die))$ $(object(A, Y) \wedge agent(A, X))$ with respect to X and Y. It should be possible, by inspecting this formula, to realise that it requires to be instantiated twice in order to become a proposition. From this we should be able to infer that it must be a transitive verb, with the syntactic subject and the complement providing the items which are to instantiate it. We should even be able to infer that the complement must be an NP, since it is going to denote the kind of entity which is capable of being the semantic object of an event of type *die*. It is the syntactic presentation of this information that seems most redundant. We definitely need the semantic presentation, since this cannot be reconstructed entirely from the syntax. We retain the redundant syntactic presentation to help with our account of phenomena such as passivisation, and the relations between (264) – (267).

We return to (264) – (267). We provide the following general frame for verbs like *open*:

(F63): Frame for instrumental agentive verb (e.g. *open*)

$structure(syntax(major(\dots,$

$$[structure(syntax(\#VP,\dots),$$
$$semantics(pre(PRE_{VP}),$$
$$content(C_{VP})))$$

$$\overrightarrow{COMP}]),$$

$$\dots),$$
$$semantics(pre(\dots),content(VERB)))$$

$IAG = \bullet[EVENT, \bullet[X, \bullet[Y, \bullet[Z, (\exists E : event(E) \wedge type(E, EVENT))$
$$(\bullet[u, object(E, u)] \in Y)$$
$$\wedge \ \bullet[u', instrument(E, u')] \in Z)$$
$$\wedge \ \bullet[u'', agent(E, u'')] \in X)]]]])))$$
$(COMP = structure(syntax(\#NP, \dots),$
$$semantics(pre(\dots), content(C_{NP})))$$
$$structure(syntax(\#PP,$$
$$minor(\dots,$$
$$local(ptype(with),$$
$$structure(syntax(\dots)$$
$$semantics(pre(\dots),$$
$$content(C_{PP})))),$$
$$semantics(\dots))]])))$$
$$\wedge C_{VP} = C_{NP} \in (C_{PP} \in (VERB \in IAG)))$$
$\vee \ (COMP = structure(syntax(\#NP, \dots),$
$$semantics(pre(\dots), content(C_{NP})))$$
$$\wedge C_{VP} = \bullet[V, \bullet[B, \exists T(T \in B)] \in (C_{NP} \in (V \in (VERB \in IAG)))]])$$
$\vee \ (COMP = structure(syntax(\#NP, \dots),$
$$semantics(pre(\dots), content(C_{NP})))$$
$$\wedge C_{VP} = \bullet[V, (C_{NP} \in (\bullet[B, \exists T(T \in B)] \in (V \in (VERB \in IAG)))]])$$
$\vee \ (COMP = \emptyset$
$$\wedge C_{VP} = \bullet[V, \bullet[B, \exists T(T \in B)]$$
$$\in (V \in (\bullet[B', \exists T'(T' \in B')]$$
$$\in (VERB \in IAG)))))))])$$

This is undeniably complex. We are trying to provide a description of a complex phenomenon, and we could hardly expect it to be simple. The essential point, however, is fairly straightforward. The expression

$$IAG = \bullet[EVENT, \bullet[X, \bullet[Y, \bullet[Z, (\exists E : event(E) \wedge type(E, EVENT))$$
$$(\bullet[u, object(E, u)] \in Y)$$
$$\wedge \ \bullet[u', instrument(E, u')] \in Z)$$
$$\wedge \ \bullet[u'', agent(E, u'')] \in X)]]]])))$$

shows us the basic structure of the reported event. It is an event of type $EVENT$, with an agent, a semantic object and an instrument. There are then four possible complements, each of which contributes a different selection of the items for the various roles. The first specifies that the complement consists of an NP and a PP headed by *with*. In this case the NP specifies the semantic object, the PP specifies the instrument, and the agent is left unspecified (to be filled in later by the subject). The second possibility is that the complement should consist of just an NP, in which case this NP supplies the semantic object. In this case the instrument is supplied by an implicit existential quantifier. The third option is just like the second except that it is the agent that is supplied by the implicit existential quantifier and the instrument that is provided later by the subject. Finally, in the fourth case the complement is empty, with the semantic object to be filled in later by the subject and both the agent and the instrument specified via existential quantifiers.

The frame for verbs such as *open*, then, specifies a range of possible complement types, and associates with each of them a way of building up the meaning of the VP in which the verb appears. This approach commits us to saying that any time anything is opened (or whatever), there is an agent that did the opening and an instrument that they used for doing it. We will see shortly that there will be cases where we cannot afford to assume that the basic semantic expression for the meaning of the verb contains all and only the relevant semantic roles. We will return to this when we come to consider PP's which provide information about the time, place or manner of the event.

It should also be noted that we have not provided enough information to distinguish between the second and third options in any particular case. If all we had was (F63) we would not be able to tell whether the subject of (264) was the agent or the instrument, and likewise for (265).

One final point relating to (F63) is that we have made no attempt to generalise over properties of the various semantic roles. It seems, for instance, that agents are generally supplied as subjects, and that semantic objects can appear either as subjects (if no agent is specified) or as syntactic objects. We have nothing to add in this area, and we simply leave it as a topic for further investigation.

5.2 Passives

The frame for instrumental verbs showed how the same verb could have a range of different complements, each of which supplied specifications for items playing different roles. We have already seen an example of this, without discussing it. Consider:

(276) *Tibbles killed a bird.*
(277) *A bird was killed by Tibbles.*

These are very similar, at least in terms of presupposition and content. There are good reasons for choosing to say one of (276) and (277) rather than the other, but their commitments, at least, are the same. It seems that the suffix *-ed* can mark a change of complement as well as putting the reported event into the past. We require the following frames:

(F64): Passive participle (semantics, with PP)
$structure(syntax(\ldots,$
$$minor(head(\ldots, vform(nonfinite(participle(passive))))),$$
$$\ldots)),$$
$$semantics(pre(\ldots),$$
$$content(\bullet[P, \bullet[X, \bullet[I, \bullet[Y, X \in (Y \in (I \in P))]]]])))$$

(F65): Passive participle (semantics, without PP)
$structure(syntax(\ldots,$
$$minor(head(\ldots, vform(nonfinite(participle(passive))))),$$
$$\ldots)),$$
$$semantics(pre(\ldots),$$
$$content(\bullet[P,$$
$$\bullet[I, \bullet[Y, [\bullet A : \exists x(x \in A)] \in (Y \in (I \in P))]]]])))$$

We will look at (F64). The main effect of this is to swap the semantic roles of the subject and the first element of the complement, as required for the relationship between (276) and (277). Using this description of the semantic effects of the passive suffix, we obtain the following description of *killed* as a passive participle:

$structure(syntax(major(n,$
$\qquad [VP$
$\qquad\qquad \longrightarrow$
$\qquad\qquad\qquad structure(syntax(NP,\ldots),$
$\qquad\qquad\qquad\qquad semantics(pre(PRE),$
$\qquad\qquad\qquad\qquad\qquad content(CONT_{NP})))]),$
$\qquad\qquad \ldots),$
$\qquad\qquad semantics(pre(\ldots),content(KILL)))$

$KILL = \bullet[B,\bullet[B',(\exists E : event(E) \wedge type(E,die))$
$\qquad\qquad\qquad\qquad (\bullet[u,object(E,u)] \in B) \wedge \bullet[v,agent(E,v)] \in B')]]$
$VERB = \bullet[T, CONTENT_{NP} \in (KILL \in T)]$
$PASSIVE = \bullet[P,\bullet[X,\bullet[I,\bullet[Y, X \in (Y \in (I \in P))]]]]$
$VP = structure(\ldots,$
$\qquad\qquad\qquad semantics(pre(PRE),$
$\qquad\qquad\qquad\qquad content(VERB \in PASSIVE)))$

The content of *VP* here simplifies to:

$\bullet[X,$
$\quad \bullet[I,$
$\qquad \bullet[Y,$
$\qquad\quad (\bullet[u,\bullet[v,(\exists A : event(A) \wedge type(A,die))$
$\qquad\qquad\qquad\qquad (object(A,u) \wedge agent(A,v))]] \in I]] \in Y) \in X]]$

This is just like the content of the active form of *kill*, except for a change in the
order in which the variables corresponding to the denotations of the subject (Y)
and syntactic object (X) and the temporal specification (I) get provided and instantiated. The change in the order of X and Y is exactly what you would expect.
We have also had to reorder the instantiation of the temporal information, since we
assume this will be provided by the temporal properties of the auxiliary. Since our
syntactic analysis suggests that the verb should be combined with its complements
before the result of this is combined with the auxiliary, we have to recognise that
the first thing to be supplied will be the description of the agent, with the temporal
specification coming next and the description of the semantic object coming last.

(F65) is very similar to (F64), except that the specification of the agent is supplied explicitly via an objectification of an existentially quantified formula. We will

say no more about (F65), since there is nothing interesting to say about it that we have not already said about (F64).

There remain two problems with the above analysis. The first is that it would only work if the complement of the passive form of *kill* were an NP, so that instead of (277) we had:

(277′) *A bird was killed Tibbles.*

The meaning of *by* in passive sentences does not seem very closely related to its normal meaning when it occurs in locative PP's. In *by half-past ten*, or *by the statue of Winston Churchill*, or even *by herself*, it seems to say something about adjacency or nearness. In passive sentences this does not seem to be the case. We propose that there should be two frames for prepositions:

(F66): Preposition (PP as modifier)

$structure(syntax(major(\ldots,$
$\qquad\qquad\qquad [structure(\ldots,$
$\qquad\qquad\qquad\qquad semantics(pre(PRE), content(PP)))$

$\qquad\qquad\qquad \longrightarrow$

$\qquad\qquad\qquad structure(\ldots,$
$\qquad\qquad\qquad\qquad semantics(pre(PRE), content(C_{NP})))]),$
$\qquad\qquad minor(\ldots,$
$\qquad\qquad\qquad local(ptype(\ldots), modifier(+)))),$
$\qquad semantics(\ldots, content(C_{prep})))$

$PP = C_{NP} \in (C_{prep} \in MODIFIER)$

(F67): Preposition (PP as complement)

$structure(syntax(major(\ldots,$
$\qquad\qquad\qquad [structure(\ldots,$
$\qquad\qquad\qquad\qquad semantics(pre(PRE), content(C_{NP})))$

$\qquad\qquad\qquad \longrightarrow$

$\qquad\qquad\qquad structure(\ldots,$
$\qquad\qquad\qquad\qquad semantics(pre(PRE), content(C_{NP})))]),$
$\qquad\qquad minor(\ldots,$
$\qquad\qquad\qquad local(ptype(\ldots), modifier(-)))),$
$\qquad semantics(\ldots))$

The first of these describes the kind of PP that can be used for providing extra information about the location or manner of some event. We will return in Section 5.6 to the semantics of the preposition itself and the value of *MODIFIER* in such cases.

The second, which is the one that interests us here, ignores the semantics of the preposition entirely. (F67) essentially says that this kind of preposition provides a kind of **case marking** on NP's — that *by Tibbles* in (277) is really an NP which is required to appear as the first complement of a passive verb, in the same way that *I* is required to appear as the subject of a verb. Syntactically, *by Tibbles* is a PP; but when it occurs as a subcategorised subgoal of a passive verb, it is semantically just like the NP *Tibbles*. We also use this analysis of PP's when they appear as ordinary subcategorised complements, such as the occurrence of *for his niece* in *He made a model boat for his niece*. The feature *modifier(...)* is used to distinguish between PP's occurring as free modifiers and ones occurring as subcategorised arguments.

The second problem with our analysis of passives is more awkward. We would like to explain the oddness of cases like:

(278) *That hat suits you.*
? (279) *You are suited by that hat.*
(280) *The farm belongs to Mary.*
? (281) *Mary is belonged to by the farm.*

We suggest that the problem with (279) and (281) is that the passive form requires the item that occupied the subject position for the active form to be the agent. Neither *suit* nor *belong* have agents, so (279) and (281) sound odd. We will rely on extra-linguistic postulates such as

$$\forall A : (event(A) \land type(A, belong)) \neg \exists X agent(A, X)$$

to rule out such examples.

The frames we have considered so far in this chapter have all been for verbs that report events. For some purposes it may be useful to distinguish these from ones that report states:

(F68): Simple stative verb (e.g. *own*)
$structure(syntax(major(\ldots,$
$$[structure(syntax(\#VP,\ldots)$$
$$semantics(pre(PRE),$$
$$content(CONTENT_{VP})))$$

$$\longrightarrow$$

$$structure(syntax(\#NP,\ldots),$$
$$semantics(pre(PRE),$$
$$content(CONTENT_{NP})))]),$$
$$\ldots),$$
$$semantics(pre(\ldots),content(VERB)))$$

$ST = \bullet[STATE,\bullet[A,\bullet[A',(\exists S : state(S) \wedge type(S,STATE))$
$$((\bullet[u,object(S,u)] \in A')$$
$$\wedge (\bullet[v,object(S,v)] \in A))]]]$$
$CONTENT_{VP} = \bullet[T,(CONTENT_{NP} \in (VERB \in ST)) \in T]$

It is unclear exactly how we should best characterise the differences between states and events. It is, indeed, not even clear that these are the right categories for our task. Perhaps we need states, events and actions. Perhaps we need natural states, volitional states, events and actions. We will arbitrarily assume that the distinction between states and events is sufficiently widespread to be included in our basic vocabulary for describing verb semantics, but that the other finer distinctions should be left to emerge from the axioms describing particular cases. The assumption here is purely for ease of presentation. To make any use of it would require us to be able to reason about what was being said, and to fit it into a broader picture of the way the world is. We might for instance have used some such distinction when considering verbs that do not have passive forms, in order to categorise the kind of event that has no agent, rather than producing a collection of individual statements to this effect for different words. Since we are not presenting any theories about how we reason, and we are not developing a broader picture of the way the world is, we cannot actually do anything with the distinction between states and events (or of any other distinction we might have made). It is in this way similar to the general rule that agents must be animate, which is true and would be useful if we had a picture of what is involed in being animate, but is no use to us here for allocating the referents of NP's to the role of agent or instrument.

5.3   Generics: Bare Plurals and Habituals

Given that verb frames now deal with each of the verb's arguments independently, so that we can supply the kind of object that represents the meaning of an NP, we can now see how to deal with sentences containing bare plural NP's. Consider the following sentence:

(282) *Martin is eating peaches.*

What can we infer on the basis of (282)? We know that Martin is eating, and we know that the things he is eating are peaches. In other words, there are some objects which Martin is eating, and these objects are in fact peaches. We can obtain an interpretation like this with the following analysis of bare plurals:

$$
\begin{aligned}
&\textbf{(R17): Bare plural NP}\\
&[structure(syntax(\#NP,\\
&\qquad\qquad\qquad minor(head(agr(\ldots,third(plural),\ldots),\ldots),\ldots)),\\
&\qquad\quad semantics(pre(PRE),\\
&\qquad\qquad\qquad content(\bullet[B,(\forall x:x\in B)(x\in CONTENT_{NN})])))\\
&\longrightarrow\\
&structure(syntax(\#NN,\\
&\qquad\qquad\qquad minor(head(agr(\ldots,third(plural),\ldots),\ldots),\ldots)),\\
&\qquad\quad semantics(pre(PRE),\\
&\qquad\qquad\qquad content(CONTENT_{NN})))]
\end{aligned}
$$

Using this analysis of the meaning of bare plural NP's, we can obtain the following description of the content (282):

$$
\begin{aligned}
AT(now,\bullet[(\exists E:event(E)\wedge type(E,eat))\\
agent(E,X)\wedge(\forall Y:object(E,Y))peach(E,Y))])
\end{aligned}
$$

This says that Martin (the value the presupposition would impose on X) is eating, and that each of the things he is eating is a peach. In other words, that he is *peach-eating*, or *eating peaches*. This analysis may not be correct in every single detail, but it does capture the essence of (282). It is, at the very least, better than suggesting that (282) states a relationship between Martin and the property of being a peach: whatever Martin is doing, he is not eating a property; and it is also better than introducing a new quantifier, *GEN*, to denote the generic property of being a peach without providing any semantics for *GEN* [Carlson 1989].

(282) introduced one kind of generic item, namely the kind of unspecified set of items referred to by bare plurals. These often occur in contexts where the time when the event took place is also unspecified:

(283) *Martin eats peaches.*

(283) would not support any inferences about what Martin is currently doing. You could say (283) even if you knew that he was in fact asleep at the moment (though probably not if you knew he was dead). It would not even support the inference that he frequently eats them, since there is no awkwardness about:

(284) *Martin eats peaches when he can get them, which is not very often.*

You can, however, infer that there are some occasions when he does so. The fact that we know there are no unicorns, for instance, makes

(285) *Martin rides unicorns.*

seem very odd. Why is it odd? Because **habitual** uses of the present tense like this do entail that the reported event does happen sometimes. The following also seem unacceptable:

(286) *Martin eats peaches (though he's never eaten one yet).*
(287) *Martin eats peaches (though he'll never eat one again).*

We propose the following alternative frame for the present tense marker:

(F60): Habitual present tense
$structure(\ldots,$
$\qquad semantics(pre(\ldots), content(\bullet[R, HABIT \in R])))$

$HABIT = \bullet[P, (\exists I : interval(I) \land CONTAIN(I, now))$
$\qquad\qquad (\exists t : instant(t) \land CONTAIN(I, t) \land BEFORE(t, now))$
$\qquad\qquad\qquad\qquad AT(t, \bullet[P])]$
$\qquad\qquad \land (\exists t' : instant(t') \land CONTAIN(I, t') \land BEFORE(now, t'))$
$\qquad\qquad\qquad\qquad AT(t', \bullet[P])]$

Again, analyses based on this frame may not correspond exactly to the meaning of sentences like (283). The content we obtain from it for (283) does, however, at least support some appropriate inferences — that Martin has eaten peaches at some time in the past and that he will do so again in the future.

There is much much more than this to understanding how habitual uses of tensed verbs operate. In particular, we have not investigated the relationship between generic NP's and tensed verbs, or the fact that it seems as though only non-stative verbs have this kind of interpretation. The following sentences, for instance, are hard to interpret as habituals:

(288) *Martin eats a peach.*
(289) *Martin lives in Bristol.*

There is nothing in (F69) which rules these out explicitly. (F69) looks like a good starting place, and it may be possible to adapt it to show why (288) and (289) do not have habitual readings. We will simply leave it that (F69) does enable us to obtain a description of the content of sentences like (283) which supports some appropriate inferences, and no inappropriate ones, and that this is better than nothing.

5.4   Sentential and Verbal Complements

We turn now to some issues associated with verbs that take VP's or sentences as their complements. We start with a simple example of a sentence with such a verb:

(290) *I know John saw Mary.*

This seems to express very much the same relationship between the speaker and the proposition that John saw Mary as

(291) *I know John.*

expresses between the speaker and John. We will not investigate the nature of that relationship in great detail here. What matters for the moment is that it seems to be much the same for (290) and (291). We would therefore expect to have very much the same frame for verbs with sentential complements, like *know* in (290), and verbs with ordinary NP complements, like *know* in (291):

(F70): Verb with sentential complement (e.g. _know_)

$structure(syntax(major(\ldots,$

$\qquad [structure(syntax(\# VP, \ldots)$

$\qquad\qquad\qquad semantics(pre(PRE),$

$\qquad\qquad\qquad\qquad content(CONTENT_{VP})))$

$\qquad\qquad \longrightarrow$

$\qquad\qquad structure(syntax(\# S, \ldots),$

$\qquad\qquad\qquad semantics(pre(PRE),$

$\qquad\qquad\qquad\qquad content(CONTENT_S)))]),$

$\qquad \ldots),$

$\qquad semantics(pre(\ldots), content(VERB)))$

$VC = \bullet[EVENT, \bullet[X, \bullet[Y, (\exists A : event(A) \wedge type(A, EVENT))$

$\qquad\qquad\qquad ((X \in \bullet[u, object(A, u)]$

$\qquad\qquad\qquad\qquad \wedge (\bullet[v, agent(A, v)] \in Y))]]$

$CONTENT_{VP} = \bullet[CONTENT_S] \in (VERB \in VC)$

With this frame for _know_, we will obtain the following description of the content of (290) (assuming that _see_ is an ordinary agentive verb and _saw_ is its past tense):

$(\exists I : interval(I) \wedge CONTAIN(I, now))$

$\qquad DURING(I, \bullet[(\exists E : event(E) \wedge type(E, know))$

$\qquad\qquad\qquad (agent(E, Z) \wedge object(E, SEEING)])$

$SEEING = \bullet[(\exists I' : interval(I')$

$\qquad\qquad\qquad \wedge (\forall T : instant(T) \wedge CONTAIN(I', T))(BEFORE(T, now)))$

$\qquad\qquad\qquad\qquad DURING(I', \bullet[(\exists E : event(E) \wedge type(E, see))$

$\qquad\qquad\qquad\qquad\qquad (agent(E, X)$

$\qquad\qquad\qquad\qquad\qquad\qquad \wedge object(E, Y))])])$

X, Y and Z here are variables appearing in the usual forms of presupposition for named individuals and pronouns. The expression above says very much what we would expect — that there is a current knowing event whose agent is the speaker and whose semantic object is the proposition that there was a past seeing event involving John and Mary. We can contrast this with:

(292) *I want John to see Mary.*

This is fairly similar to (290), except that the complement in (292) contains a *to*-form main verb rather than a tensed one. (290) reports a specific event, located at a particular time and place. (292), on the other hand, is concerned with the general state of affairs in which John sees Mary, rather than with any particular occurrence. We will assume for now that *to*-form verbs are like present participles, so that their interpretation is unspecified as to time. We suggest that the following frame is appropriate for verbs taking NP-VP(*to*-form) complements:

(F71): Verb with NP and *to*-form VP complement

$structure(syntax(major(\dots,$

$\qquad\qquad [structure(syntax(\#VP,\dots)$
$\qquad\qquad\qquad\qquad semantics(pre(PRE_{NP} \wedge PRE_{VP}),$
$\qquad\qquad\qquad\qquad\qquad content(C_{GOAL})))$

$\qquad\qquad\longrightarrow$

$\qquad\qquad structure(syntax(\#NP,\dots),$
$\qquad\qquad\qquad\qquad semantics(pre(PRE_{NP}),$
$\qquad\qquad\qquad\qquad\qquad content(C_{NP}))),$
$\qquad\qquad structure(syntax(\#VP,$
$\qquad\qquad\qquad\qquad minor(head(\dots,$
$\qquad\qquad\qquad\qquad\qquad\qquad vform(nonfinite(to),$
$\qquad\qquad\qquad\qquad\qquad\qquad\qquad \dots),$
$\qquad\qquad\qquad\qquad\qquad \dots)),$
$\qquad\qquad\qquad\qquad semantics(pre(PRE),$
$\qquad\qquad\qquad\qquad\qquad content(C_{VP})))]),$

$\qquad \dots),$
$\qquad semantics(pre(\dots), content(VERB)))$

$VC = \bullet[EVENT, \bullet[X, \bullet[Y, (\exists E : event(E) \wedge type(E, EVENT))$
$\qquad\qquad\qquad\qquad\qquad (X \in \bullet[u, object(E, u)])$
$\qquad\qquad\qquad\qquad\qquad\qquad \wedge \bullet[v, agent(E, v)] \in Y))]]$
$COMP = \bullet[P, (\exists t : instant(t))(AT(t, \bullet[P]))] \in C_{VP}$
$C_{GOAL} = \bullet[(C_{NP} \in COMP)] \in (VERB \in VC)$

With this we obtain the following description of the content of (292) (with X, Y and Z constrained by the usual presuppositions for sentences involving proper names and pronouns):

$$(\exists I : interval(I) \wedge CONTAIN(I, now))$$
$$DURING(I, \bullet[(\exists E : event(E) \wedge type(E, want))$$
$$(agent(E, Z) \wedge object(E, SEEING)])$$

$$SEEING = \bullet[(\exists t : instant(t))$$
$$AT(t, \bullet[(\exists E' : event(E') \wedge type(E', see))$$
$$(agent(E', X) \wedge object(E', Y))])])]))])$$

This is similar to the analysis of (290), except that there is now no indication of the relation between the time of utterance and the instant at which the event is to take place. It might be argued that the seeing event referred to in (292) should be located in the future. The exact details of when things which are wanted should happen are rather complex. Consider for instance:

(293) *I want Mary to have seen John.*

This seems to place the desired event in the past — that at some past instant Mary should have seen John. It is very easy to add modifiers to this to make it also refer to a future state of affairs instead:

(293') *I want Mary to have seen John before I talk to her.*

This hint of a future state of affairs seems to be an idiosyncracy of the verb *want*, rather than a general characteristic of NP+VP complement verbs. We therefore choose to omit any temporal specifications from the general frame for such verbs, relying on specific information about particular verbs to supply it as appropriate.

Verbs that take an NP and a present participle VP as complement are clearly very similar. We will in fact take them to be identical, with the choice between *to*-form and present participle simply an idiosyncracy of the verb. This will ultimately turn out to be inadequate, since we will be unable to distinguish between:

(294) *I want you to play tennis (this evening).*
(295) *I want you playing tennis (by the time I arrive).*

This, however, is more a problem with our account of the meanings of nonfinite VP's in general than with the way we treat them when they occur as complements. We decline to provide a formal account of the distinction between (294) and (295), since we do not have a clear intuitive account of it and hence do not know what we would be formalising.

We turn now to some further complications associated with sentential and NP+VP complements. The first of these is that, as we saw in Chapter 3, some such verbs can take either an NP+VP or just a VP:

(296) *I like seeing John.*

When we considered this phenomenon in Chapter 3 we referred to it as "subject control". This name reflects the fact that the NP is not just omitted. It is rather assumed that it is the same as the subject of the main verb (*like* in this case). (296) is taken to be the correct way of saying:

*(296') *I like myself seeing John.*

To account for this we need to adapt the frame for NP+VP verbs to describe controlled subject versions:

(F72): Subject-control verb with present participle VP complement
$structure(syntax(major(\ldots,$
$$[structure(syntax(\# VP, \ldots)$$
$$semantics(pre(PRE_{VP}),$$
$$content(CONTENT_{GOAL})))$$

$$\longrightarrow$$

$$structure(syntax(\# VP,$$
$$minor(head(\ldots, VFORM)),$$
$$\ldots)),$$
$$semantics(pre(PRE),$$
$$content(CONTENT_{VP})))]),$$
$$\ldots),$$
$$semantics(pre(\ldots), content(VERB)))$$

$VFORM = vform(nonfinite(participle(present)), \ldots)$
$VC = \bullet[EVENT, \bullet[X, \bullet[Y, (\exists E : event(E) \wedge type(E, EVENT))$
$$(((A \in X) \in \bullet[u, object(E, u)])$$
$$\wedge(\bullet[v, agent(E, v)] \in Y))]]$$
$CONTENT_{GOAL} = \bullet[A,$
$$A \in (\bullet[P, (\exists t : instant(t)) AT(t, \bullet[P])] \in CONTENT_{VP}))$$
$$\in ((VERB \in VC) \in T)$$

The only difference between (F72) and (F71), apart from the change in the specification of the *vform*, is that in (F72) the specification of the agent, A, of the main event is also used to instantiate the agent of the reported event. The syntactic object is a VP, though the semantic object needs to be a proposition. Using the subject of the main verb enables us to turn the content of the VP into a proposition, as required.

The relationship between (F71) and (F72) provides a simple and plausible account of the semantic effects of subject control. It is clearly not a complete account of this phenomenon. The worst problem with it is that it says nothing about why some verbs permit it and others do not:

(297) *I want to be good at tennis.*
*(298) *I want myself to be good at tennis.*
(299) *I know myself to be bad at tennis.*
*(300) *I know to be bad at tennis.*

Nonetheless, (F71) and (F72) do at least provide a descriptively adequate account of what is going on in those cases where it applies. We leave an account of the reasons why some verbs permit it and others do not for another time.

5.5   Intensional Objects

We now reconsider the interpretation of (292), and in particular the semantic object of the main event. This semantic object is an objectified proposition. What exactly is an objectified proposition? We have said very little about the nature of such things, and we do not intend to say any more now. The most we want to say is that there is some correspondence between propositions and ways the world might be. We will not equate propositions with ways the world might be, or to use an alternative terminology, with sets of possible worlds. And we will not take any position on the reality or otherwise of alternative worlds. We take the least committed position we can, namely that (i) propositions exist, and can play the role of semantic object, or of instrument, or whatever, and (ii) there is a way of thinking about propositions which makes them seem to correspond to sets of possible worlds. We will use the terms "way the world might be", "state of affairs" and "set of possible worlds" interchangeably.

In the case of (292), the proposition which appears as the semantic object corresponds to the state of affairs in which John sees Mary. What about the following?

(301) *I want to find a unicorn.*

The frames and rules we have developed so far would provide the following content for this:

$$(\exists I : interval(I) \land CONTAIN(I, now))$$
$$DURING(I, \bullet[(\exists E : event(E) \land type(E, want))$$
$$(agent(E, Z) \land object(E, FINDING)])$$

$$FINDING = \bullet[(\exists t : instant(t))$$
$$AT(t, \bullet[(\exists E' : event(E') \land type(E', find))$$
$$(agent(E', Z)$$
$$\land (\exists Y : unicorn(Y))object(E', Y))])]))])$$

This seems perfectly reasonable. If I want to find a unicorn, I presumably have a preference for states of affairs in which there is a unicorn which I find. Suppose, however, that (301) were part of a more extended discourse:

(302) *I want to find a unicorn. It was in the courtyard of the castle this morning, but it seems to have escaped.*

This seems to say that there is some unicorn which I want to find. The usual approach to cases like this is to suggest that the scope of the existential quantifier that introduces the unicorn should be taken to include the rest of the statement, resulting in a content like:

$$(\exists I : interval(I) \land CONTAIN(I, now))$$
$$DURING(I,$$
$$\bullet[(\exists Y : unicorn(Y))(\exists E : event(E) \land type(E, want))$$
$$(agent(E, Z)$$
$$\land object(E, FINDING)])$$

$$FINDING = \bullet[(\exists t : instant(t))$$
$$AT(t, \bullet[(\exists E' : event(E') \land type(E', find))$$
$$(agent(E', Z) \land object(E', Y))])]))])$$

Why might we want such a **wide-scope** interpretation? We want to capture the fact that (302) seems to entail extra information about the unicorn I want to find, namely that it was in the castle garden. We can, however, place (301) in a discourse which also entails extra information about the unicorn, but which does not seem to require wide-scope interpretation:

(303) *I want to find a unicorn. It must be young and tender, since I need it for the king's unicorn pie.*

We need to be able to refer to the unicorn mentioned in the first sentence in order to be able to make sense of the second, which provides additional information about it. Yet we would not expect a wide-scope interpretation of the first sentence in (303).

We also need to distinguish between

(304) *I believe you found a unicorn.*

which seems to admit either kind of interpretation, and

(305) *I know you found a unicorn.*

which only seems to have a wide-scope reading.

We suggest that only the narrow-scope interpretation is ever appropriate. The wide-scope one seems to be necessary because in certain contexts the extra information we can obtain about the object in question is that it really exists. We want the wide-scope interpretation of (302), for instance, because the follow-up sentence allows us to infer that there really is some particular unicorn which the speaker is looking for. This is, however, a consequence of the follow-up sentence, not of the statement that the speaker wants to find a unicorn. Similarly, the fact that (305) can only be true if there really is a unicorn which you found is a consequence of the meaning of *know*. Since you can only know true things, you can only know someone found a unicorn if they really did, in which case there must really be one.

The issues which have been addressed under the headings of **opaque contexts** and **quantifying in**, then, are non-issues, and there is no need for wide-scope readings. All we need are the following two principles: (i) If an existentially quantified statement is true then there must be an object of the type indicated by the existential quantifier. (ii) Certain verbs which correspond to relations between entities and propositions carry the extra information that the relevant proposition is true. Neither of these principles is very controversial, and between them they solve all the problems of narrow-scope/wide-scope quantification.

We end the discussion of verbs that take sentential and NP+VP complements by considering their semantics in situations where they take simple NP's instead:

(306) *I want a unicorn.*

We do not want to treat *want* here as though it were an ordinary transitive verb, since that would lead us to an interpretation under which there is some particular unicorn which I want. We suggest that it is better to treat it as though it were an abbreviation for something like:

(307) *I want to own a unicorn.*

The appropriate frame for this is a partially filled in version of the frame for the controlled subject version of the verb:

(F73): Verb with implicit proposition

$structure(syntax(major(\ldots,$

$\qquad [structure(syntax(\#VP, \ldots)$

$\qquad\qquad semantics(pre(PRE_{VP}),$

$\qquad\qquad\qquad content(CONTENT_{GOAL})))$

$\qquad\qquad \longrightarrow$

$\qquad\qquad structure(syntax(\#NP, minor(\ldots),$

$\qquad\qquad\qquad semantics(pre(PRE),$

$\qquad\qquad\qquad\qquad content(CONTENT_{NP})))],$

$\qquad \ldots),$

$\qquad semantics(pre(\ldots), content(VERB)))$

$CONTENT_{VP} = A' \in (CONTENT_{NP} \in \bullet[B, \bullet[B', (OWNING \in B) \in B')]])$

$OWNING = \bullet[C, \bullet[C', (\exists t' : instant(t'))$

$\qquad\qquad AT(t', \bullet[(\exists E' : state(E') \wedge type(E', own))$

$\qquad\qquad\qquad (\bullet[u'agent(E', u')] \in C]$

$\qquad\qquad\qquad\qquad \wedge \bullet [v', object(E', v')] \in C'])]]]$

$AG = \bullet[EVENT, \bullet[X, \bullet[Y, (\exists E : event(E) \wedge type(E, EVENT))$

$\qquad\qquad\qquad ((\bullet[u, object(E, u)] \in (A' \in Y))$

$\qquad\qquad\qquad \wedge (\bullet[v, agent(E, v)] \in X))]]$

$CONTENT_{GOAL} = \bullet[T,$

$\qquad\qquad (\bullet[P, (\exists t : instant(t)) AT(t, \bullet[P])] \in CONTENT_{VP}))$

$\qquad\qquad \in ((VERB \in AG) \in T)]$

This will produce exactly the same analysis of (306) as the controlled subject frame would for (307). In particular, it avoids any supposition that there is some particular unicorn which I want, since the existential quantifier only covers the embedded proposition, not the entire sentence.

The same sort of analysis will also provide an interpretation for

(308) *John seeks a unicorn.*

as though it were:

(309) *John wants to find a unicorn.*

In all these cases, it may subsequently be established that the quantifier refers to an object which is known to exist, and which the speaker may even be able to identify.

This is, however, a matter for subsequent context, and not for the interpretation of the sentence in question.

5.6   Free Modifiers: Prepositional and Adverbial Phrases

Consider the prepositional phrase *in the park*. This PP specifies something about the location of some object. Phrases like this can occur in a wide variety of contexts:

(310) *The man in the park was feeding the ducks.*
(311) *I went running in the park.*
(312) *In the park I saw someone feeding the ducks.*

In (310) *in the park* is saying something about the man who was feeding the ducks. In (311) it says something about the kind of running I did. In (312) it describes where the event consisting of me seeing someone feeding the ducks took place. As usual, we want to use the same analysis of *in the park* in all three contexts, and in any others in which it might occur, though the *way* we use it may be different in each case. We start by considering (310).

In (310) the phrase we are interested in seems to be doing much the same job as a restrictive relative clause. Its function is to provide information about the individual who performed the action, in order to help pick them out. We would therefore like to combine it with the contribution made by the NN *man*, in order to construct a more elaborate property to be combined with the determiner. We start by seeing how to expand our treatment of the kind of PP that functions as a general modifier so that it denotes a property.

(F74): Preposition (PP as modifier, expanded)
$structure(syntax(major(\ldots,$

$$[structure(\ldots,$$
$$semantics(pre(PRE),$$
$$content(\bullet[X, (X \in C_{prep}) \in C_{NP}])))$$

$$\longrightarrow$$

$$structure(\ldots,$$
$$semantics(pre(PRE), content(C_{NP})))]),$$
$$minor(\ldots,$$
$$local(ptype(\ldots), modifier(+)))),$$
$$semantics(\ldots, content(C_{prep})))$$

Given this general frame for prepositions, we need specific frames for particular prepositions such as *in*. The following frame corresponds to the notion that *in* says something about the location of some item:

> **(F75): Specific preposition, e.g.** *in*
> $structure(syntax(\ldots),$
> $\qquad semantics(\ldots, content(\bullet[u, \bullet[v, loc(v, u)]])))$

Combining these we obtain

$$\bullet[X, (X \in \bullet[u, \bullet[v, loc(u, v)]]) \in C_{NP}]$$

as the content of the preposition *in*. This simplifies to:

$$\bullet[X, \bullet[v, loc(X, v)] \in C_{NP}]$$

Suppose the NP here is *a park*, i.e. we are trying to interpret the PP *in a park*. The result of supplying the appropriate interpretation of *a park* produces:

$$\bullet[X, \bullet[v, loc(X, v)] \in \bullet[B, (\exists z : park(z))(z \in B)]]$$

This in turn simplifies to

$$\bullet[X, (\exists z : park(z))(z \in \bullet[v, loc(X, v)])]$$

and thence to:

$$\bullet[X, (\exists z : park(z))loc(X, z)]$$

In other words, *in a park* denotes the property of being something whose location is some park. If we consider *in the park* we obtain

$$\bullet[X, loc(X, z)]$$

where z is some item which is constrained by a presupposition to be a unique salient park. This kind of semantic object looks very like the descriptions we have for relative clauses. A PP acting as a modifier denotes a property, just as a relative clause does. In order to use such a PP as part of an NP, we combine the property it denotes with the property of the NN that contributes to the NP, just as we did for restrictive relative clauses:

(R18): NN + PP
$[structure(syntax(\#NN, minor(\ldots)),$
$\qquad semantics(pre(PRE_{NN} \cup PRE_{PP}),$
$\qquad\qquad content(\bullet[X, X \in CONT_{NN} \wedge X \in CONT_{PP}])))$

$\longrightarrow$

$structure(syntax(\#NN, minor(\ldots)),$
$\qquad semantics(pre(PRE_{NN}),$
$\qquad\qquad content(CONT_{NN})))$
$structure(syntax(\#PP,$
$\qquad\qquad minor(\ldots, local(\ldots, modifier(+))),$
$\qquad semantics(pre(PRE_{PP}),$
$\qquad\qquad content(CONT_{PP})))]$

With this rule we would obtain

$structure(syntax(\ldots),$
$\qquad semantics(pre(\{(\exists!y : salient(y))(park(y))\}),$
$\qquad\qquad content(\bullet[B, (\exists x : (man(x) \wedge loc(x, y)))(x \in B)])))$

---

as the interpretation of *a man in the park*. This has a single presupposition, which should be verified when the free occurrence of y in the content is encountered. The content is just like the content of any other indefinite NP, except that the restriction on the existential quantifier refers to x's location as well as the fact that x is a man.

The same rule leads to

$structure(syntax(\ldots),$
$\qquad semantics(pre(\{(\exists!x : salient(x))(man(x) \wedge loc(x, y)),$
$\qquad\qquad\qquad (\exists!y : salient(y))(park(y))\}),$
$\qquad\qquad content(\bullet[B, x \in B])))$

---

as the interpretation of *the man in the park*. This is slightly less straightforward, since one of its two presuppositions is required to fix a variable y which occurs free in the other. This is unusual, but it does not require any extension to our basic framework.

We can clearly use the same rule for dealing with other cases such as *a man in a park* and *the man in a park*. How do we deal with cases where a PP of this kind is modifying some other structure such as a VP (311) or an S (312)?

We suggested above that the PP in (312) describes where the event consisting of me seeing someone feeding the ducks took place. The ordinary semantics of

(313) *I saw someone feeding the ducks.*

introduces a "seeing" event. All we need, therefore, is to say that this event has the property specified by the PP. Consider the following rule:

(R19): PP + S
$[structure(syntax(\#S, minor(\ldots)),$
$\qquad semantics(pre(PRE_S \cup PRE_{PP}$
$\qquad\qquad\qquad \cup \{(\exists! E : salient(E))(state(E) \vee event(E))\}),$
$\qquad\qquad content(CONT_S \wedge (E \in CONT_{PP}))))$
$\longrightarrow$
$structure(syntax(\#PP,$
$\qquad\qquad minor(\ldots, local(\ldots, modifier(+))),$
$\qquad\quad semantics(pre(PRE_{PP}),$
$\qquad\qquad\quad content(CONT_{PP}))),$
$structure(syntax(\#S, minor(\ldots)),$
$\qquad\quad semantics(pre(PRE_S),$
$\qquad\qquad\quad content(CONT_S)))]$

This rule simply says that there is some unique salient state or event and that the PP adds some information about it. Suppose we use it to analyse:

(314) *In the park I saw John.*

(R19) will lead to the following description of (314):

$$structure(\dots,$$
$$semantics(pre(\{\exists!X(speaker(X)),$$
$$(\exists!Y : salient(Y))(name(Y, [\![John]\!])),$$
$$(\exists!Z : salient(Z))([\![park]\!](Z)),$$
$$(\exists!E : salient(E))(state(E) \vee event(E))\}),$$
$$content((\exists I : interval(I))$$
$$(\forall T : instant(T) \wedge CONTAIN(I, T))$$
$$(BEFORE(T, now))$$
$$\wedge\ DURING(I, SEEING)$$
$$\wedge\ loc(E, Z))))$$

$$SEEING = \bullet[(\exists E' : event(E') \wedge type(E', see))(agent(E', X) \wedge object(E', Y))]$$

The presupposition here introduces the variables X, Y and Z to stand for the speaker, John and the relevant park as usual, and E to stand for some event. The first part of the content says that an event E', of X seeing Y, took place during some past interval; the second part of the content says that the location of the event E (the one introduced by the presupposition) was Z.

The second part of the content contains a free occurrence of E. E is introduced appropriately in a presupposition, so this is acceptable. In order to verify this presupposition we need to draw on the introduction of E' in the first part of the content. We can do this, since we assume that the first component of a conjunction will have been "conceded" in the semantic game before the second component is investigated. Hence when we need to verify the presupposition involving E, in order to establish that we know what E is, we have access to the introduction of E' as an event.

We could have dealt with the PP in (314) by objectifying the content of *I saw John* and then saying that this objectified proposition was located in the park. Doing this would have required us to treat *loc* as a relation between propositions and places. It seems preferable to treat it as a relation between events and places, particularly since we have already interpreted it as a relation between individuals and places in order to deal with NP's containing modifying PP's. It would also have led to trouble in the interpretation of sentences involving PP's which specify temporal relations. Consider:

(315) *I saw John on Sunday.*

Using (R19) we would arrive at an interpretation like:

$structure(\ldots,$
$\qquad semantics(pre(\{\exists!X(speaker(X)),$
$\qquad\qquad\qquad (\exists!Y : salient(Y))(name(Y, [\![John]\!])),$
$\qquad\qquad\qquad (\exists!E : salient(E))(state(E) \vee event(E))\}),$
$\qquad\qquad content((\exists I : interval(I))$
$\qquad\qquad\qquad\qquad\qquad ((\forall T : instant(T) \wedge CONTAIN(I,T))$
$\qquad\qquad\qquad\qquad\qquad\qquad (BEFORE(T, now))$
$\qquad\qquad\qquad\qquad \wedge\ DURING(I, SEEING)$
$\qquad\qquad\qquad \wedge\ (\exists Z : (date(Z) \wedge name(Z, [\![Sunday]\!]))$
$\qquad\qquad\qquad\qquad\qquad\qquad temploc(E, Z))))$

$SEEING = \bullet[(\exists E' : event(E') \wedge type(E', see))(agent(E', X) \wedge object(E', Y))]$

This says that E' happened in the past, and that the temporal location of E was called *Sunday*. Once we have realised, using the first component of the content and the appropriate presupposition, that E and E' are in fact the same event, we will have a more precise specification of when that event took place than either of them provides by itself. If we had treated the PP as a relation between a temporal location and a proposition, we would have arrived at an analysis which said that on Sunday the event of my seeing John was a past event, which is clearly not what (315) says. This seems compelling evidence in favour of saying that the PP modifies the central event referred to in the proposition, rather than the proposition itself.

We note here that it would be surprising if we required a radically different analysis for

(316) *I saw John recently.*

from the one for (315). We will simply assume that adverbs are just like prepositions whose NP complement has been implicitly supplied, so that an adverb produces a PP whose semantic description is just like the semantic description of a PP. Given this assumption, we can use the same analysis for adverbial phrases as we have used for PP's without further comment.

We can adapt (R19) so that it covers cases where the PP is a post-modifier on a VP:

$$(\mathbf{R20})\text{: } \mathbf{VP + PP}$$
$$[structure(syntax(\#\,VP, minor(\ldots)),$$
$$semantics(pre(PRE_{VP} \cup PRE_{PP}$$
$$\cup \{(\exists!E : salient(E))(state(E) \vee event(E))\}),$$
$$content(\bullet[B, (B \in CONT_{VP}) \wedge (E \in CONT_{PP}))]))))$$
$$\longrightarrow$$
$$structure(syntax(\#\,VP, minor(\ldots)),$$
$$semantics(pre(PRE_{VP}),$$
$$content(CONT_{VP})))),$$
$$structure(syntax(\#PP,$$
$$minor(\ldots, local(\ldots, modifier(+))),$$
$$semantics(pre(PRE_{PP}),$$
$$content(CONT_{PP}))))]$$

This is slightly more complex than (R19), since the content of the PP is being combined with something — the content of a VP — which is not itself a proposition. It is, however, essentially the same. When a subject is added in order to produce a sentence then the abstraction over B will absorb the subject without affecting the contribution made by the PP.

The similarity between the treatment of PP's that modify whole sentences and the treatment of ones that modify VP's is a consequence of our decision to make the semantics of the PP introduce a state or event. This state or event is then identified with the central state or event referred to by the S or VP by the same mechanism that interprets definite references.

Once we have rules which allow PP's to post-modify either NP's or VP's, we run into trouble with sentences like:

(317) *I saw John feeding the ducks in the park.*

The PP *in the park* might be a modifier on the *the ducks*, on *feeding the ducks*, or on *saw John feeding the ducks*. As it happens in this case it makes very little difference. If I was in the park when I saw him feeding the ducks then he was probably doing it in the park; and if he was feeding them in the park then they were probably in it themselves. It can, however, be important:

(318) *I saw the man in the park with a telescope.*

To say that I used a telescope to see him is very different from saying that he was in some park which contained a telescope. To say that he is the man who was in the park which contains a telescope, rather than the one who was in the park which contains a lake, is very different from saying that he was the man who was carrying a telescope in the park rather than the one who was carrying an umbrella there. There is no way for us to decide which of the myriad interpretations of this sentence is the correct one in any given situation unless we know more about the situation — are there several parks, so we need more information about the park, or several men in the same park, so we need more information about the man, or ...? It seems futile to try to find *a priori* grounds for preferring one reading. They are all acceptable, but they mean different things. To decide which is correct in a given situation we need to know about the speaker's and hearer's knowledge of that situation.

5.7 Meaning Postulates

The discussion so far describes what someone who sincerely utters some sentence must believe about the world and about their hearer. We have couched the descriptions of what sentences entail in a formal language, PT, in order to help us investigate whether we have got them right. By couching them in a formal language we can appeal to the semantics of that language in order to see whether our descriptions do in fact entail the right constraints on the world and the hearer; and we may have an automatic inference engine which can help us enumerate these constraints.

We are *not* suggesting that native English speakers translate into and out of some similar formal language when they use their native tongue. There would be little point in suggesting this, since we would then have to explain how they dealt with expressions in this formal language. If we were to do this by appealing to some further internal translation we would be on the road to an infinite regress. If we had some way out of this vicious circle for a formal language, then we could presumably use the same way out when considering natural language itself. Our descriptions of what the speaker must believe are just that: descriptions. The formal translation helps us see what facts about the world, what regularities, the speaker must be attuned to. It does not explain what it means for a speaker to be attuned to some aspect of the world, or what it means for them to believe that their hearer is.

When we investigate the consequences of descriptions, we may need to use real world knowledge. Suppose we have the following sentences:

(319) *I believe there is a unicorn in the garden.*
(320) *I know there is a unicorn in the garden.*
(321) *I believe there is a unicorn with two horns in the garden.*

We know that (320) cannot be true, though (319) could be. How do we know that (320) cannot be true? We need access to the real-world fact that there are no unicorns, and to the property of knowledge that anything which is known must be true. The fact that there are no unicorns is simply an accident, a contingent fact about the world. There *could* have been unicorns, if evolution had taken a different path. The fact that anything which is known must be true is an intrinsic property of knowledge.

In just the same way, (321) is also less acceptable than (319). Having one horn is an intrinsic part of being a unicorn, so that the NP *a unicorn with two horns* simply does not seem to make any sense. This kind of knowledge of the intrinsic properties of objects seems to be part of what it means to say that someone is a native speaker of some language. You could be a native English speaker without knowing that there are no unicorns, so that you could sincerely utter (319). If, however, you were to say (321) you would betray the fact that your knowledge of the language was imperfect.

We will not attempt to provide a detailed discussion of either the general world knowledge shared by most adult native speakers of English or the knowledge of intrinsic relationships possessed by *any* native speaker. We simply remark that a complete analysis of a natural language like English does seem to require a set of **meaning postulates** to account for the latter. You will use language more effectively if you have a good idea of what your speaker knows and believes about the world in general, and knowing things about the world in general will help with that. But you will not be able to use a natural language at all unless you have a grasp of the intrinsic connections between the concepts that users of that language are attuned to.

6 LINGUISTIC ACTION

The analysis so far is concerned with what a speaker must believe, about the world in general and about the listener in particular, in order to be able to utter a sentence sincerely. We have developed a set of rules which build descriptions of the meanings of utterances out of descriptions of the meanings of words. This set of rules is incomplete in two obvious ways. It is incomplete simply because we have not dealt with all possible ways of putting words together to form complex utterances; and it is incomplete because we have not developed a set of meaning postulates [Carnap 1936] to capture the relations between the underlying concepts. We could try to improve it by covering more cases, or by saying more about the intrinsic relations.

It is also, however, incomplete in a more radical way. The rules we have been developing deal with the relations between utterances and what speakers believe. This fails to explain why speakers produce utterances at all. Language is hardly going to be less complex than is implied by the theory outlined so far. It looks, therefore, as though the task of constructing an utterance which is appropriate in a situation is going to be really quite difficult. Why should a speaker undertake this difficult task? To complete our theory, we would like to know how to relate a speaker's action in uttering some sentence to the rest of their behaviour.

In attempting to deal with this, we make two assumptions: (i) people's behaviour is generally rational, i.e. directed towards achieving their goals; (ii) linguistic action is not intrinsically different from other kinds of action. Thus any attempt to explain why speakers say things is going to depend on a general analysis of rational behaviour. The details of linguistic behaviour will then have to fit into this general analysis.

6.1 Rational Behaviour and AI Planning Theory

We are going to base the discussion of the way language is used on the theory of rationality embodied in AI planning theory. This is not to say that we believe that this theory is right, or that we do not believe that other ways of looking at rationality have anything to offer. In Chapter 1 we committed ourselves to embodying our theory as a program, partly because we believe this makes it more testable and partly because we fondly hope that someday the program that embodies the theory may turn out to be useful. AI planning theory is the only model of rationality available within this framework.

By AI planning theory we mean the extensive body of work arising from Mc-Carthy and Hayes' [1969] **situation calculus** and Fikes and Nilsson's [1971] implementation of the situation calculus in their **STRIPS** planning algorithm. We will restrict our attention to STRIPS, since this is all that is used in most attempts to apply planning theory to language. We will ignore extensions that make the STRIPS algorithm more efficient or more robust [Sacerdoti 1977], or that improve the expressive power of the situation calculus [Steel 1985]. If we wanted to deal with language use in terms of AI planning theory then these improvements to the basic theory would be invaluable. The main argument in this chapter, however, will be that it is very hard to see that STRIPS-like planning is relevant at all. The problem with using this kind of planning is very basic, and is unlikely to be solved by improving the algorithm or the representation language. We therefore concentrate on STRIPS itself, rather than its extensions.

The essence of the STRIPS approach to planning is that actions can be characterised in terms of the conditions that have to be met before they can be performed and the effects that they produce. Actions have all sorts of other properties. They take time, they require resources, they may be broken down into smaller sub-actions, and so on. Nonetheless, in working out what to do in order to achieve some goal, what matters is the effects that actions produce and the conditions that have to hold before they can be performed. Thus the quintessential AI action of picking up a block from a table can be characterised as:

$$
\begin{aligned}
&pickup(X) \\
&preconditions : \forall Y \neg on(Y, X) \\
&\qquad\qquad\qquad \forall Y' \neg holding(Y') \\
&effects : holding(X), \forall Y'' \neg on(X, Y'')
\end{aligned}
$$

In other words, you can't pick something up unless your hand is empty (you are not *holding* anything) and the thing you want to pick up is clear (there is nothing *on* it). Once you have picked it up you are *holding* it and it is not *on* anything.

We have changed the basic STRIPS notation a little here by allowing arbitrary formulae of FOPC as preconditions and effects. This makes descriptions clearer, at considerable extra computational cost. We are not particularly interested in computational efficiency at this point, so the extra clarity seems worth having.

Given a set of descriptions of this kind for actions like putting things down and moving your hand around, how can we construct a plan to achieve some configuration of blocks? Suppose my goal configuration included the fact that I should be holding some particular block, c. If this is not true in the world as I see it now, I must find some action which will produce this as an effect. I therefore try to match the effects of actions against my goals. In the present example, I would find that $holding(c)$ matches one of the effects of picking something up. Furthermore, matching this against the effects of picking something up will instantiate the free variable in the description of this action, resulting in the specific action:

$$pickup(c)$$
$$preconditions : \forall Y \neg on(Y, c)$$
$$\forall Y' \neg holding(Y')$$
$$effects : holding(c), \forall Y'' \neg on(c, Y'')$$

In other words, I would like to perform $pickup(c)$. I can only do this if the preconditions of this action are met. I have therefore swapped my original goal, $holding(c)$, for two subgoals, namely $\forall Y \neg on(Y, c)$ and $\forall Y' \neg holding(Y')$. These are the same kind of thing as the original goal, and the same mechanism should enable me to achieve them. The STRIPS algorithm essentially chains back through the effects and preconditions of action descriptions in this way until it arrives at actions whose preconditions are actually true. At this point it has a plan for achieving its original goals.

This simple story about how to construct plans turns out to be inadequate. The major problem is that actions often have unforeseen side-effects which cancel out the effects of other actions. Avoiding this problem makes the basic algorithm much more complex, but the basic idea is the same. In order to get your actions to lead to your goals (i.e. in order to act rationally), think of actions that will bring them about and then try to make sure that you can actually perform those actions.

6.2   Speech Act Theory

AI work on using language to achieve goals has concentrated on a set of seemingly anomalous cases. Consider the following examples:

(322) *Do you know the time?*
(323) *Can you pass the salt?*
(324) *The milk's boiling.*

(322) and (323) look like questions which invite the answers *Yes* or *No*. (324) looks like a simple statement of fact. If we take it that utterances have some sort of face-value effect, then you would expect someone to utter (322) if they wanted to know

whether their hearer knew the time, and you would expect them to utter (324) if they wanted their hearer to know that the milk was boiling.

There are two problems here. The first is that if the hearer took (322) at face-value, they would assume that the appropriate thing for them to do would be to reply *Yes* or *No*. In most cases, however, simply replying *Yes* in response to the question *Do you know the time?* is not acceptable (though there is nothing wrong with replying *No*). (322) looks like a request for information about the user's knowledge of the time but it is not. It is really a complicated way of asking what the time is.

The second problem is that the reply *Yes* is an inappropriate answer *in most cases*. If I'm standing underneath the clock on Waterloo station, and I point to it and say to you *Do you know the time?* I probably do expect you to say *Yes*. Or rather, I expect you to say something like *Yes, the first train was cancelled and after that they were all full and I had to wait an hour before I could get on one.* I would be just as irritated in this case if you said *Yes, it's quarter to nine* as I would have been if you had just said *Yes* in the more normal situation.

It seems, then, as though the intended effects of utterances can often be different from their face-value effects. Furthermore, they can be different in different ways. (322) can be a request to be told the time, a complaint about the hearer's lateness, even a request to be told about the hearer's knowledge (e.g. in a situation where an army patrol are synchronising their watches). (324) can be a comment on the efficiency of the cooker, a request that the milk be poured into a jug, ... It seems as though we need a mediating level of description to connect the surface effect of an utterance and its intended effect in a situation.

Most AI work in this area [Allen & Perrault 1980, Cohen & Perrault 1979, Appelt 1985] has followed [Searle 1969] and [Austin 1962] in proposing a range of **speech acts**. A speech act is an action which is characterised partly in terms of the production of some utterance, partly in terms of changes in the knowledge and beliefs of the speaker and hearer. We might, for instance, introduce an action of "requesting polar information":

$$
\begin{aligned}
&request-polar-inf(X,Y,P) \\
&preconditions: \neg(KNOW(X,P) \vee KNOW(X,\neg P)) \\
&\qquad\qquad BELIEVE(X, \bullet[KNOW(Y,P) \vee KNOW(Y,\neg P)]) \\
&effects: BELIEVE(Y, \bullet[want(X, \bullet[KNOW(X,P) \vee KNOW(X,\neg P)])])
\end{aligned}
$$

In other words, X can request Y to provide information about P if X does not know whether P is true or not, and X believes Y does. The effect is that Y knows that X wants to know whether P is true.

We can attach such actions as face-value effects to particular kinds of utterance. We might say, for instance, that *request-polar-inf* is the face-value effect of questions with initial auxiliaries, or that some action called *inform* is the face-value effect of simple declarative sentences. The problematic **indirect** cases that have concerned AI workers can then be characterised as situations where the standard face-value effect has no utility.

(322) is a prime case. Suppose we've been playing badminton, we have just finished a game, and I say to you *Do you know the time?*. You recognise this as a case of me performing an instance of *request-polar-inf*. You believe me to be a rational agent, so you assume that I have performed this action because I expect it to help me attain some goal. Being a helpful, cooperative person you wonder what my goal might be. Why might I want to know whether you know the time?

You may be helpful, but you are also practical. You cannot imagine anything I might want to do which requires me to know whether you know the time. You consider all the actions I might perform, trying to think of *anything* I might do which requires that I know whether you know the time. The only thing you can think of is that I cannot successfully ask you what the time actually is unless you do know it. This leads you to anticipate that I am going to follow up my initial question with *Well then, what is it?*. You could decide to anticipate me and reply *Yes, it's quarter to seven*.

Being *very* helpful, however, you wonder why I want to know what the time is. What plan could I have that requires me to know what the time is? Again you consider all the actions I might perform, trying to think of something I might do which requires that I know the time. This time you realise that I cannot try to get my revenge for losing the last game if it's after seven, since we have to stop playing at seven. So you say *It's OK, we've got time for another set*. You have not told me explicitly that you know the time; you have not answered the question I was preparing to ask; but you have enabled me to perform the action I really wanted to perform all along.

This kind of story about how language is used is irresistible. Utterances have some conventional connection to face-value actions. Hearers identify the face-value actions, look at their effects, and try to infer the reasons why these effects might be desirable. One response will be better than another if it is based on a more extended analysis of the speaker's requirements.

In order to turn this from a story to a computationally realised theory, we need to provide descriptions of surface-value actions and associate them with utterance types. Once we have such descriptions, the task of working out what to say (as a speaker), or of anticipating the needs of the speaker (as a listener), is simply a matter of applying standard planning theory. It will be a hard planning task, since the preconditions and effects are complex expressions involving quantification over propositions. Recognition by the hearer of the speaker's goals will be particularly hard, since the hearer will have to work forward trying to anticipate what desired action the effects some observed action might facilitate. This is a more open-ended task than the usual task where we have to chain backwards to find actions $A_1, A_2, \ldots$ which achieve our principal goals, and then find further actions which will enable us to perform $A_1, A_2, \ldots$. Furthermore, since the speaker has to ensure that the hearer will be able to do this forward inference successfully, the speaker's own task is more complex than the usual planning task. Nonetheless, both speaker and hearer are performing ordinary planning. All we need is a set of descriptions of action schemas.

Consider the following schema for the action of *inform*ing someone of something (adapted from Appelt [1985]):

$inform(X, Y, P)$
$preconditions : KNOW(X, P)$
$\qquad\qquad\qquad \neg KNOW(X, \bullet[KNOW(Y, P)])$
$effects : \mu(X, Y, P)$

In other words, X can only properly inform Y of P if X knows P, and does not know that Y knows it. The effects of this action are that X and Y should be mutually aware of P. If I inform you that I feel unwell and am going home, I should be able to assume that you know I feel unwell, that you know that I know you know I feel unwell, that I know that ... It may be that some of these are too complicated for you to believe that they are pre-requisites of my real goal, but they should all be available to either of us.

Suppose I have managed to inform you that I feel unwell, in other words that I have successfully performed an instance of the above action schema. If we are to have acquired mutual knowledge of $[[I feel unwell]]$, we must both have recognised that I performed this action. Suppose I tried to inform you of it, and you heard me but thought I was talking to my boss. Then we will both know that I feel unwell, but since you thought I was talking to someone else you will not realise I was informing you. Hence you will not know that I know you know it. It could even happen that I tried to inform you, you heard me but thought I was talking to someone else, and I realised that you had heard me. Then I would know that you knew how I felt, but we would not have mutual knowledge. Suppose you realised I realised you had heard me. Then you would know that I knew you knew how I felt. And *still* we would not be mutually aware of the fact that I felt unwell. The only way for mutual awareness to be achieved is if we are both aware that I have informed you about it.

If we are both aware that I performed this action, then we will both know that its preconditions must have held. In other words, we will both know that before the action was performed I knew I felt unwell and I did not know you knew it. It is notable, however, that anything which is known must be true. We have remarked on this property of knowledge before, and we built it into our epistemic logic. To convince yourself that this is so, consider the following sentences:

(325) *I used to believe the earth is flat, but I now realise it is not.*
(326) *I used to know the earth is flat, but I now realise it is not.*

(326) seems extremely odd — much odder than (325). The reason is that *knowing* P entails that P is true, so that to say you used to know something but that it is not true is self-contradictory. Anything which is known must be true.

If anything which is known must be true, then anyone who is aware that I informed you that I felt unwell must know that I felt unwell. This follows from the fact that anyone who is aware that I performed this action will know that its preconditions held, and in particular that I knew I felt unwell. But if I knew I felt unwell then it must have been true, so that anyone who knew I knew I felt unwell must themselves have known how I felt. If our claim that informing only works properly if the speaker and hearer are mutually aware that it has happened, then if I successfully informed you that I felt unwell then we must be mutually aware of my state of health.

This leads to the conclusion that X and Y can infer their mutual awareness of P simply from their knowledge of the preconditions of *inform* and the fact that if X has successfully informed Y of P then the preconditions must have held. In other words, there is no need for *inform* to have any effects! The description of *inform* thus becomes:

$$inform(X, Y, P)$$
$$preconditions: KNOW(X, P)$$
$$\neg KNOW(X, \bullet[KNOW(Y, P)])$$
$$effects :$$

We now consider a different simple declarative sentence:

(327) *You've been in the pub.*

Suppose X utters (327) to Y. It is virtually impossible for this to constitute an *inform*. Y may have been in the pub so long that she cannot understand the utterance at all, in which case X will not *inform* her of anything by uttering it since she will not understand what was said. Suppose, on the other hand, that she is still capable of understanding simple utterances. She can hardly be unaware of where she has been, and X can hardly be unaware of this. Scenarios where X knows that Y has been in the pub and Y does not are conceivable, but they will generally be very contrived. In almost any reasonable context, Y will know where she has been, and X will know this. This violates the preconditions of *inform*, which say that X must not know that Y already knows P.

We therefore require a different action:

$$
\begin{array}{l}
nag(X, Y, P) \\
preconditions: KNOW(X, P) \\
\qquad\qquad\qquad KNOW(X, \bullet[KNOW(Y, P)]) \\
effects:
\end{array}
$$

Nagging is just like informing, except that informing requires that X does not know that Y knows P and nagging requires that X does know that Y knows P. In particular, neither action has any effects beyond mutual awareness that the action has been performed; and there is no syntactic marker which indicates whether something was an instance of nagging or an instance of informing. Both are typically realised via simple declarative sentences, and simple declarative sentences can easily be interpreted either way.

We conclude from this that the action schemas for *inform* and *nag* are not going to help us work out what is going on in any given situation. (i) The only way that we can tell which action was performed is to see which of them had its preconditions satisfied. If I say *I feel unwell* then I am probably trying to *inform* you of something, since until I say this I do not know that you know how I feel. If I say *You've been in the pub* then I am probably nagging you, since I must assume that you would know where you have been. (ii) The only effects that are produced by actions like *inform* and *nag* are consequences of their preconditions. Putting (i) and (ii) together, we see that we have to check the preconditions of *inform* and *nag* in order to infer that their preconditions hold. This does not seem like a sensible way to proceed.

We are therefore driven back to a rather simpler action:

$$
\begin{array}{l}
declare(X, Y, P) \\
preconditions: KNOW(X, P) \\
effects:
\end{array}
$$

If X successfully declares P to Y then X and Y will be mutually aware of P. Any extra effects that X wants to produce will have to be based on information which is available to both parties already. If X wants to inform Y of P then X and Y must already be mutually aware that X does not know that Y knows P. If, on the other hand, X wants to nag Y about P then they must be mutually aware that Y does know P.

6.3 Epistemic Planning

The argument above suggests that subtly different linguistic actions such as *inform* and *nag* do not help us understand the use of declarative sentences in various situations. The extra information that such actions seem to provide over the information provided by simpler actions such as *declare* turns out to be illusory. In order to identify which such action has been performed, the speaker and hearer must already be aware of the extra information, so there is no point in identifying the action.

The effect of *declare* is exactly what we have embodied as the *content* of a simple declarative sentence. We claim that this is as it should be. All that is present in the words which someone utters is the information we considered in Chapters 4 and 5. Any further information that a speaker wants to draw upon must already be available. It does not matter where it comes from — whether it comes from general background knowledge, or from earlier utterances, or from meaning postulates such as the fact that anything which is known must be true. The important point is that there is nothing to be gained by positing an extra layer of linguistic actions and associating them with particular utterance types. Speakers produce utterances in order to make their *contents* available, and nothing more.

This does not mean that we have abandoned our story about the way language gets used. We cannot possibly explain how

(328) *It's OK, we can have another game.*

could possibly be a response to

(329) *Do you know the time?*

without considering the way the hearer might reconstruct the speaker's plans and goals. What it does mean is that we cannot use standard STRIPS-like planning theory, with descriptions of action schemas that embody information beyond what is literally available in the utterance. We are left with an extremely difficult planning problem. How can I reason about your plans when my observation of your actions only provides the kind of information embodied in the description of *declare*? This is, indeed, much harder than trying to reason with actions like *inform* and *nag*. Unfortunately we do have to solve it. We might be able to manipulate the more subtle actions more effectively, but manipulating them will not get us anywhere.

We will not present a theory of epistemic planning from first principles here. Such a theory will be required before we can explain how to use language, but we do not have one. All we can say is that we need one. We end this chapter on a slightly more positive note. Consider again the "donkey sentence":

(330) *If Pedro owns a donkey he beats it.*

We have had to work extremely hard to explain the connection between *Pedro* and *he*, and between *a donkey* and *it*. We had to introduce the notion of presuppositions; we had to explain that in a semantic game about a formula of the form $P \rightarrow Q$ the defence of Q could draw upon P; we had to specify that presuppositions get evaluated when they are required for fixing values of free variables, and that their evaluation can invoke any information that is available at that point.

Suppose we tried to express the same information in predicate calculus. We would just write:

$$(\forall X : donkey(X))(own(P, X) \rightarrow beat(P, X))$$

All the difficulties of the English version have been side-stepped by using the same term to denote the same object throughout — X for the hypothetical donkey, P for Pedro. Why does natural language not work the same way?

We have noted several times in the current chapter that effective use of language depends on the speaker and hearer being mutually aware of various propositions. We also noted, when discussing epistemic logic, that mutual awareness is not in fact attainable. This is rather awkward. Language users have to act as though they had mutual knowledge, but they never do. They therefore have to continually check with each other that the conversation is still working properly, that they are both aware of the things that they believe themselves to be mutually aware of.

It would be extremely tedious to continually interject explicit utterances aimed at checking these assumptions about mutual knowledge. Sometimes it is unavoidable. At the start of a conversation, for instance, you may have to negotiate in order to make sure that you are starting off with sound assumptions about each other:

- *You know the restaurant we went to last week?*
- *The one where we saw a rat, or the one where we saw cockroaches?*
- *The one where we saw a rat.*
- *Yeah.*
- *Well it's been closed down.*

The above dialogue is a fairly extreme case, since nearly all of it is concerned with setting up the right assumptions about mutual knowledge. As far as possible we avoid explicit negotiations of this kind. We suggest that the real function of presuppositions is to carry the burden of ensuring that the conversation is proceeding correctly. A presupposition is something that the speaker believes the hearer is aware of. If the hearer does not explicitly indicate that this is not true, the speaker can assume that their belief is correct. Any other information carried by presuppositions, such as the information required for fixing references, is a purely fortuitous side-effect.

EPILOGUE

We now have a description of how to obtain an interpretation of an utterance by combining the interpretations of its constituents. The rules in Chapters 4 and 5 specify this description in some detail, at least for declarative sentences (see [Groenendijk & Stokhof 84] for the difficulties involved in extending this kind of description to questions). We have thought briefly about the reasons which a speaker might have for producing an utterance, suggesting that any detailed analysis of this requires a great deal of sophisticated epistemic planning. We thus have some idea of how to compute the presupposition and content of an utterance, and of what we would have to do in order to compute its effects. We end by reconsidering Humpty Dumpty's verse:

> *'Twas brillig, and the slithy toves*
> *Did gyre and gimble in the wabe.*
> *All mimsy were the borogoves,*
> *And the mome raths outgrabe.*

We will look in particular at one sentence from it:

    (331) *The slithy toves did gyre and gimble in the wabe.*

Thorne et al. [1968] showed that you can parse quite effectively simply using the information provided by closed class words and by the suffixes which get applied to open class words. In (331) the closed class words *the*, *did* and *in* provide us with a great deal of information, since the occurrences of *the* can only introduce NP's, the occurrence of *did* must introduce a VP, and *in* must introduce a PP. We do not get much information in this example from word endings, since only one word (*toves*) appears to have a suffix at all. We cannot even be sure about this, since we have never seen this word before and hence we cannot actually tell whether its root is *tove*, with *toves* as the plural, or *toves* itself. Very few English words have root forms which end in *-es* (if any do), so we will assume that *toves* is in fact *tove* + *-s*. Given this assumption, our rules of Chapter 5 permit a small number of analyses of (331), including:

$structure(syntax(\#S, minor(\ldots)),$
$\qquad semantics(pre(\{((\exists!X : salient(X))((X \subseteq [\![tove]\!]) \wedge (X \subseteq [\![slithy]\!])),$
$\qquad\qquad\qquad (\exists!Y : salient(Y))([\![wabe]\!](Y)),$
$\qquad\qquad\qquad (\exists!Z : salient(Z))(state(Z) \vee event(Z))\}),$
$\qquad\qquad content((\exists I : (interval(I)$
$\qquad\qquad\qquad\qquad\qquad \wedge (\forall T : (instant(T) \wedge CONTAIN(I, T))$
$\qquad\qquad\qquad\qquad\qquad\qquad\qquad (BEFORE(T, now)))$
$\qquad\qquad\qquad\qquad\qquad\qquad\qquad DURING(I, ACTIONS)$
$\qquad\qquad\qquad \wedge loc(Z, Y))))$

$ACTIONS = \bullet[(\exists E : event(E) \wedge type(E, [\![gyre]\!]))(agent(E, X)$
$\qquad\qquad \wedge (\exists E' : event(E) \wedge type(E, [\![gimble]\!]))(agent(E', X))])]$

The presuppositions here introduce a set of slithy toves X, a wabe Y, and a state or event Z. The content specifies that X was involved as agent in two events, one of type $[\![gyre]\!]$ and the other of type $[\![gimble]\!]$, and that the location of Z was Y.

The only way that the other interpretations allowed by the rules of Chapter 5 differ from this is that they allocate different roles to X in the two events. The possible ambiguity in the scope of the PP *in the wabe* is covered by the fact that this PP requires the presupposition $(\exists!Z : salient(Z))(state(Z) \vee event(Z))$ to be verified. This verification might connect it to the simple *gimbling* event or to the compound event of *gyring and gimbling*.

It is now clear why Humpty Dumpty concentrates on unpacking the content of the new words, confident that Alice will realise that *slithy* denotes a property, *toves* denotes a set of objects, and so on. Alice, being a native speaker of English, can infer this generic information from the structure of (331). All she needs to be told is *what* property, *what* class of objects, and so on. In particular she needs to be told *what role* the X play with respect to the two events.

And why did Lewis Carroll put this verse in his book? Presumably to provoke the sort of speculation that has led us to here. But recognising *that* requires us to undertake complex epistemic planning.

BIBLIOGRAPHY

Aczel P. (1980): Frege Structures and the Notions of Proposition, Truth and Set, in *The Kleene symposium* (ed. J. Barwise): North Holland, Amsterdam: 31–39.

Allen J.F. (1984): Towards a General Theory of Time and Action, *Artificial Intelligence* 23(2): 123–154.

Allen J.F. & Perrault C.R. (1980): Analysing Intention in Utterances, *Artificial Intelligence* 15: 148–178.

Appelt D. (1985): *Planning English Sentences*: Cambridge University Press, Cambridge.

Austin J. (1962): *How to Do Things with Words*: Oxford University Press, Oxford.

Barwise J. & Perry J. (1983): *Situations and Attitudes*: Bradford Books, Cambridge, MA.

Bibel W. (1982): *Automatic Theorem Proving*: Vieweg & Sohn, Braunschweig.

Bresnan J.W. & Kaplan R. (1982): Lexical Function Grammar, in *The Mental Representation of Grammatical Relations* (ed. J.W. Bresnan): MIT Press, Cambridge, MA.: 173–281.

Calder J., Klein E. & Zeevat H. (1988): Unification Categorial Grammar: a Concise, Extendable Grammar for Natural Language Processing, *Proc. 12th Int. Conf. on Computational Linguistics*, : 83–86.

Carlson G. (1989): On the Semantic Composition of Engish Generic Sentences, in *Properties, Types and Meaning II: Semantic Issues* (eds. G. Chierchia, B.H. Partee & R. Turner): Kluwer Academic Publishers, Dordrecht: 167–192.

Carnap R. (1936): Testability and Meaning, *Philosophy of Science* 3: 401–467.

Chierchia G., Partee B.H. & Turner R. (1989): *Properties, Types and Meaning I: Foundational Issues & II: Semantic Issues*: Kluwer Academic Publishers, Dordrecht.

Chomsky N. (1957): *Syntactic Structures*: Mouton, The Hague.

Cohen P.R. & Perrault C.R. (1979): Elements of a Plan-based Theory of Speech Acts, *Cognitive Science* 7(2): 171–190.

Dowty D.R (1989): On the Semantic Content of the Notion of 'Thematic Role', in *Properties, Types and Meaning II: Semantic Issues* (eds. G. Chierchia, B.H. Partee & R. Turner): Kluwer Academic Publishers, Dordrecht: 69–130.

Dowty D.R (1989): On the Semantic Content of the Notion of 'Thematic Role', in *Properties, Types and Meaning II: Semantic Issues* (eds. G. Chierchia, B.H. Partee & R. Turner): Kluwer Academic Publishers, Dordrecht: 69–130.

Eco U. (1976): *A Theory of Semiotics*: Indiana University Press, Bloomington.

Fikes R.E. & Nilsson N.J. (1971): STRIPS: a New Approach to the Application of Theorem Proving to Problem Solving, *Artificial Intelligence* 3(4): 251–288.

Fillmore C. (1968): The Case for Case, in *Universals in Linguistic Theory* (eds. E. Bach & R.T. Harms)): Holt, Rinehart & Winston, Chicago: 1–90.

Gazdar G., Klein E., Pullum G. & Sag I. (1985): *Generalised Phrase Structure Grammar*: Basil Blackwell, Oxford.

Gazdar G., Pullum G.K., Carpenter R., Klein E., Hukari T.E. & Levine R.D. (1988): Category Structures, *Computational Linguistics* 14(1): 1–19.

Ginsberg M.L. (1987): *Readings in Non-monotonic Reasoning*: Morgan Kaufman, Los Altos.

Girard J.Y. (1987): Linear Logic, *Theoretical Computer Science* 50: 1–102.

Groenendijk J. & Stokhof M. (1984): *Studies on the Semantics of Questions and the Pragmatics of Answers*, diss., Department of Philosophy, University of Amsterdam.

Gupta A. (1982): Truth and Paradox, *Journal of Philosophical Logic* 11: 1–60.

Hendriks H. (1987): Type Change in Semantics: the Scope of Quantification and Coordination, in *Categories, Polymorphism and Unification* (eds. E. Klein & J. van Benthem): Centre for Cognitive Science, University of Edinburgh & Institute for Language, Logic and Information, University of Amsterdam, Edinburgh & Amsterdam: 169–200.

Herzberger H. (1982): Notes on Naive Semantics, *Journal of Philosophical Logic* 11: 61–102.

Hintikka J. & Kulas J. (1985): *Anaphora and Definite Descriptions: Two Applications of Game Theoretic Semantics*: D. Reidel, Dordrecht.

Hughes G. & Cresswell M. (1968): *Introduction to Modal Logic*: Methuen, London.

Jackendoff R.S. (1977): *X-bar Syntax: a Study of Phrase Structure*: MIT Press, Cambridge, MA.

Jech T.J. (1971): *Lectures in Set Theory, with Particular Emphasis on the Method of Forcing*: Springer Verlag (Lecture Notes in Mathematics 217), Berlin.

Kamp H. (1984): A theory of Truth and Semantic Representation, in *Formal Methods in the Study of Language* (eds. J. Groenendijk, J. Janssen & M. Stokhof): Foris Publications, Dordrecht: 277–322.

Koskiennemi K. (1985): A General Two-level Computational Model for Word-form Recognition and Production, *COLING-84*: 178–181.

Lorenz K. (1961): *Arithmetik und Logik als Spiele*, Ph.D. thesis, Kiel.

Lorenzen P. (1959): Ein Dialogisches Konstructivitatskreiterium, *Proceedings of the Symposium on the Foundations of Mathematics*, Warsaw.

Manthey R. & Bry F. (1988): SATCHMO: a Theorem Prover in PROLOG, *CADE-88*.

Matsumoto Y., Hozumi T., Hirakawa H., Miyoshi H. & Yasukawa H. (1983): BUP: a Bottom-up Parser Embedded in PROLOG, *New Generation Computing* 1: 145–158.

McCarthy J. (1980): Circumscription: a Form of Non-monotonic Reasoning, *Artificial Intelligence* 13: 27–39.

McDermott D.V. (1982): A Temporal Logic for Reasoning about Processes and Time, *Cognitive Science* 6: 101–155.

Milne R. (1986): Resoving Lexical Ambiguity in a Deterministic Parser, *Computational Linguistics* 12(1): 1–12.

Moortgat M. (1987): Lambek Theorem Proving, in *Categories, Polymorphism and Unification* (eds. E. Klein & J. van Benthem): Centre for Cognitive Science, University of Edinburgh & Institute for Language, Logic and Information, University of Amsterdam, Edinburgh & Amsterdam: 169–200.

Pereira F.C.N. & Warren D.H.D. (1980): Definite Clause Grammars for Language Analysis — a Survey of the Formalism and a Comparison with ATNs, *Artificial Intelligence* 13(3): 231–278.

Pollard C. & Sag I.A. (1988): *An Information Based Approach to Syntax and Semantics: Vol 1 Fundamentals*: CSLI lecture notes 13, Chicago University Press, Chicago.

Pulman S. (1987): Events and VP-modifiers, in *Proceedings of the Alvey Sponsored Workshop On Formal Semantics in Natural Language Processing* (ed. B.G.T. Lowden): University of Essex, Colchester.

Quillian M.R. (1968): Semantic Memory, in *Semantic Information Processing* (ed. M. Minsky): MIT Press, Cambridge, MA: 216–270.

Quine W.v.O (1960): *Word and Object* MIT Press, Cambridge, MA.

Ramsay A.M. (1988): *Formal Methods in Artificial Intelligence*: Cambridge University Press, Cambridge.

Ramsay A.M. (1990): Disjunction Without Tears, *Computational Linguistics* [in press].

Reichenbach H. (1956): *The Direction of Time*: University of California Press, Berkeley.

Reiter R. (1980): A Logic for Default Reasoning, *Artifical Intelligence* 13(1).

Robinson J.A. (1965): A Machine-oriented Logic Based on the Resolution Principle, *Journal of the ACM* 12(1): 23–41.

Rounds W.C. (1988): LFP: a Logic for Linguistic Descriptions and an Analysis of its Complexity, *Computation Linguistics* 14(4): 1–9.

Sacerdoti E.D. (1977): *A Structure for Plans and Behaviour*: Elsevier North-Holland, Amsterdam.

Schank R.C. (1972): Conceptual Dependency: a Theory of Natural Language Understanding, *Cognitive Psychology* 3(4): 552–631.

Searle J.R. (1969): *Speech Acts: an Essay in the Philosophy of Language*: Cambridge University Press, Cambridge.

Stalnaker R.C. (1984): *Inquiry*: Bradford Books, Cambridge, MA.

Steel S. (1985): Refinements of Operator-based Action Representation, *AISB-85*, Warwick: 98–107.

Stegmuller W. (1964): Remarks on the Completeness of Logical Systems Relative to the Validity-concepts of P. Lorenzen and K. Lorenz, *Notre Dame Journal of Symbolic Logic* 2: 81–112.

Thorne J.P., Bratley P. & Dewar H. (1968): The Syntactic Analysis of English, in *Machine Intelligence 3* (ed. D. Michie): Edinburgh University Press, Edinburgh.

Turner R. (1987): A Theory of Properties, *Journal of Symbolic Logic* 52(2): 455–472.

Turner R. (1990): *Truth and Modality for Knowledge Representation*: Pitman, London.

Whitehead A.N. & Russell B. (1925): *Principia Mathematica*: Cambridge University Press, Cambridge.

Winograd T. (1983): *Language as a Cognitive Process*: Addison Wesley, Reading, MA.

RULES AND FRAMES

F1: basic description of sentence (p. 63)
F2: basic description of VP (p. 64)
F3: basic description of verb (includes embedded rule) (p. 64)
F4: basic description of NP (p. 65)
F5: basic description of nominal group (NN) (p. 65)
F6: description of lexical item, with HFC (p. 66)
F7: determiner, with skeletal embedded rule (p. 69)
F8: preposition (p. 72)
F9: -∅ as singular noun suffix (p. 74)
F10: -*s* as plural noun suffix (p. 75)
F11: basic frame for noun (p. 75)
F12: noun with possessive marker (p. 78)
F13: preposition with possessive NP ruled out (p. 79)
F14: adjective with adjectival phrase as goal (p. 80)
F15: adjective with NP as goal (for complement to *be*, etc.) (p. 80)
F16: adverb (p. 81)
F17: -*s* as third person singular present tense verb suffix (p. 83)
F18: -*ing* as present participle suffix (p. 83)
F19: lexical entry for *prove* (p. 85)
F20: -*ed* as past tense verb suffix (p. 86)
F21: -*ed* as passive verb suffix, without PP complement (p. 86)
F22: -*ed* as passive verb suffix, with PP complement (p. 88)
F23: auxiliary and modal (p. 89)
F24: ditransitive verb (*give, tell,* ...) (p. 90)
F25: controlled subject form of NP+VP verb (p. 91)
F26: aux-inversion for auxiliary and modal verb (p. 93)
R1: rule for simple declarative sentence (p. 95)
R2: NP without determiner (p. 97)
R3: NP with possessive NP as determiner (p. 97)
R4: slash elimination (p. 100)
R5: topicalisation (p. 100)
R6: relative clause with "missing element" (p. 101)

F58: semantics of infix conjunction (p. 149)
R16: semantics of infix coordination (p. 149)
F59: simple agentive verb (e.g. *kill*) (p. 155)
F60: simple agentless verb (e.g. *die*) (p. 156)
F61: lexical entry for *kill* (p. 156)
F62: lexical entry for *die* (p. 156)
F63: instrumental agentive verb (e.g. *open*) (p. 158)
F64: semantics of passive with PP complement (p. 160)
F65: semantics of passive without PP complement (p. 160)
F66: preposition where the PP is a modifier (p. 162)
F67: preposition where the PP is a verbal complement (p. 162)
F68: stative verb (e.g. *own*) (p. 164)
R17: bare plural NP as generic (p. 165)
F69: habitual interpretation of present tense (p. 167)
F70: verb with sentential complement (e.g. *know*) (p. 168)
F71: verb with NP and *to*-form VP complement (p. 169)
F72: controlled subject form of NP+VP complement verb (p. 171)
F73: verb with implicit proposition (p. 175)
F74: expanded version of preposition with PP as modifier (p. 176)
F75: lexical entry for *in* (p. 177)
R18: nominal group + PP (p. 178)
R19: PP + sentence (p. 179)
R20: VP + PP (p. 182)

INDEX